Answering Atheism

Trent Horn

Answering Atheism

How to Make the Case for God with Logic and Charity

Catholic Answers Press

San Diego
2013

Published by Catholic Answers, Inc.
2020 Gillespie Way
El Cajon, California 92020
888-291-8000 orders
619-387-0042 fax
www.catholic.com

Printed in the United States of America

ISBN 978-1-938983-43-6
ISBN 978-1-938983-44-3 (Kindle)
ISBN 978-1-938983-45-0 (ePub)

For Laura

Acknowledgments

This book would not be possible without the aid of the pro-life organization Justice for All (JFA). Through their outreach events I gained valuable experience in real-world dialogue with students that held a wide variety of worldviews. I would also like to thank Eric Westby, Fr. Matt Lowry, Fr. John Parks, Ryan Howe, and the St. Theresa parish Life Teen program for forming my Catholic faith. I also am indebted to the many scholars and authors (past and present) who artfully defend the Christian faith. In particular, I am grateful for the work of Dr. William Lane Craig, which has immeasurably helped my journey as an apologist. I am also grateful to my fellow apologists and the staff at Catholic Answers, especially acquisitions editor Todd Aglialoro and the director of apologetics Tim Staples, who helped me to refine this manuscript. I feel that this combination of influences will allow this book to benefit both Catholic and non-Catholic readers who are interested in learning how to answer arguments for atheism. And I am thankful for my parents as well as my wife, Laura. She patiently helped me during the writing process and is always an excellent source of inspiration. Above all, I thank God for his grace, which makes all that I do possible. A.M.D.G.

Contents

Can You Give Me a Good Reason?

From 2009 to 2011, I traveled the country as a pro-life missionary engaging students at public universities in dialogue about abortion. I remember one student I met, named Violet, who said that she resented pro-lifers' "pushing their religion" on her. I said that my case against abortion didn't rely on religion, but that even if it did, why should that matter? Violet retorted, "Because I'm an atheist! I bet you can't even give me one good reason to believe that God exists."

I responded, "I can give you more reasons than that," and we talked for several minutes. Violet was amazed that I was willing to listen to her, that I didn't think her questions were stupid, and that I could give her interesting answers to think about. From one objection to the next, whether it was evolution, faith versus science, or the obnoxiousness of her Christian friends, I helped her see that she actually didn't have any compelling reason to think there was no God. As our conversation ended, Violet became sad, and said to me, "If only I had met someone like you when I had so many questions, maybe I wouldn't be an atheist today."

Since that encounter, I've met many "Violets," or people who struggle to have faith in God because they have so many unanswered questions. You've probably met people like this and wished you had good answers for their thoughtful questions. Or you might be like Violet and have questions no one is willing to answer. I can't promise this book has all the answers you're looking for, but I have done my best to present the best reasons to think God exists. With the task of equipping believers and engaging skeptics in mind, I have set out two goals in my critique of atheism.

Take atheism seriously, but confront it charitably

In recent years, the notoriety of pro-atheism books like *The God Delusion, God Is Not Great,* and *The End of Faith* has led Christian authors to write popular pro-theist apologies in response. Unfortunately, some of these books not only argued against atheism, but mocked it as "delusional," "incomprehensible," and "childish." Others went so far as to attack the character of atheists and accuse them of promoting anti-social behavior, or even genocide! Needless to say, showing them to my atheist friends was not an option, at least if I wanted to still be friends with them.

So how *should* Christians respond to atheists? First, we must recognize that there are powerful arguments that can be raised in defense of atheism, and those arguments need to be confronted. Secondly, even if the "New Atheists" like Richard Dawkins or Christopher Hitchens have been less than respectful when writing about religion, that doesn't give Christians a license to be just as disrespectful when writing about atheism. The book of Proverbs puts it well, "A soft answer turns away wrath, but a harsh word stirs up anger."[1]

We should also keep in mind that many people who are non-religious don't even call themselves "atheists"—they just don't think about God much. The term "apatheist" has been used to describe people who don't believe in God because they are just too apathetic to think about if he exists or not.[2] These atheists are content to let religious people live their lives without criticism as long as they are granted the same courtesy. Of course, some non-religious people, whether they consider themselves atheists or not, enjoy debating Christians. So whether the person we encounter is a curious questioner or an apostle for atheism, as Christians we should, in the words of St. Peter, "Always be prepared to make a defense to anyone who calls you to account for the hope that is in you, yet do it with gentleness and reverence."[3]

Make the truth accessible both to scholars and laymen

Several years ago when I hosted an "answering atheism" seminar, I found that I could not recommend to the participants any one book defending the existence of God. Like Goldilocks, who found her porridge either too hot or too cold, I struggled between recommending books that were either too simple or too complex. The benefit of giving someone a simple apologetics book is that he is more likely to read it. The downside is that a shallow book may under-prepare him for the questions that skeptics will inevitably ask. Conversely, a long book by a professional philosopher will be great at preparing people for the tough questions. The downside is that readers who do not have adequate preparation in science or philosophy can become frustrated as they read such dense material. Rather than read such a book, it may just stay in a bookshelf gathering dust.

My approach is a compromise between these two positions. I have included a large number of arguments so that the reader is prepared for a wide variety of conversations, but I've also explained those arguments with simple illustrations so that the reader is not overwhelmed by them. The more technical or complicated arguments can be found in the appendices.

What to expect

This book is divided into three parts. Part I examines the different views involved in the debate over the existence of God. It also addresses the bad attitudes both theists and atheists sometimes bring to the discussion, and how we can avoid them.

The remainder of the book sets out to defend the following statement: "There are no good reasons to think atheism is true, and many reasons to think it is false." In Part II, I answer the question, "Should I be an atheist?" by examining arguments that attempt to show there is no God. Some of my atheist readers will think this is a backward approach. Why not first prove God exists? That would be the best answer to atheism! But I want to treat atheism with a high level of respect by examining it as a worldview that could be either true or false.

In that regard, I will examine atheists' arguments and show that there are in fact no good reasons to think atheism is true. Of course, disproving the arguments for atheism does not prove God exists; we could always be agnostics who just don't know if there is a God. That is why in Part III I will answer the question, "Should I believe in God?" by examining the arguments for God's existence. These include the arguments from necessity, first cause, design, morality, and personal experience. Finally, I go "Beyond the God Debate" and tackle the more existential or practical objections to belief in God.

My goal is to show that there are good reasons to think that God exists and no equally good reasons to think that atheism is true. As a result, the rational person has nothing to fear in embracing a personal relationship with the God of the universe.

PART I

The God Debate

Theism, Atheism, and the God Debate

I was once reading a defense of atheism while waiting to be served in a restaurant. The hostess looked over at my book, with its bold ATHEISM in the title, and asked, "How could someone ever be an atheist? I mean, everybody has to believe in something, don't they?" Unfortunately, this woman confused *nihilism* (the belief that nothing matters) with *atheism* (the belief that God does not exist). It's true that nihilists are usually atheists, but many atheists are not nihilists. They would say they believe in many things that matter, God just isn't one of them.

Misconceptions, like the one held by this woman, can derail fruitful conversations about God and turn them into heated arguments. Instead of fighting, we should clear away misconceptions so that even if people disagree, they can feel respected, and both parties can move closer to finding true beliefs. Before I defend my beliefs about God, let's define our terms so that the people who disagree about God's existence can at least talk *to* one another instead of talking *past* one another.

What do we mean by God?

While various concepts of God differ across the world, they all usually describe God as the supernatural creator of the universe. In the Western philosophical tradition, God is a being that is necessary (cannot fail to exist), eternal (not bound by time), immaterial (not bound by space), all-powerful, and all-knowing. Finally, most Western theologians and philosophers claim that God is all-good, or he is the perfect embodiment of the virtues of love, justice, and every other good we know.[4] He is, as St. Anselm of Canterbury declared, the being "than which no greater can be thought." This definition of God is consistent with the God worshipped by Christians, Jews, and Muslims, who believe that God revealed himself to mankind. Of course, if atheism is true, then we don't have to wonder which people God has revealed himself to, because God doesn't exist. So before we can find out if a certain *kind* of God exists, we should find out if God exists at all.

If God could be proven to exist, would it be possible to understand such an infinite being? Here we must distinguish between "basic understanding" and "advanced comprehension." I don't *fully comprehend* how every part of a nuclear reactor works, because I'm not a nuclear engineer. But the facts provided by nuclear engineers that are printed in encyclopedias allow me to have a *basic understanding* of how a nuclear reactor works. I understand (at a basic level) that using nuclear energy to heat water creates steam, which spins turbines, which create electricity. Similarly, I may not comprehend how God knows all truths or how he created the world, but I can understand that such tasks are not impossible for an infinite being like him. According to the *Catechism of the Catholic Church*:

> God transcends all creatures. We must therefore continually purify our language of everything in it that is limited, image-bound or imperfect, if we are not to confuse our image of God—"the inexpressible, the incomprehensible, the invisible, the ungraspable"—with our human representations. Our human words always fall short of the mystery of God.[5]

We must remember too that a good teacher can take a very complex topic and break it down into a framework that even a simple person can understand. So if God is an infinite being, then he is also the universe's infinitely greatest teacher. He is able to "come down to our level" and reveal himself through both nature and human experience.

Getting our terms right: Theism

Theists believe that a personal God exists who interacts with the world. Monotheists, like Christians, Muslims, or Jews, believe that only one God exists. Polytheists, like the followers of Greek and Roman mythologies, believe that many gods exist. Deists believe that one God created the universe, but unlike theists, they believe this God no longer interacts with the world he created. Some Founding Fathers, such as Thomas Jefferson, were deists: They rejected Christianity, but they did not reject what they called "nature's God."[6]

Monotheists, deists, and polytheists believe that at least one God exists, and he is not identical to the world he created. Pantheists, on the other hand, believe God exists but he (or she, or even it) is identical to the universe itself. The Catholic theologian Jean Daniélou called these pantheistic beliefs "cosmic religions" because their followers considered the cosmos itself to be divine.[7] When Albert Einstein said, "God does not play dice," he was most likely referring metaphorically to the laws of nature as having a divine quality about them. Einstein explicitly claimed on several occasions that he did not believe in the existence of a personal God.[8]

Getting our terms right: Atheism

Atheism literally means "without God" and can be divided into either strong or weak types. I remember once asking a student at Northern Arizona University if he believed in God. He responded, "Hell, no! I'm not just an atheist, I'm a super-atheist!" At first I was expecting him to show off his x-ray vision or super strength, but what he meant was that he was 100 percent confident that God does not exist. This view, also known as *positive atheism* or *strong atheism*, claims that it is a fact that "God does not exist." In contrast, negative atheism or weak atheism merely claim that there is insufficient evidence to prove that God exists.

Another name for atheism is *naturalism,* or the view that only the natural world exists.[9] Naturalists may admit that there are things in our universe we cannot detect (like particles that are smaller than atoms) or natural objects outside of our universe (like "multiverses"), but they deny the existence of a supernatural being that transcends nature. Atheism is also sometimes called *materialism,* or the belief that only matter exists, and therefore an immaterial being like God does not. But atheism is not the same thing as materialism, because some atheists believe in the existence of immaterial things that are not God (like minds or numbers).

Getting our terms right: Non-religious

It's also important not to confuse atheists with people who have no religion, or as they're sometimes called, "nones."[10] No, these aren't the women who wear habits, pray the rosary, and are quick to discipline unruly Catholic schoolchildren. These "nones" may believe God exists, but they don't follow any particular religion. Sometimes the God "nones" believe in is not a person but something like the Force from *Star Wars.*

As a friend of mine once told me, "I believe in God, but not the Christian God. God is love. That's all we need." C. S. Lewis has an answer to this idea:

> Of course, what these people mean when they say that God is love is often something quite different: they really mean "Love is God." They really mean that our feelings of love, however and whenever they arise, and whatever results they produce, are to be treated with great respect. Perhaps they are: but that is something quite different from what Christians mean by the

statement "God is love." They believe that the living, dynamic activity of love has been going on in God forever and has created everything else.[11]

The other common conception of God among the religiously unaffiliated is what sociologists Christian Smith and Melinda Denton call *moralistic therapeutic deism,* which claims that:[12]

1. God exists and watches over the world.
2. God wants people to be nice, and good people go to heaven.
3. God is not needed in life unless there is a problem he can solve, because the purpose of life is to be happy.

Although such bland forms of deism are the majority belief among unaffiliated Americans, atheism is on the rise. The so-called "New Atheists" are putting forward arguments and attitudes that they hope will convert the "nones" to their side.

Getting our terms right: New Atheism

In his 2004 book *The End of Faith,* American atheist Sam Harris argued that religion is a mental illness and cannot be part of a rational worldview.[13] British biologist Richard Dawkins followed in 2006 with *The God Delusion,* in which he claimed that religious education is a form of child abuse.[14] Then came similarly bold anti-theism books from journalist Christopher Hitchens (*God Is Not Great*) and philosopher Daniel Dennett (*Breaking the Spell: Religion as Natural Phenomenon*). Before Hitchens passed away from cancer in 2011, these four were collectively known as the Four Horsemen of the "New Atheism." What made these atheists "new" was not their arguments but their *attitude* that religion should be reviled. Secular humanist Tom Flynn wrote:

> The triumph of Harris, Dennett, Dawkins, and Hitchens was to take arguments against religion that were long familiar to insiders, brilliantly repackage them, and expose them to millions who would never otherwise pick up an atheist book. Let me say that again in bolder type. **There's nothing *new* about the New Atheism.**[15]

Getting our terms right: Agnosticism

Agnosticism (from *gnosis,* the Greek word for knowledge) is the position that a person cannot know if God exists.[16] A strong agnostic claims that no one is able to know whether God exists. A weak agnostic merely claims that while *he* doesn't know if God exists, it is possible that someone else may know.[17] Agnosticism and weak atheism are similar in that both groups claim to be "without belief in God."[18] Pope Benedict XVI spoke sympathetically of such people in a 2011 address:

> In addition to the two phenomena of religion and anti-religion, a further basic orientation is found in the growing world of agnosticism: people to whom the gift of faith has not been given, but who are nevertheless on the lookout for truth, searching for God. Such people do not simply assert: "There is no God." They suffer from his absence and yet are inwardly making their way towards him, inasmuch as they seek truth and goodness. They are "pilgrims of truth, pilgrims of peace."[19]

Because agnosticism seems more open-minded than atheism, many atheists are more apt to describe themselves like agnostics even though they call themselves "atheist." They say that an atheist is a person who lacks a belief in God but is open to being proven wrong. But saying you lack a belief in God no more answers the question, "Does God exist?" than saying you lack a belief in aliens answers the question, "Do aliens exist?" This is just agnosticism under a different name. For example, can we say agnosticism is true? We can't, because agnostics don't make claims about the world; they just describe how they feel about a fact in the world (the existence of God). Likewise, if atheists want us to believe that atheism is true, then they must make a claim about the world and show that what they lack a belief in—God—does not exist.

An illustration might help explain the burden of proof both sides share. In a murder trial the prosecution must show beyond a reasonable doubt that the defendant committed the murder. But if the prosecution isn't able to make its case, then the defendant is found not guilty. Notice the defendant isn't found innocent. For all we know, he could have committed the crime, but we just can't prove it. Certain kinds of evidence, like an airtight alibi, can show the defendant is innocent. But it is the responsibility of the defense to present that evidence.

Likewise, even if the theist isn't able to make his case that God exists, that doesn't show God does not exist and therefore atheism is true. As atheists Austin Dacey and Lewis Vaughn write, "What if these arguments purporting to establish that God exists are failures? That is, what if they offer no justification for theistic belief? Must we then conclude that God does not exist? No. Lack of supporting reasons or evidence for a proposition does not show that the proposition is false."[20] If he wants to demonstrate that atheism is true, an atheist would have to provide additional evidence that there is no God. He can't simply say the arguments for the existence of God are failures and then rest his case.

The following flowchart should help you sort out what the different terms so far mean:

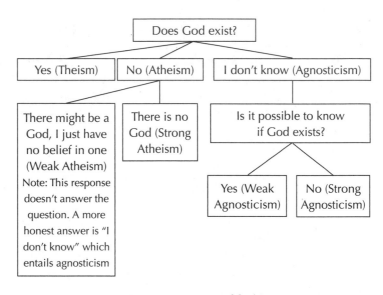

Is it just a matter of faith?

When most people think of proof, they think of mathematical proofs that cannot be doubted, like the proof for 2+2=4. With that idea of "proof" in mind, some people claim that since so many people doubt that God exists, his existence must be beyond the realm of "proof" and is just a matter of "faith." Now, God's existence (along with many other things we think are true) cannot be demonstrated with 100 percent psychological certainty. Faith helps us overcome emotional doubt. But that doesn't mean belief in God is *solely* a matter of faith. Instead, saying one can prove God's existence is shorthand for saying that the balance of evidence in favor of God's existence outweighs the evidence against God's existence. The *Catechism* says that the proofs for God are a series of "converging and convincing arguments which allow us to attain certainty about the truth."[21]

It's like saying we can "prove" someone is guilty of a crime by using cumulative pieces of evidence that converge toward a particular verdict. In a trial, the prosecutor doesn't prove the defendant's guilt with a long mathematical equation on a chalkboard. Instead, he presents pieces of evidence to the jury that are best explained by the defendant's guilt. No one piece of evidence may prove the defendant is guilty, but taken as a whole they may very well accomplish that task.

Likewise, a theist can present evidence from the natural world that is best explained by the existence of God.[22] While personal experience of God (what some people call faith) can be a part of this evidence, this does not show that belief in God is just the result of wishful thinking or mere "blind faith."

Atheists will also become annoyed when they are told their belief in atheism is just a "matter of faith." They will respond that they have the same faith in the nonexistence of God as theists have in the nonexistence of Santa Claus. Some atheists will define faith as "belief in spite of the evidence," or more charitably as "belief in the absence of evidence."[23] But according to most traditional Christians, faith is not a belief in spite of or in the absence of evidence. Instead it is, as the *Catechism* defines it, "the theological virtue by which we believe in God and believe all that he has said and revealed to us."[24] Although we live in a culture that equates faith with "blindly accepting something as true," it may be more helpful to think of faith instead as a kind of "trust" that is based on good reasons.

Most of what we believe is taken on this kind of trust-ing faith, because as limited human beings we cannot directly research the truth about everything. We need to have con-fidence (or "faith") in the authority of teachers, textbooks, maps, schedules, parents, and Internet websites, among many other things. Sometimes this faith is misplaced, and we end up believing false things. But if that happens, and if we are presented with good evidence that our beliefs are not true, we simply give up those false beliefs. An atheist might complain that there is a difference in having faith in people and having faith in God. We *know* people exist because we can experi-ence them with our five senses and can investigate to see if what they say is true. But the same is not true for God, whose very existence is disputed.

But who says that the only way we can know if something exists is through the use of our five senses? If God existed, then he could reveal himself to a human being by causing that person to have an internal awareness of God. If that person does not doubt his own sanity, then why shouldn't he trust this personal experience?[25] Along with this personal, subjec-tive knowledge, the First Vatican Council taught that God can also be known objectively, by reasons accessible to everyone. It said that God "can be known with certainty from the con-sideration of created things, by the natural power of human reason."[26] Now, this doesn't mean that everyone will come to know God by reason but only that it is possible for anyone to come to know God with certainty in this way.

The diagram on the opposite page may help. On the far left, we see that there are some truths (like mathematical truths) that are known only through reason. On the far right, there are other truths that can only be known if they are revealed by God and accepted through faith (like the Christian belief that God is a Trinity). But some truths, those in between the

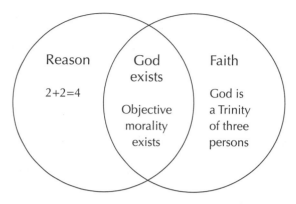

overlapping circles, can be known by either faith or reason. These include the truth that God exists or the truth that some actions are objectively right or wrong.[27]

Both atheists and theists have "faith" in the sense that they believe statements that cannot be proven with certainty. For example, almost everyone believes that the world is not a computer simulation like the Matrix, or that the laws of nature that operate today will operate the same way tomorrow. We don't carefully reason our way to these truths. They are merely assumptions we think are true because they just appear to be true. But calling belief in these basic truths "faith" would stretch the meaning of the word beyond recognition. Theists have religious faith while atheists have confidence in truths that cannot be absolutely proven.

Should we just keep to ourselves?

Some atheists, and even some theists, claim that discussing religion is too emotional and not worth the trouble. They say arguments don't change anyone's mind and that we should all just focus on being nice to one another. But it is simply not true that no one ever changes his mind on this issue. Several books in just the last few years, for example, relate conversions to theism as well as "de-conversions" to atheism.[28]

Furthermore, if an all-powerful, all-knowing, all-good creator of the universe *does* exist, that would have a profound impact on our lives—well worth any emotional responses that come from the discussion. Cambridge logic professor Arif Ahmed, himself an avid atheist, once said in a debate, "We're discussing probably the most important question any of us will ever have to face in our life. If God exists, then you and I should change our lives. If I really believed it . . . then I would change my life."[29]

In a 2009 YouTube video, atheist and magician Penn Jillette described how a Christian approached him after one of his magic shows and gave him a Bible. Instead of being offended, Penn said the Christian was "a good man" and that if Christians actually believe their faith was true, then they should have no problem sharing it with other people. After all, if sharing what you believe dramatically affects someone's eternal destiny, then, as Jillette says, "How much do you have to hate somebody to not proselytize? How much would you have to hate somebody to believe that everlasting life is possible and not tell them that?"[30]

Being open to what's true, as opposed to what we want to be true, is exactly the right attitude we all should have concerning the existence of God. In the next chapter, we will examine certain bad attitudes that theists and atheists both must overcome if we are to have fruitful conversations.

2

Getting Rid of Bad Attitudes

Norman Vincent Peale, who wrote *The Power of Positive Thinking*, once said, "The trouble with most of us is that we would rather be ruined by praise than saved by criticism." It's hard to honestly face criticism, but it's the only way we can grow as human beings, since we are notoriously good at deceiving ourselves about our own competence and knowledge.[31] That is why I hope theists and atheists will consider shedding attitudes we might unknowingly possess that can hinder productive dialogue. Let's start with three bad attitudes people who believe in God sometimes exhibit.

Bad Theistic Attitude #1: "No rational person can be an atheist! Do you think we just came from monkeys or something?"

In his book *Introduction to Christianity*, Joseph Cardinal Ratzinger (the future Pope Benedict XVI) writes, "Just as the believer is choked by the salt water of doubt constantly washed into his mouth by the ocean of uncertainty, so the non-believer is troubled by doubts about his unbelief, about the real totality of the world which he has made up his mind to explain as a self-contained whole."[32] Theists do their cause a great disservice by ridiculing atheists or saying that it is obvious atheism is false. If atheism were simply irrational, then why would believers have to guard against being "drowned" by unbelief? Likewise, atheists should know that many people have wrestled and struggled with the question of God's existence before they converted to religious faith. Both sides should accept each other's doubts and journey toward the truth together in a spirit of mutual humility.

In regard to the theory of evolution, atheists will probably find an origin from monkeys to be more likely than an origin from God—because at least we have seen monkeys and know they exist. Even if a theist doesn't believe in the theory of evolution, if he can create a case for God's existence that does not come across as anti-science, most atheists will find that position to be more reasonable.[33] Indeed, scientific ignorance—real or perceived—only reinforces the negative stereotypes that atheists have about Christians. St. Augustine worried about this kind of attitude in the fourth century when he wrote:

> Usually, even a non-Christian knows something about the earth, the heavens, and the other elements of this world. . . . Now, it is a disgraceful and dangerous thing for an infidel to hear a Christian, presumably giving the meaning of Holy Scripture, talking nonsense on these topics; and we should take all means to prevent such an embarrassing situation.[34]

There's no need to insult someone's intelligence just because he does not believe in God. In a debate at Cambridge University on the subject "Is God a Delusion?", William Lane Craig said,

> [Atheists] recognize that the existence of God is a difficult question on which rational opinion can vary. Peter and I haven't indicted our opponents tonight as being deluded. We think they're mistaken, but we wouldn't say they're deluded. Why can't they return the favor? People can disagree without calling each other names.[35]

Sensible atheists also have this agreeable attitude. Scott Aiken and Robert Talisse write in their book *Reasonable Atheism: A Moral Case for Respectful Disbelief:*

We think that religious beliefs are false and that religious believers are mistaken in their religious beliefs. We do not "respect" religious beliefs. We do, however, respect religious believers. We hold that religious believers can be intelligent, rational, and responsible, despite the falsity of their religious beliefs; in short, we hold that religious believers can be *reasonable*.[36]

Bad Theistic Attitude #2: "Atheists are immoral."

Once when I was taking questions from an audience after one of my presentations, a gentleman asked me, "Why would anyone ever be an atheist? Don't they know that Hitler and Stalin were atheists?" I told this man that saying someone is like Hitler usually starts a conversation off on the wrong foot, but there was an even more fundamental problem with this attitude. Whether Hitler was an atheist is unclear,[37] but even if he was, so what? Maybe Hitler liked kittens and sunsets, too, but that doesn't make those things evil by association. The immoral, even heinous, lives of some atheists do not invalidate the truth of atheism any more than the lives of immoral Christians invalidate theism. Any religion or belief system can have immoral people who hold to it. This does nothing to prove whether its beliefs are true or false.[38]

Some theists say that if God does not exist, then what reasons would an atheist have to be good, since there is no life beyond the grave? But atheists have many practical reasons to be moral and would be offended by the idea that they are, as a whole, not morally good people.[39] An atheist might cite her desire to make the human community more stable, or her need to follow her own conscience, or her belief in a principle like the Golden Rule as a reason to be moral. In any case, the real question we should ask is not why *individual* atheists would be moral, but why *objective* moral truths exist if God does not (more on that in chapters 14-16).

Bad Theistic Attitude #3: Failing to empathize with atheists

In her 2012 book *Why Are You Atheists So Angry?*, Greta Christina catalogues nearly 100 grievances atheists have against the followers of various religions. Christina's complaints can be grouped under a few common themes:

- Atheists are compelled by the state to endorse or practice religion against their will (such as being forced to participate in public prayer).
- The state endorses a particular set of religious beliefs (like the teaching of creationism in public schools or prohibitions on marriage between people of the same sex).
- Religious people have ridiculous beliefs that cause them to hurt or dehumanize other people through acts like medical malpractice, bullying, social rejection, and even murder.
- Religious people believe things for stupid reasons.

In one example, Christina writes, "I'm angry at preachers who tell women in their flock to submit to their husbands because it's the will of God, even when their husbands are beating them within an inch of their lives."[40] Some theists will reply defensively that such examples don't reflect their religion, or that their religion is being misrepresented as being unreasonable. But sometimes atheists don't want to know if your religion is reasonable. Sometimes they just want to know if *you* are reasonable. Aren't you at least angry at Christians who use religion as an excuse to bully children?[41] Wouldn't you agree that laws related to marriage or abortion should be based on reason and not religion? Isn't it okay to be angry when religious hypocrites hurt others? If atheists think theists are just "out to get them" and aren't concerned by these injustices like they are, then there can be little hope for theistic beliefs to get a fair hearing among non-believers.

Likewise, atheists should realize that although theists and Christians are a majority in the United States, there are many particular places where they are the minority and can be pushed around. According to the Social Science Research Council, while only about one in five people think the Bible is a book of fables and myths, nearly three out of four professors at elite universities hold that view.[42] Instead of bullying, both sides of this debate should protect each other's right to discuss and disagree without the fear of violence or persecution.

Now, in the spirit of mutual correction, let's examine three bad attitudes atheists sometimes bring to the debate over the existence of God.

Bad Atheistic Attitude #1: "All religion contradicts science."

Certainly, there are some religious beliefs that contradict science. Some Hindu creationists think modern human beings have existed for billions of years, while some Christian creationists think modern humans are only 6,000 years old. Both of these estimates are far off the mainstream scientific view.[43]

But just because *some* religious beliefs don't line up with certain widely accepted scientific conclusions doesn't mean that religion—or theism—is in itself anti-science. In fact, Catholic scientists like Fr. Georges Lemaitre (who discovered the Big Bang) and the friar Gregor Mendel (who discovered genetic inheritance), followed the medieval motto *fides quaerens intellectum*, or "faith seeking understanding," and were among those who contributed to the flourishing of modern science.

Belief in a God who carefully made the world and watches over it is one of the reasons Christians have desired to explore how the world works through the natural sciences.[44] If the world had no intrinsic order or design, then trying to explain how it works would be like trying to assemble a puzzle that was the result of an exploding toy factory. There would be no guarantee that rational explanations could even be discovered.

The allegation that religion contradicts science usually refers to religious beliefs that contradict the age of the universe or the theory of biological evolution. But once again, there are many theistic belief systems that explain only non-scientific truths, like the ultimate origin of reality itself, and do not try to replace the natural sciences that are focused on determining how reality functions. For example, the majority of Catholics, Eastern Orthodox, and mainline Protestant Christians accept the theory of evolution.[45] When I told a group of atheists in New York that I believed in evolution as well as the teachings of the Catholic Church, they questioned me not in a spirit of hostility but in a spirit of curiosity. These students were intrigued because they had never met a practicing Christian who did not deny the theory of evolution.

The Catholic Church teaches that the first chapters of the book of Genesis are primarily concerned with expressing theological truths, like that God created the world and man's immortal soul, and not scientific truths about the earth's physical history.[46] As Cardinal Caesar Baronius is reported to have said, "The Bible teaches us how to go to heaven, not how the heavens go."

Bad Atheistic Attitude #2: "Religion is just a product of geography."

Some atheists say that if you were born in India, you would be a Hindu, but since you were born in America, you are probably a Christian. Therefore, your religion has little to do with objective truth and depends only on where and when you were born. But just because someone is born in a place where they fail to discover the right answer about life's important questions does not mean there is no right answer. This goes for any kind of truth claim.

If you were born in the year 1713 as opposed to the year 2013, you probably would have supported the enslavement of native Africans. If you were born in 2013 B.C., you probably would have denied the Earth revolved around the sun. If you were born in modern North Korea, you probably would believe that democracy was evil. But none of these facts proves that slavery is moral, the sun revolves around the Earth, or that dictators are a great idea. All they prove is that large numbers of people can be wrong.

For all of our political, scientific, and ethical beliefs we would say that even if other people disagree with them, and do not live in places that teach these beliefs as truths, that does not mean these beliefs are false. We can put forward rational arguments to defend these beliefs and then say that those other cultures who disagree are simply mistaken. If we can do this for disputed scientific, political, and ethical beliefs, then why not say we can put forward rational arguments for religious beliefs that are not universally believed but are nonetheless true?

Bad Atheistic Attitude #3: "All religion is a 'God of the gaps' fallacy."

If our argument for God is that he explains what is currently unexplainable in the universe, then once science does explain a mystery (whether it's the cause of lightning or the complexity in the human cell), then it will have erased part of our evidence for God. As the Lutheran pastor and Holocaust victim Dietrich Bonheoffer once wrote,

[H]ow wrong it is to use God as a stop-gap for the in-completeness of our knowledge. If in fact the frontiers of knowledge are being pushed further and further back (and that is bound to be the case), then God is being pushed back with them, and is therefore con-tinually in retreat.[47]

However, atheists should not presume that "gaps" are the only evidence a theist can muster. The philosophical argu-ments from necessity, first cause, design, and morality don't start from what we don't know and say, "God must have done it." Instead, they start from what we *do know* and conclude that God is the best explanation for certain features of the universe we observe.

For example, the kalām cosmological argument (see chap-ters nine and ten) uses philosophical and scientific evidence to demonstrate the non-religious truth that the universe began to exist from nothing. Then the argument joins that evidence with the philosophical truth "Whatever begins to exist has a cause for its existence." It follows logically from these two known truths that a cause brought the universe into existence.

An atheist may claim at this point that the theist is saying, "I don't know how the universe was caused to exist, therefore God did it" and thus is still committing the God-of-the-gaps fallacy. However, the theist doesn't reason this way. Instead, he reasons about what it means to be a "cause of the universe" and arrives at the conclusion that a being like God is the best answer. This is similar to the reasoning a scientist might use if he discovered the ruins of an ancient civilization on the moon and concluded that aliens existed. The theist arrives at the logical conclusion that the cause of space and time cannot be bound by those things, and thus the first cause must have the divine properties of eternal, immaterial existence.

The God-of-the-gaps objection also seems to commit an equivalent "science-of-the-gaps" fallacy, which presupposes that *any question* about *anything* can be filled in with the answer, "Science knows or will know some day." But this seems to rule out theistic explanations right from the start. For example, many atheists say they would believe God exists if a Christian could perform some publicly verifiable miracle, or if God appeared to everyone on Earth at the same time. But consider the following exchange:

> **Theist:** Look, a giant being proclaiming to be God just resurrected every man named Brian and caused them all to sing "Don't Stop Believin'," by Journey.

> **Atheist:** Well, one day science will be able explain this supposed miracle. Maybe there is a natural principle that explains it, or an alien species that can perform this feat using advanced technology. Ancient people used to be impressed by thunder just as we are impressed by this event. If we say this happened because God did it . . . well . . . that doesn't explain anything!

Since it is restricted to explaining the natural world, science can't answer every claim about reality. If there is a supernatural world, it is beyond the means of science to explore it. But if supernatural proofs for God are always dismissed in this way, then no evidence could falsify atheism, and atheism would be as unprovable as the religious beliefs it wants to criticize.

What's wrong with arguments?

If even miracles can be considered "God-of-the-gaps" reasons insufficient to prove that God exists, then what reasons could the theist offer for belief in God? That is why the proofs for God in this book focus on major aspects of reality, like the evidence of design in the universe or the presence of moral truths, which would be nearly impossible for aliens to cause but would be expected if God exists. Atheists may yet reply, "Stop with the philosophy and show me the hard evidence for God's existence." But what is so bad about using philosophical proofs to show that basic facts about the world are true? After all, philosophers use complex arguments to demonstrate truths about free will, the reality of the external world, and the nature of time and space. Most ordinary people believe in these things because they experience them, while philosophers put forward complex arguments in order to defend the same truths.

For example, most people who are not exposed to an undergraduate philosophy class will tend to believe in free will, or the idea that human beings can choose to act in certain ways. Many philosophers reject free will and say that human beings are completely determined by factors like genetics and environment and can no more choose to act or not act than a can of Coca-Cola can choose to fizz or not fizz.[48] Those philosophers who defend genuine free will (also called libertarian free will) tend to use sophisticated arguments to make their case.[49] But I don't think philosophers would consider someone to be *irrational* because he believes in free will without studying the complex arguments that are used to defend the idea. For most people it just seems obvious they can freely choose to do or not do certain things. The arguments merely serve to confirm this basic belief.

If something as basic as the existence of free will can be confirmed via philosophical debate, then why not take the same approach with the existence of God? Most people believe in God without studying complex arguments, but those arguments can serve to objectively prove the validity of the faith they personally experience. We will examine arguments for the existence of God in part three. But, before doing so, we must see that atheism can be considered "true" only insofar as it makes a claim about the world: specifically, the claim "There is no God." So even if the theist had no arguments for the existence of God (and hang tight, because we're going to look at several), this would not show that atheism was true. To do that, the atheist will have to make arguments to show that God does not exist—arguments we will consider in the following chapters.

PART II

Should I Be an Atheist?

3

Is Atheism True?

There are two words that can instantly set my wife and me against each other: *Santa Claus*. If we are blessed with children in the future, should we tell them the traditional story about an omniscient man in red who dispenses gifts at Christmas? Laura thinks that it's a fun, magical part of childhood that causes no real harm. I think encouraging belief in a mythical figure comes perilously close to lying to children. Even worse, what if our child grows up and decides that God is just a made-up story like Santa?

Some atheists see God as no different from Santa Claus. There's no real evidence for either one, they say; and since no one feels obligated to prove that Santa Claus does not exist, why should anyone feel obligated to prove that God does not exist? The lack of evidence is proof enough.

No Evidence = No God

One of the most entertaining debates on the existence of God I've ever seen was the 2003 debate between biologist Lewis Wolpert and philosopher William Lane Craig.[50] Craig offered five arguments for the existence of God, including the kalām cosmological argument, the fine-tuning argument, the argument from objective moral values, the argument from personal experience, and the argument from the Resurrection of Christ. After he made these arguments, the following exchange took place:

Wolpert: A tiny bit of evidence would be a good beginning.
Moderator: He's offered you evidence.

> **Wolpert:** Oh, that's not evidence!
> **Craig:** Certainly, that's more than a tiny bit of evidence . . .
> **Wolpert:** Noooooo!
> **Craig:** . . . that God exists.
> **Wolpert:** That's total speculation!

Wolpert said that although no argument could convince him that God exists, sufficient "evidence" could convince him that theism was true. Of course, what Wolpert meant by "evidence" was empirical evidence: that which can be observed with the five senses. This presupposes the idea that unless there is empirical evidence for something, then that thing can't be proven to exist. But consider the following three examples.

Beyond the reach of science

The *existence of other minds* is not proven by direct scientific evidence alone. The mind, which is a collection of immaterial thoughts, cannot be observed like the brain, which is a three-pound lump of tissue that resides in your skull (though observing the brain will require surgery or dissection). Since I can't observe other people's thoughts, I must *assume* that they actually have thoughts and therefore have a mind like I do. Only with this unscientific assumption can I believe that they have a mind and aren't just sophisticated robots or mental illusions.

Secondly, the *existence of moral truths* such as "It is wrong to cause suffering simply to increase suffering in the world" cannot be proven scientifically. These statements are also not true by definition like the statement "All triangles have three sides." The only part science plays in proving this particular statement is true is by telling us what suffering is like and how it occurs. Science does *not* tell us if (or when) suffering should not be caused.[51]

Finally, the *existence of abstract objects* cannot be proven scientifically. As Jim Holt writes in the *New York Times*, although most mathematicians are atheists, the majority of them still believe in heaven. Here's what they mean: If you erased everything in the universe except for forty-seven particles, would numbers like forty-eight still exist even though there could never be forty-eight of anything? According to Holt, most mathematicians think numbers would still exist, but instead of existing in the physical universe these numbers and mathematical objects exist in an abstract "heavenly" realm.[52] Detection of these real but abstract objects does not use the scientific method but instead uses a kind of "extrasensory perception," or intuition. As Holt concludes, "You might say that mathematicians are no strangers to belief in the unseen."[53]

Other minds, moral truths, and abstract objects cannot be proven with science, yet most people, including atheists, agree they exist. So an atheist can only say, "There is no evidence for God" if he narrowly restricts the word *evidence* to mean direct, empirical evidence. Of course, there is no empirical evidence or scientific experiment that can prove the belief that all true beliefs must be validated with the scientific method! This is a philosophical viewpoint called *scientism*, and it is ultimately self-defeating.[54]

A universe that looks godless

Some atheists argue that God does not exist simply because the universe seems like the kind of place we would expect if there was no God. Nicholas Everitt, in his book *The Non-existence of God,* makes what he calls an "argument from scale." He claims that if God existed, then the universe would not be billions of years old and billions of light years across.

He says that "given the central role of humanity, what would be the point of a universe which came into existence and then existed for unimaginable aeons without the presence of the very species that supplied its rationale?"[55] I empathize with Everitt that the immensity of the universe does make humans, supposedly God's crowning achievement, look pretty insignificant. But looks can be deceiving.

After all, the inefficiency of creating a grand universe would be a problem only for a being that is limited in time and resources. For example, after I completed my graduate studies I drove across the country without stopping, because I didn't have a lot of time or money to spare and needed to get back to a regular job as soon as possible. But if I wasn't starting a job for six months and had just received a large inheritance, I might have gone on a long, scenic trip instead. In the same way, since God has unlimited time and resources, he has no problem making a grand cosmos for human beings. It's not as if God "loses track of us" in the expansive universe he created.

Moreover, the human brain is the most complex thing in the universe, so why not think that God made a grand universe for these brains to explore? Who hasn't been out in the middle of nowhere at night and just looked at the stars? I think billions of years of cosmic evolution were worth it for a view like that.

Moreover, how does Everitt know with such confidence that God would *not* create a world like ours? Suppose God made a universe with only our solar system in it. Would the typical atheist think, in contrast, that such a world proves God exists? He might just as plausibly argue that if God existed, surely he would have created something grander. A small and simple universe, he might argue, is precisely what we would expect if it simply popped into existence from nothing, without a cause. As C. S. Lewis put it, "We treat God as the policeman in the story treated the suspect; whatever he does will be used in evidence against him."[56]

A planet that looks godless

An atheist might also argue that our planet looks godless, because if God existed, why are there so many different religions and so many people who don't believe in him? If God existed, would we even need books and arguments to defend him?

This objection assumes that God would not have morally sufficient reasons for allowing false religions—and even atheism—to exist. One reason may be that he does not want to override our free will. If your parents monitored you with security cameras everywhere you went, it is unlikely you would ever develop a genuine desire to be good or please them. If God made his existence just as obvious, we might behave out of fear of punishment, not for the joy of doing good in order to please God and fulfill our purpose in life.[57]

Or, if God made his existence obvious, it's possible humans might resent him and actually choose to not worship him. The late Christopher Hitchens once said that even if God existed he would not worship him because such a being would, in his mind, differ little from an earthly dictator.[58] If God constantly watched over us from the sky like a towering Goliath, this might only reinforce the attitude held by people like Hitchens that God has put us in a police state.

Finally, this "divine hiddenness" gives believers the opportunity to lead other people to God, which would be impossible if God's existence were as obvious as the noonday sun.[59] The philosopher Richard Swinburne writes:

> The agnosticism of the agnostic also makes possible a great good for the religious believer. It allows the

believer to have the awesome choice of helping or not helping the agnostic to understand who is the source of his existence and of his ultimate well-being (helping the agnostic not merely by verbal preaching but by an example of what living a religious life is like).[60]

Absence of evidence and evidence of absence

Sam Harris is so indignant about the irrationality of belief in God that he wonders why we even need to debate atheism at all. He says "Atheism is not a philosophy; it is not even a view of the world; it is simply an admission of the obvious. In fact, 'atheism' is a term that should not even exist. No one ever needs to identify himself as a 'non-astrologer' or a 'non-alchemist.'"[61] But Harris's attempt to lump theism together with other false beliefs won't succeed, because he still needs an argument to show that the proposition "God exists" is false.

Yes, there are no "non-astrologers" or "non-alchemists." That is because those of us who deny these things just say we believe in psychology and chemistry instead. But how would the atheist fill in the following statement: "I don't believe in God, I believe in _____?" He can't fill it in with "science," because God exists outside of the realm of experimental science.[62] There is no science whose methods, when used properly, show God does not exist. An atheist must use principles in philosophy in order not only to refute theism but to prove atheism as well. Atheism has a burden of proof that is not discharged by saying, "Well, it's just obvious that my view is right."

But what about the atheist who says, "I can't prove that leprechauns don't exist, but the failure to prove they do exist gives us good reason to say leprechauns don't exist—and the same is true for God"?

To answer this argument, let's consider another statement: "Aliens exist." Is this statement true or false? Based on my knowledge of the world, I would honestly say, "I don't know." I've never seen a UFO nor had the experience of being abducted by aliens, but other people claim to have experienced those things. Even if all of those experiences were debunked and disproved, it would still be possible that aliens existed somewhere in the universe. Therefore, I must be agnostic when it comes to the question "Do aliens exist?" I cannot give a definite answer.

What is the lesson to be learned? *Absence of evidence is not necessarily evidence of absence.* Just because there is no evidence for the existence of X, it doesn't follow that X does not exist.

Proving a negative

Is it even possible to disprove the existence of God? Atheist critics will sometimes claim, "You can't prove a universal negative." Mathematician John Paulos uses a colorful example to make this point:

> No matter how absurd the existence claim (there exists a dog who speaks perfect English out of its rear end), we can't look everywhere and check everything in order to assert with absolute confidence that there's no entity having the property.[63]

But, contra Paulos, it *is* possible to disprove the existence of some beings. I would say the proposition "Santa Claus exists" is false. How do I know this? First, there is no good evidence that he exists. Second, if Santa existed, then good evidence would be available all around us. We would expect to locate Santa's workshop at the North Pole. We would expect parents to rely on Santa and not place presents under the tree themselves. We would expect NORAD to track Santa's sleigh on radar. In this case, absence of evidence *is* evidence of absence because if Santa did exist, then we would reasonably expect to see certain evidence of his existence. When we look for Santa Claus in places where we expect to find him, he is not there. Therefore, we can say he doesn't exist.

To make a similar argument against God, an atheist would have to demonstrate that if God existed then the world would look a certain way, and since it doesn't look that way, God does not exist. But as we saw earlier, the examples that atheists prefer (like a small universe, abundant miracles, and unanimous belief in God) would not automatically be expected if God did exist. The absence of these things does not show there is no God. In Part III we will see that there are in fact features of the universe—like its coming into being from nothing, and the existence of objective moral truth—that we would expect if God existed, and their presence serves to confirm that God does exist.

An atheist might object that proving Santa Claus does not exist is not the same as proving a universal negative like "God does not exist," since we can check the North Pole to see if Santa is there but we can't search an entire universe in order to prove there is no God in it. But we do know that there are no "square circles" or "shapeless colors" anywhere in the universe, since those things are impossible and could not exist at all. So it is possible to prove a "universal negative," and arguments that try to describe God as a kind of logical contradiction that could not possibly exist will be examined in chapter five.

The Celestial Teapot

At this point, an atheist may respond, "So are you saying that along with God you believe that there are unicorns, dragons, and celestial teapots? Just because something can't be disproved doesn't mean it exists." The "celestial teapot" is an example from Bertrand Russell, and is a good example to help understand this objection. Russell once said:

> I ought to call myself an agnostic; but, for all practical purposes, I am an atheist. I do not think the existence of the Christian God any more probable than the existence of the gods of Olympus or Valhalla. To take another illustration: nobody can prove that there is not between the Earth and Mars a china teapot revolving in an elliptical orbit, but nobody thinks this sufficiently likely to be taken into account in practice. I think the Christian God just as unlikely.[64]

An atheist may use this analogy to argue that even though he can't disprove the existence of the celestial teapot, that doesn't mean he has to take the teapot seriously. He could claim that no one believes in the teapot because there's no good reason to think such an object exists. This is enough evidence to justify being an "a-teapotist," or a person who says celestial teapots don't exist and isn't just agnostic about the question—as I am not agnostic about the existence of Santa Claus.

Russell's teapot seems compelling until we replace it with a less absurd example. Let's instead consider the question, "Is there an invisible alien probe orbiting the sun between Earth and Mars that provides information about us to potential invaders?" Unlike the celestial teapot, the idea of a secret alien probe is not utterly implausible, even though there is no evidence for it. Though they might be skeptical, most people would not say with total confidence that such a thing couldn't exist. This shows that we reject Russell's teapot not because there is no evidence for it (because otherwise we would have the same dismissive attitude toward the invisible alien probe), but because of its sheer implausibility: Russell's example violates what we know about teapots and their tendency to stay on Earth.[65]

At this point, the theist should be careful to not make an argument like this one: "Atheism is doomed to failure because no one can possibly prove that God does not exist. Therefore, theism stands undefeated and is the most rational position to hold." This is called the argument from ignorance. It's like someone saying, "No one has proven there is no Loch Ness monster by draining Loch Ness and searching every inch of it. Therefore there is a Loch Ness monster." But atheists can also be guilty of using the argument from ignorance in order to justify their beliefs. Compare the following two statements:

1. Since you can't prove God exists, that means atheism is true.
2. Since you can't disprove atheism, that means atheism is true.

These two statements appear identical, since proving God exists would disprove atheism. But as formulated in statement two, this line of reasoning commits the argument from ignorance. Failing to prove God exists does not entail that God does not exist. At best, the atheist could only say the following, "Since you can't prove God exists, that means *there is no objective reason* to say God exists." As atheist philosopher Kai Nielsen remarks, "Even if all the proofs for God's existence fail, it may be still be the case that God exists."[66]

Do we live in a Godless world?

Theist: So you call yourself an atheist?
Atheist: That's right.
T: Okay, what does it mean for you to be an atheist?

A: I just don't think God exists.

T: Okay, how do you know God does not exist?

A: Well, there's no evidence that God exists.

T: I would disagree with that, but let's say you're right. How would that show there isn't a God? Would you say that even if there is no credible evidence for aliens, it's still possible that aliens exist somewhere in the universe? Is it at least possible God exists?

A: Sure, it's possible, but the answer is probably no.

T: Isn't your view really agnosticism, or the view that we can't know if God exists?

A: Well, I don't think the terms matter. I just think if God existed then it would be obvious, and since it's not obvious, it's a safe bet to say God doesn't exist.

T: What do you think the universe would look like if God existed?

A: For starters, it would be a lot smaller. I mean, it's just a bunch of useless space where bacteria evolved for billions of years until we accidentally showed up. Even worse, the humans that evolved seem to create God to fulfill their own needs. I mean, they can't even agree on which God exists.

T: But how does any of this show there is no God? Let's look at each one of your examples. Yes, the universe is very large, but who's to say God would not want to create a large universe for us to enjoy? Haven't you ever heard lovers say they would "move the stars and the moon" for each other if they could? Well, God can, so I don't see the big deal.

A: But think about all the billions of years when nothing was happening. What a waste!

T: Are you the kind of kid who couldn't wait for Christmas and had to have presents right now?

A: Huh?

T: Just a joke. But what's wrong with God, who exists outside of time and is not constrained by it, taking a while to make humans? If that is a possible way for God to make the world, then how would that fact show he does not exist? Even Darwin said that the process of evolution provided "grandeur in this view of life." Plus I think the world also has features that make sense if there was a God, but I'll save that for later. What else shows there definitely isn't a God?

A: I think it's obvious the idea of God was something people came up with. Man created God in his image.

4

Did Man Invent God?

The ancient Greek philosopher Xenophanes claimed that the popular gods of his time, such as Zeus, were myths because they were clearly modeled after the appearances and moral weaknesses found in human beings. He claimed this was true for all mythic gods and wrote, "Ethiopians say that their gods are snub–nosed and black. . . . Thracians that they are pale and red-haired. . . . But if cows, horses and lions had hands or could paint and sculpture with their hands like humans, then the horses would represent the gods as horses and bullocks as bullocks, and they would create bodies in the same way as their own bodies."[67]

Xenophanes did believe there was "one god, greatest among gods and humans, like mortals neither in form nor in thought" that was not a mere projection.[68] However, contemporary atheists approach even this ideal conception of God with the attitude that he is a myth invented by humans.[69] So are there any good reasons to think atheism is true because God is just a made-up story?

God is just a trick of our brains

Some atheists claim that evolution had caused our brains to form beliefs that help us survive, regardless of whether or not they are true. For example, evolutionary psychologists might claim that the reason we fear snakes more than cars (even though cars kill many more people than snakes) is because for millions of years our ancestors who feared snakes were less likely to be killed by them. Over time, the population of humans without a fear of snakes died out (because they were bitten so much), and today the humans who are left are the descendants of those who feared snakes and thus lived to reproduce.

In the same way, evolutionary psychologists claim religious belief is the result of a survival mechanism gone overboard.[70] They say that our ancestors had an "overactive agency detection system" (or an OADS) that caused them to imagine things that didn't exist. An OADS was beneficial for ancient humans, because when they overreacted to imaginary tigers in rustling bushes they were less likely to be eaten when there was a real tiger. This OADS was passed on to modern humans, who imagine a God exists who isn't actually there.

However, even some atheists criticize evolutionary psychology as being untestable. Biologist Jerry Coyne writes in his book *Why Evolution Is True,* "Imaginative reconstructions of how things might have evolved are not science; they are stories."[71] Our collective brains fooling us into thinking God exists is one possible story to account for religious belief, but another possible story is that we "detect" God, since he has given us an instinct to find and worship him. Both of these stories explain religious belief, and the atheist would have to provide an additional argument to justify preferring his story over the theistic one. As Michael Shermer, the editor of *Skeptic* magazine, writes in his book *The Believing Brain,* "Whether or not belief in God is hardwired into our brains, the question remains: does God actually exist?"[72]

Fooled by the God helmet

If evolutionary psychology is unable to show that God is a trick of our brains, perhaps neuroscience can. Canadian neuroscientist Michael Persinger claimed that magnets within a special helmet could cause some people to believe that another person, or even God himself, was present in a room with them (Richard Dawkins tried on the helmet and felt no extra presence).

In 2004, a team of researchers in Sweden attempted to replicate Persinger's results and discovered a problem with his original study: Some test subjects experienced presences even when the helmet's magnets were turned off. They concluded that magnetic fields have little to no effect in stimulating religious experiences—instead people's *predisposition* to religious beliefs coincided with their observations of an external presence in the room. This would explain why an atheist like Richard Dawkins did not feel any presence when wearing the helmet.[73]

Furthermore, our experience of an external world can be simulated in a laboratory using virtual-reality goggles. But this fact would not show that the external world didn't exist. The self-described skeptical atheist John Shook writes:

> If science did try to conclude logically that nothing divine could be involved [in a religious experience], only because it could induce religious experiences by natural methods, that logical argument could be equally applied to human experiences of everything else. Could a powerful brain-science figure out how to induce a visual experience of your friend? If so, does that henceforth mean that your friend never really exists when you think you have contact with her by seeing her?[74]

I believe in one less God than you

Some atheist critics say, "When it comes to the extinct gods of mythology like Zeus or Thor or Quetzalcoatl, we're *all* atheists. I just believe in one less god than you." The roots of this argument go back to the journalist H. L. Mencken, who described something he called the "graveyard of the gods":

> Where is the graveyard of dead gods? What lingering mourner waters their mounds? There was a time when Jupiter was the king of the gods, and any man who doubted his puissance was ipso facto a barbarian and an ignoramus. But where in all the world is there a man who worships Jupiter today?[75]

This argument tries to show that theists are hypocrites because they accept their own version of God while rejecting every other religion's version of God. But just because *some* conceptions of God are fictional, how does it follow that *all* conceptions of God are fiction? Ancient philosophers like Plato and Aristotle did not believe in anthropomorphic deities like Zeus and Hercules, but they did believe in a supreme being, or god, that created all of reality.[76]

Another problem with this argument is its reasoning, "Some of X are bad, therefore all of X are bad." Imagine an anarchist saying that since everyone rejects *some* forms of government, whether it is communism, feudal monarchy, or direct democracy, therefore "All of us are anarchists. I just reject one more form of government than you do." No, the anarchist must prove that no governments should exist at all, not simply that most forms of government are no longer used today.

I could understand an atheist's frustration if modern theists believed in a God exactly like Zeus except in trivial ways— if theists said something like, "God exists and Zeus doesn't because God wears a hat and Zeus doesn't." But the theist doesn't reason in this way. Rather, the theist simply believes that a God exists. Then, through acts of reason or revelation, he narrows the scope of his investigation and chooses to believe in the God that most probably exists. The atheist can't just trot out the graveyard of dead gods and goddesses and say that an infinite, personal, perfect God necessarily belongs there as well. He must provide evidence that the God of classical theism has suffered the same fate as his mostly forgotten mythological competitors.

God is a silly idea, therefore he doesn't exist

In 2005, high school student Bobby Henderson wrote a letter to the Kansas state school board, opposing the board's decision to require public high schools to teach the theory of intelligent design. Intelligent design (ID) uses scientific evidence to show that certain features in the natural world are best explained by the existence of an "intelligent designer." In court, ID advocates frequently deny they know the identity of the intelligent designer and even go so far as to say that the designer could be an ancient alien race. However, in private, most ID advocates seem to believe that the designer is the Judeo-Christian God.[77]

In his letter, Henderson demanded that, should ID (which he saw as a religious belief) be taught as a theory of biological origins, then his belief in the Flying Spaghetti Monster—an all-powerful creature composed of spaghetti, two meatballs, and two protruding eyes—should be taught as well. The Flying Spaghetti Monster (or FSM) and its accompanying parody religion, Pastafarianism, quickly became Internet phenomena. Henderson received a grant to fund his book, *The Gospel of the Flying Spaghetti Monster*, which claims, among other things, that the world was created 5,000 years ago with the appearance of a much older age, that the decline of pirates and the rise in global sea levels is evidence of the FSM, and that gravity is nothing more than the FSM's "noodly appendages" pushing people down.[78] Atheists have seized upon the FSM, as well as related ideas like invisible pink unicorns, to argue that religious faith should be ridiculed like these ideas are ridiculed. So how should the theist respond to an argument like this?

First, theists must resist the urge to say, "That's stupid" and ignore FSM arguments. People like Henderson would simply respond, "I agree it's stupid, but how is your belief in a traditional God any less stupid?" Just because the arguments are silly does not mean they do not have a serious point. Instead, we should consider the FSM to be an *argument from parody*. This argument can be broken down into the following premises:

1. Our quasi-religion (like the Gospel of the Flying Spaghetti Monster) is silly and unfounded and therefore false.
2. Other religions are just as silly and unfounded as our religion.
3. Therefore, other religions are false.

The key premise to challenge in this argument is premise two, or the idea that other religions are just as silly as Pastafarianism. It is beyond the scope of this book to defend biblical Christianity, which seems to be the main target of parody attack. Instead, we can ask whether belief in the God of the philosophers is as silly as belief in the Flying Spaghetti Monster. Part three of this book presents cosmological, design, moral, and personal experience arguments for the existence of God. Although these arguments may not convince everyone, most philosophers don't consider them on an intellectual par with the Gospel of the Flying Spaghetti Monster. Instead, Pastafarianism seems to rely on *ad hoc explanations*.

Ad hoc explanations occur when a person starts with a conclusion he wants to be true and then finds reasons to support his conclusion. When Pastafarians jokingly claim that because modern people are taller than previous generations this proves the FSM exists (because there are now too many people for the FSM to hold down with his "invisible noodly appendages," and so they grow taller), they are using an ad hoc explanation because there is no logical connection between people's height and "invisible noodly appendages." The explanation is simply made up to fit the facts and could easily be changed if the facts were different. For example, if people were shorter than their ancestors, this might show that there are too many people for the FSM to stretch and make taller via his invisible noodly appendages.

The FSM argument from parody claims that all other religions use similar ridiculous ad hoc explanations that should be rejected just as the FSM explanations are rejected. But theists don't start with the belief that God exists and add irrelevant details about the world in order to prove it. Instead, they follow facts about the world to their logical conclusion that God exists. The fact that the world doesn't have to exist implies that the world exists because of something that has to exist. The fact that there is an objective moral law implies there is an objective moral lawgiver. Theists don't start with God and then manufacture evidence that has nothing to do with his existence but instead follow the evidence in the natural world that points to a being that exists beyond it.

Defending what Mom told us

A critic could object that most theists first believe in God for emotional reasons when they are gullible children. Only after that emotional assent do believers seek logical reasons that justify their belief. Some clever atheists will quote St. Paul who said, "When I was a child, I spoke like a child, I thought like a child, I reasoned like a child; when I became a man, I

gave up childish ways."[79] The implication made by these atheists is that faith in God is a childish belief we should simply
"give up."

But this argument, as well as Paul's admonishment, is an
indictment of the *psychology* of believers; it does not show
that the believer's *argument* is ad hoc. Such a pattern of reasoning does not disprove religious belief any more than it
would disprove the rationalization we have for other beliefs
that originated in childhood. After all, most of us believe the
Holocaust happened because our parents or teachers told us
about it when we were children. As adults, perhaps if we are
challenged by Holocaust deniers, we might seek out reasons
to justify or deepen our belief that the Holocaust occurred.
Those reasons—as long as they are logical and are not ad
hoc—are not invalidated because we first simply believed
what we were taught as children. St. Paul even told Timothy
to "continue in what you have learned and have firmly believed, knowing from whom you learned it."[80] If the source
of a belief is reliable, then it is irrelevant at what age we
believe it.

Parody can be a powerful rhetorical device, but we should
not reject an argument just because someone can make its
conclusion look silly. If we found objects on the moon that
appeared to be designed, it would be absurd for someone to
say that they must be natural objects, because any reference
to alien designers could lead us to believe that the aliens are
made of spaghetti. Since spaghetti aliens are a silly idea, should
we believe there can be no aliens at all? We should just accept
that the alien designers exist and then argue later (maybe at
a local pub) about what they're made of. Likewise, we can
use philosophical arguments to show that a cosmic creator of
some sort exists. After that, we can debate whether or not this
creator is made of spaghetti.[81]

God as a magic trick

Some critics maintain that saying God created the universe, or morality, or anything else, doesn't tell us anything. They say that making God the cause or source of things is no better than saying, "It was magic," because we don't know how, or by what process, God created the world.

But this confuses the role of explanations. Richard Swinburne says that there are two kinds of explanation: scientific and personal.[82]

For example, let's say I go outside in the morning to find my car, which was previously dusty, is now clean. I might ask, What explains my car being clean? In this case, a scientific explanation is that water dissolves dust and has certain physical properties that cause it to evaporate off my car, leaving the car clean. The other explanation is that someone washed my car. Both explanations validly answer the question "Why is my car clean?" Even if we lack the complete causal or scientific explanation of an event, that doesn't mean the explanation is invalid (especially if we have a compelling personal explanation).

In 1971, *Humanist* magazine published a rebuttal of astrology, the pseudoscience that claims people's personality traits can be predicted based on the alignment at the time of their birth of objects in outer space such as the moon.[83] One hundred eighty-six scientists signed the rebuttal. But Carl Sagan, who has become something of a cult celebrity in the atheist community, refused to sign it, because even though he did not believe in astrology he did not consider its lack of a mechanism to be enough to refute the entire field. Sagan writes, "The statement stressed that we can think of no mechanism by which astrology could work. This is certainly a relevant point but by itself it's unconvincing."[84] Sagan goes on to remind his readers that the theory of continental drift had no mechanism to explain itself when it was first proposed, but it still turned out to be a correct geological theory.

Lack of a causal explanation does not mean we should give up a valid personal explanation. For example, when a magician pulls a rabbit out of a seemingly empty hat, we may not know *how* he did it, but we certainly know *he* did it. Similarly, if God's existence is demonstrated and his personal intentions explain the world around us, there is no harm in accepting that conclusion even though we can't provide a step-by-step explanation of how God functions in the universe.

But, of course, the critic will object that while we're familiar with magicians and understand how they perform illusions through trickery, we're unfamiliar with God, so he is a bad explanation. Swinburne's reply is that of the two kinds of explanations, scientific and personal, scientific ones require the application of natural laws. Since there were no natural laws prior to the beginning of the universe, only a personal explanation will adequately account for the universe and its various features.[85]

Just because God has never been observed empirically in a laboratory experiment does not make God a bad explanation for the universe. What would make God a bad explanation would be if the idea of God were illogical and so could not explain the universe even if he did exist. We'll examine those kinds of arguments for atheism in the next chapter.

Did man invent God?

T: What else shows there definitely isn't a God?
A: Well, look at the humans he created. I mean, *you* don't believe in most of the ancient gods that people used to worship, like Zeus. You are an atheist like me. I just believe in one less god than you.

T: Hold on a minute. I think I have good reasons for not believing in Zeus, as well as good reasons for believing in an infinite God of the philosophers. How does it follow that just because I don't believe in some gods, therefore all gods don't exist?

A: But just think about it. Doesn't it make more sense to say that man created God in his image so he would not feel lonely in the universe? That explains why every culture has a different idea of what God is like.

T: Even if human beings came up with the idea of God to fulfill their needs, that wouldn't show God did not exist. Imagine a primitive tribal chief telling children to stay out of the ocean because a huge monster with razor sharp teeth that can smell them a mile away will eat them. The chief just made it up, but such a creature does exist: We call them sharks. Just because the source of an idea is a bad one doesn't prove the idea is false.

A: But doesn't it just seem like God is something that was made up so people would feel better?

T: This argument could be applied to atheism as well. I could say people made up atheism so that they would feel better and not have to worry about pleasing an all-good God. That might be true, but it wouldn't show God exists. In order to do that I'd need to show you evidence God exists. Likewise, I won't become an atheist unless you can prove atheism is true.

A: But how can I prove that there isn't a God anywhere in the whole universe?

T: In order to show God could not exist, an atheist would have to show that the idea of God wasn't just weird, like flying purple people-eaters, but impossible, like a married bachelor or a square circle. A God who is contradictory could not possibly exist, and therefore atheism would be true.

A: Okay. I'm willing to give that a shot.

5

Is God a Contradiction?

When I was a senior in high school, we used to play a joke on the incoming freshmen. Most of the classrooms were in a circular two-story building, and when a student would ask where something was, we would reply, "It's in the first corner of the circle." As the student walked away from us, we would wonder how long it would take for him to figure out that a circle with corners is a logical contradiction, and so our directions were meaningless. Likewise, the only way to show that God could not possibly exist would be to show that the idea of God involves a logical contradiction. If an atheist can demonstrate that the idea of God is as nonsensical as a circle with a corner, then he will have proven atheism true.

Can it be done? First, we should provide a definition of God; then we can examine the major types of arguments that try to show that definition involves a logical contradiction.

Understanding the argument

One useful but incomplete definition of God comes from the *Baltimore Catechism*: "When we say that God is the Supreme Being we mean that He is above all creatures, the self-existing and infinitely perfect Spirit. I am the First, and I am the Last, and besides me there is no God."[86] Because God is so beyond us, we can understand him only in indirect ways. We can know what God is *not*, for example: God exists beyond space, so he is not made of matter (the stuff that occupies space). God is morally perfect, so he does not sin. God is beyond time, so he has no beginning or end.

We can understand God in a positive way as the perfection of goods we are familiar with here on earth. For example, we can say that God is perfect love, or that God has perfect knowledge. St. Thomas Aquinas argued that God is the simplest being imaginable: not divided into any parts but merely one perfect "act" of being that has no potential. So God's knowledge is actually his goodness, which is his power, which is his justice, and so on. Thanks to this lack of division, God has no separate parts, so he can't contradict himself in any way, and thus the argument from logical contradiction cannot succeed. But even if the critic were to reject this Thomistic understanding of God, we shall see that even a definition of God that lists separate attributes does not entail a contradiction.

Atheists typically make either single-property arguments or multiple-property arguments from contradiction against the existence of God. Single-property arguments claim that if God must have a certain property, and that property is contradictory by its own nature, then God is also contradictory and does not exist. For example, some atheists claim that no being could be all-powerful or all-knowing, and therefore if God must have one of these properties, then he does not exist. Multiple-property arguments claim that if God must have certain properties that conflict with one another, then God does not exist. For example, some atheists claim God cannot be both all-just and all-merciful.

Let's first examine some of the single properties God must possess to see if they involve contradictions.

Omniscience

When we say that God is omniscient, or all-knowing, we mean he knows all true statements and does not accept as true anything that is false. He knows how many hairs are on your head and every moment a sparrow drops to the ground.[87] He even knows more complex truths, right down to the number, location, and activity of every sub-atomic particle in the universe. God knows not just everything that is presently true but every real thing about the past (such as how many steps Alexander the Great took in his lifetime) and even every real thing about the future (such as whether you will finish reading this book).[88]

Some critics contend that God is not all-knowing, because he doesn't know what it is like for God to be afraid, even though you and I know what it is like to be afraid.[89] However, God's inability to know imperfect emotions does not count against his omniscience. God knows how *I* feel when *I* am afraid, but God simply cannot be afraid, because such a condition is meaningless. God is a perfect being who cannot suffer pain, loss, or any diminishment, so he can never be afraid. Since the statement "God is afraid" (and others like it) is meaningless, it can't be true. If it can't be true, it can't be known. And if it can't be known, then it can't contradict God's omniscience, which involves his knowledge of only all real or potentially real things.

Omnipotence

Omnipotence means that God has infinite power, or God is able to do anything that is possible.[90] Some critics respond to this definition with the age-old challenge "Can God make a stone so heavy that even he could not lift it?" Fortunately, Aquinas helps us answer this apparent paradox.

He says that being omnipotent means God has all the power to do anything that is *logically possible*. God cannot do something that is logically impossible, because such a task is meaningless. God's making a stone he can't lift is as nonsensical as God committing a sin or God creating a square circle.[91] God can't do these "things" because they are contradictions that violate his perfect nature. Aquinas writes, "To sin is to fall

short of a perfect action; hence to be able to sin is to be able
to fall short in action, which is repugnant to omnipotence."[92]
God can do anything, but some actions are meaningless contradictions that don't even count as "things" to be included
in a set of actions we call "anything that can be done." St.
Augustine says that God "cannot do some things for the very
reason that he is omnipotent."[93]

God can do anything that is doable, but since things like
square circles or perfect beings who act imperfectly (such as
creating objects they cannot control) involve contradictions,
they do not fall under the category of "anything that is doable." Therefore, God's omnipotence is not contradicted by
his inability to actualize these impossible states of affairs.

Omnipresence

While on the campus of Northern Arizona University
conducting an evangelism outreach, I met a student who presented this objection to God: "God just doesn't make sense.
I mean, how can he be everywhere? Is he like an invisible
gas or something?" The attribute of omnipresence means that
God is always fully present at every location in the universe.
This does not mean that God is identical to everything in the
universe and thus "present" everywhere (which is called pantheism), nor does it mean he is dispersed through the universe
like a gas, because he exists beyond space and time. As I stated
earlier, God is not composed of separate parts, so he does not
have to be extended in space or time. So how can God be
everywhere and also exist beyond everything?

An analogy might help. Imagine a security guard who
observes an entire mall through a closed circuit television
system. If there is a problem, he can radio to another guard
in any section of the mall to investigate. Thus, the guard is
"present" everywhere without being made up of the mall's

building materials. In an analogous way, God's omnipresence means that God can observe every part of the universe and he acts within all of it to change and sustain it. Now, all analogies fail to perfectly describe the incomprehensible essence of God. God doesn't "observe" the universe as you or I might observe goldfish in a tank. Rather, God is immediately aware of all that takes place in the universe because his knowledge of real things is unlimited and a part of his infinite nature.

Furthermore, God is able to both cause events to occur at any place in the universe and to sustain every part of the physical universe. Rather than being present in the universe by being made up of matter (which would make God an imperfect pantheistic being), God is present in the universe by sustaining and affecting every part of it according to his divine will.[94] But is omnipresence even logically possible? Atheist Theodore Drange writes:

> What sorts of things might be omnipresent, anyway? Perhaps a gravitational field would serve as an example. They would all appear to be items in a different category from persons, so to try to assimilate them would be to commit a category mistake. Persons can no more be omnipresent than they can be odd or even (in the mathematical sense).[95]

Drange's argument seems to assume that the only kinds of beings that can be persons are humans. But science fiction writers can conceive of computers being persons who exist in energy fields dispersed over computer lines or wireless networks. Drange hasn't provided us a reason to think that a mind without a body, that is consequently not limited in space like a human body is, could not be omnipresent. Of course, one could conceive of a mind without a body, such as an angel, that is not omnipresent. My point is that Drange has not given us a reason to think that a person, or a being with intentions and abilities, must exist in one particular spatial location.

Now let's examine some multiple-property arguments, which claim that God can't exist because two or more of his properties contradict one another.

Immaterial and eternal vs. personal

Some atheists claim that the idea of God as an immaterial person is contradictory, because the persons we know are all made of matter and all act in time. They say a person who lacks a body or exists outside of time wouldn't be a person at all and so would not exist. But this observation doesn't force us to conclude that all persons *must* be made of matter and exist in time. Let's examine the first objection that all persons must be material.

Some philosophers claim that everything we know about the mind, or an individual's collection of immaterial thoughts, makes it either identical to or causally dependent upon the brain. Since God is immaterial and thus has no brain, these philosophers argue that God cannot be a person, and so he does not exist. The theist can offer some examples to challenge that idea:

1. If the concept of a human being with free will is coherent, then a person can't merely be chemical reactions in a brain. If he were, then he could not freely choose a course of action any more than a rock at the mercy of gravity and friction can choose which way to roll down a hill. If humans are free, then they must have an "immaterial mind" that is the source of their free will that allows them to act without being completely determined by their biological functions.[96]

2. Our minds are able to think about things, but a clump of matter can't be "about" anything. For example, if our brains were just lumps of matter, then how could anything about frozen Antarctica be inside my brain cells, which have never been there? Atheistic philosopher Alex Rosenberg writes:

> Consciousness is just another physical process. So, it has as much trouble producing *aboutness* as any other physical process . . . it's got to be an illusion, since nothing physical can be about anything . . . the clumps of matter that constitute your conscious thoughts can't be about stuff either.[97]

As a result, Rosenberg rejects the idea that our "selves" really exist and argues that our consciousness is just an illusion. But if our self really is "real," then we have good evidence that our mind is not the same thing as our brain.

Since there is no reason to think that a person *must* have a body, and there are reasons to think that we are our minds and not just our brains, there is no contradiction in God being an immaterial mind that exists without a body. But if God is eternal and exists outside of time, then can he be a person? Persons move and think and make decisions all in the passage of time. But if God is outside of time, wouldn't that make him more like a frozen stained-glass window and not a reacting person with thoughts and feelings?

This objection assumes that persons must act a certain way. When we are asleep or incapacitated, we cannot act like a person, and yet we are still persons. We have an *intrinsic* capacity to act in a rational way, and God could be a person with those intrinsic capacities for all of eternity. Since God is omniscient, he doesn't have to think, reason, or change his

mind. He doesn't "react," because he already knows everything. God's capacities as a rational and moral being simply
exist in one timeless, perfect "moment" that does not progress
into anything else. God would know all truths in a timeless
way and would simply *be*.

One popular way to define time is "that which is used to
measure change." Without any change on God's part, there
would be no passage of time, and God would exist timelessly.
God may have, as part of his perfect nature, ordered himself
toward the creation of time-bound creatures even as he existed in a changeless and timeless state without the world.[98]

All-just vs. all-merciful

God's perfect goodness means that he is also infinitely
virtuous. God doesn't satisfy some list of virtues; rather, the
morally good behavior we recognize in the world flows from
God's perfect nature. God embodies perfect compassion, love,
tenderness, justice, wisdom, mercy, and every other virtue.
But don't some of these virtues contradict one another? After
all, part of justice involves giving someone the punishment he
deserves, while mercy involves giving someone less punishment than he deserves.

However, Christ's death on the cross satisfies the demands
of justice without contradicting God's merciful embrace of
sinners who don't deserve to spend eternity with such a perfect and holy being.[99]

An atheist might say I cannot invoke the Christian God
because I haven't shown that Christianity is true. That's a fair
point. But the Christian God shows that there exists at least
one conception of God who is all-just and all-merciful, and
so those two properties are not logically contradictory. The
Christian conception of God may not be the correct one, but
it is at least possible.

Perfect being vs. creator of the world

Drange also argues that God's perfection contradicts his being the creator of the universe, because God would have created the universe only because he lacked something, and if he lacked something then he would not be perfect. Such a being might be a very powerful supernatural creature or alien, but it wouldn't be God.

But Drange is wrong in presuming that God would only have created the universe out of some imperfection, such as loneliness or boredom—like an immature parent who has a child to fill a void in his life. If God is the perfection of virtues, including love and selflessness, then his creation is a logical result of his superabundant love and self-giving. He created the universe not for his good but for ours.[100] So, being the creator of the universe does not contradict God's perfection but in fact flows from it. *Because* God is perfect love, he gives being and life to his creation.

The reform of theology

This survey of God's attributes shows that the idea of God is not a contradiction.[101] Therefore, atheists have not demonstrated that it is impossible for God to exist. It's not surprising that many atheists express skepticism at these arguments from contradiction. Richard Carrier in his book *Sense and Goodness without God: a Defense of Metaphysical Naturalism*, writes:

> To be fair, most arguments from Incoherence, as they are called, are often frivolous. A typical example is the taunt "If God is all-powerful, can he make a rock so big even he can't lift it?" This is supposed to prove that omnipotence is illogical and therefore God (who is supposed to be omnipotent) doesn't exist. There are

many arguments like that. But I don't buy them. These are generally not valid, since any definition of god (or his properties) that is illogical can just be revised to be logical. So in effect, Arguments from Incoherence aren't really arguments for atheism, but for the reform of theology.[102]

So there is no good reason to think that God is a contradiction. But is there another way to defend the argument from contradiction? Yes. If God could be shown to contradict a fact about the world we know to be true, then God would have to be rejected in lieu of this already proven fact. For many atheists, the fact that evil and suffering exist shows God does not exist.

It is this well-known and powerful argument against the existence of God that we will consider in the next two chapters.

Does God make sense?

Atheist: Okay, I've got one for you. If God is all-powerful, then can he make a rock so big that not even he can lift it?

Theist: How original.

A: Excuse me?

T: I apologize—I was being snarky. I think you don't understand what it means to be all-powerful, or omnipotent. It doesn't mean God can do anything, it only means that God can do all logically possible things. Since God is perfect in his omnipotence, he can't make something that he can't control, like the rock in your example.

A: But it seems like there's a lot that a supposedly all-powerful God *can't* do. I can lie or steal, but since God is all-good, he can't do those things. So it turns out I'm more powerful than God: I can do things he can't. **T:** God isn't a super-powered man in the sky. He is perfection itself, and his power is not weakened because he can't be imperfect. Saying "God is weak" because God can't do something imperfect is like saying God is not omnipotent because he can't make a square circle. Of course he can't; such tasks are meaningless. **A:** Okay, but now think about this: How can God be all-knowing if he doesn't know what it's like to sin or make a mistake?

T: This is sort of like omnipotence. Saying God is all-knowing, or omniscient, just means that God knows all real or possibly real things. God knows how *I* feel when *I* sin or make a mistake, so he's not ignorant of what it means to be afraid or fallible. He knows them perfectly, even though he doesn't know what it's like for God to be those things. Since situations such as God being afraid are neither real nor even possibly real, then God's omniscience doesn't require him to know those contradictions.

A: This is hopeless. Anytime I try to show that God is contradictory, you just redefine him so he makes sense. **T:** But isn't that a good thing? If our beliefs don't make sense, shouldn't we try to fix them? Shouldn't we believe in a God who makes sense?

A: But you're just making up your definition of God as you go.

T: Not at all. I'm starting with the commonsensical view that God is the infinitely perfect source of being. How else would you even define God? It follows from what God is at his very essence that he would be unlimited in power, knowledge, and goodness.

A: Okay, the goodness one I can disprove.

T: How so?

A: Well, just look at the world around us. It doesn't seem very good to me.

6

Does Evil Disprove God?

I remember one time I got really mad with God. I was in high school, and my family was being crushed under the weight of a relative's mental illnesses. I went out into the driveway and looked up at the night sky and shouted, "Hey! I'm talking to you! Why do you let these things happen?" Silence. Then I got angrier. "Give me an answer! Get down here!" I burst into tears, and it was still quiet.

In hindsight, I was lucky. The evil and suffering I've encountered in life is trivial compared to the horrendous evils people around the world and throughout history have endured. Even faithful Christians are not immune to the debilitating effects of evil and suffering. C. S. Lewis, one of the greatest Christian apologists of the twentieth century, once remarked after the death of his wife:

> Have I forgotten the moment of bitterness when she cried out, "And there was so much to live for!" ... Fate (or whatever it is) delights to produce a great capacity and then frustrate it. Beethoven went deaf. By our standards a mean joke; the spiteful trick of a monkey imbecile.[103]

It's hard to imagine such a devoted Christian referring to God as a "monkey imbecile," but one should never underestimate the power of suffering to wear down people's souls. Why does God allow his creation to undergo such intense suffering? Why does God allow serial killers, terrorists, disease, starving children? Doesn't that contradict his goodness or power? Philosophers and theologians call this the *problem of evil*.

This is one of the oldest and most emotionally powerful arguments for atheism. According to some historians, it goes all the way back to the fifth-century philosopher Epicurus. The philosopher David Hume described Epicurus's formulation of the problem of evil in this way: "Is God willing to prevent evil, but not able? Then he is impotent. Is he able, but not willing? Then he is malevolent. Is he both able and willing? Whence then is evil?"[104]

We might restate it like this:

P1. God must be all-powerful, all-knowing, and all-good.
P2. An all-powerful, all-knowing, and all-good being could eliminate evil.
P3. Evil exists.
C. Therefore, God does not exist.

God is not so great

A theist could escape the problem of evil by denying one of God's key attributes in premise one. For example, some theists believe that, although God is very powerful, he is not *all*-powerful. Rabbi Harold Kushner, in his book *When Bad Things Happen to Good People*, claims that God hates evil as much as we do, but he is just not powerful enough to stop it all. Kushner came to this conclusion as he coped with his son dying from a rare disease at the age of fourteen.

Another escape route would be to deny that God is all-knowing. Even if God were all-good and had the power to stop evil, it could be that he is just not smart enough to know *how* to stop it. According to so-called process theology, God changes and grows as the universe changes and grows. "Don't blame God. He is just learning how to do his job!"

Finally, one could deny that God is all-good, and so doesn't have to care about suffering.

But a traditional theist cannot deny any of God's key attributes without denying God himself. To say God is not all-powerful, all-knowing, or all-good would be akin to saying a triangle can exist and not have three sides. It's possible to draw a shape with more than three sides, but it wouldn't be a triangle; it's possible for there to be a powerful being that lacks the perfection of certain attributes, but this being could not be God. Atheist B. C. Johnson says, "Such a God, if not dead, is the next thing to it. And a person who believes in such a ghost of a god is practically an atheist. To call such a thing a god would be to strain the meaning of the word."[105]

Two bad answers

There are two extremes that theists should avoid when answering the problem of evil. The first is what I call "punting to mystery." This involves the Christian instantly throwing up his hands and simply saying, "God works in mysterious ways" before ending the conversation. After the devastating 2011 Japanese tsunami, MSNBC's Martin Bashir asked Evangelical pastor Rob Bell, "Which of these is true? Either God is all powerful but he doesn't care about the people of Japan, or he does care about the people of Japan but he's not all powerful."[106]

Bell rambled about God shedding tears and God's desire to renew the Earth, which prompted Bashir to forcefully ask his question again. Bell responded, "I think that this is a paradox at the heart of the divine, and some paradoxes are best left exactly as they are." Even if suffering is a mystery, or a "paradox" as Bell put it, the pain that people endure and their honest questions about God's goodness deserve a more rigorous explanation.

The other extreme is to act as if we know exactly why God allows evil and pretend that there really is no mystery.

God's zealous defender might say that "evil comes from free will" or "God can bring good from evil" and then act as if the problem of evil is not so hard to explain.

And yet it *is* hard to explain. God could have caused Hitler to have a heart attack or he could have nudged off course the iceberg that struck the *Titanic*. Free will and greater goods explain some aspects of evil, but we still feel empty inside when this overconfident approach is employed.

This way of answering the problem of evil was lampooned in Voltaire's 1759 novella *Candide,* which was written in response to another disaster that shook people's faith. Four years earlier, the city of Lisbon, Portugal, was devastated by an earthquake and tsunami that killed thousands of people on All Saints' Day. *Candide* references these disasters and critiques heartless, overly philosophical answers to the problem of evil through the character of Dr. Pangloss.

In one scene, Pangloss tries to reassure the title character after their friend James drowns in a storm that the harbor where he drowned was designed by God for him to drown in. Echoing the philosopher Gottfried Leibniz, Pangloss says God must have intended the disaster because this is "the best of all possible worlds."[107] Pangloss tells Candide in an insufferably optimistic tone, "All this is for the very best end, for if there is a volcano at Lisbon it could be in no other spot; and it is impossible but things should be as they are, for everything is for the best."[108] Like Leibniz, modern theists who try to solve the problem of evil in a paragraph in an online comment box don't seem to fully appreciate how deep the problem really is.

A better approach to the problem of evil is offered by my friend and fellow apologist Jimmy Akin. He says, "It is a mystery why God allows us to suffer, but there are reasons for our suffering that can help us endure it."

What is evil?

Before we examine the reasons for the existence of evil, it's important that we understand what "evil" is. When we think of evil, we must distinguish between two kinds. The first is moral evil, or an agent acting against the good (such as a man poisoning his wife in order to marry another woman). The second is natural evil, or bad effects that follow from morally good or non-moral causes (such as a woman accidentally drinking poison and dying). Moral evils are privations of the good and represent a defect in the one who is causing the moral evil. These evils cannot be directly created by God, for he has no defects (though he may create beings who do evil and thus he may indirectly cause moral evil to exist).[109] God can, however, directly create physical evils, such as pain. This should come as no surprise, since physical evils, such as pain, can ultimately serve the good—as your personal trainer might say, "No pain, no gain."

Theists must be careful not to push the "privation" argument too far and say that since moral evil is not directly created by God it does not exist, and as a result there is no problem of evil to solve, since evil isn't real. Someone might say a hole doesn't exist since it is just an absence of dirt; but it does exist, because you can fall into it! An absence isn't always a vacuum; something can still be present. For example, blindness involves the eye lacking something that allows for vision, but the blindness represents a real corruption of what the eye is supposed to be. Therefore, this physical evil is very real to those who suffer from it.

The problem of evil now becomes this: "Why does God allow or permit such a lack of good in the world?" After all, if you visited my house and said, "Hey, Trent, it's dark and cold in here; you're not being a good host," how would you respond if I said, "Well, I didn't cause the darkness or cold, since those things don't really exist; they're just absences of heat and light." You would probably wonder why I, the host, did not supply the needed light and heat. Just the same, people concerned about the coexistence of God and evil might wonder why God doesn't provide needed good in places where it is lacking.

Divide and conquer

The best way to answer the problem of evil is to divide the problem into three sub-problems. These can be considered the logical problem of evil, the evidential problem of evil, and the emotional problem of evil.[110]

When someone says that evil and suffering show there is no God, you should ask if he is struggling with a personal problem or a philosophical problem. If it is a personal problem, then a strictly rational approach may not be the best way to confront what's bothering him. Instead, this person needs sympathy and compassion. But if evil represents a kind of intellectual puzzle that the person wants answered, then you should first find out if the person thinks evil makes the existence of God *impossible* or if it just makes his existence *unlikely*.

Among philosophers, the first claim is called the "logical problem of evil," while the second is called the "evidential problem of evil."

What is the logical problem of evil?

The logical problem of evil attempts to show that God is a contradiction. Instead of showing that God contradicts himself, it attempts to show that God contradicts a known fact about the world. To understand this, let's review Epicurus's argument again:

P1. God must be all-powerful, all-knowing, and all-good.

P2. An all-powerful, all-knowing, and all-good being could eliminate evil.

P3. Evil exists.

C. Therefore, God does not exist.

According to the argument, if God exists, then evil would not exist. But evil does exist. Therefore, God does not exist. J. L. Mackie, historically one of the most famous defenders of the logical problem of evil, puts it this way:

> [A] good thing always eliminates evil as far as it can, and that there are no limits to what an omnipotent thing can do. From these it follows that a good omnipotent thing eliminates evil completely, and then the propositions that a good omnipotent thing exists, and that evil exists, are incompatible.[111]

But in order for the argument to work, it would have to disprove a key premise that is not included in the original argument:

P1. God must be all-powerful, all-knowing, and all-good.

P2. An all-powerful, all-knowing, and all-good being could eliminate evil.

P3. Evil exists.

P4. *God can have no good reason to allow evil to exist.*

C. Therefore, God does not exist.

If God has morally sufficient reasons to allow even one act of evil or suffering, then the argument falls apart, because then this would show that God and the existence of evil are not logically contradictory.[112]

Let's return to my example of inviting you over to my cold and dark house to get a better idea of what it means to have good reasons to permit evil. Maybe I am allowing this "evil," or privation of good because I just received a call from the power company that my home's electrical system is damaged and that turning on the lights or heater could short the fuses and cause a fire. In this case, I am allowing a minor evil to occur in order to prevent an even greater evil. Likewise, God may allow some evils to exist because by doing so he is preventing even greater evils from coming about in the future. Or, by allowing some evils to exist, God is able to allow some goods to exist that would not exist otherwise.

The gift of free will

The question now becomes: Are there any good things that God can achieve that would justify allowing some evil to occur? At first, this may seem like an odd thing to ask. It's understandable that *I* might have to allow evils to occur (like the cold and darkness in my house) in order to prevent an even worse evil from happening. But what would stop an omnipotent God from eradicating evil? One thing might be God's overriding goals for mankind, such as the goal of giving human beings free will.

Ask yourself, "Do I love my car for getting me to work every morning? Am I grateful to my toaster for making me breakfast? Am I proud of my DVR for recording my favorite show last night?" Those would be strange emotions to have toward machines. Granted, we can be impressed by machines, but we don't say they acted courageously or compassionately.[113] But when a person offers a stranger a ride, or makes his grandmother toast in the morning, or gets up in the middle of the night to record a program for his brother, we find those actions praiseworthy.

Conversely, we don't think cars or toasters are evil when they break and don't do what we want. But a person may be evil if he breaks a promise to give someone a ride or throws the toast in Grandma's face. It seems that the world is a better place because humans exist who have the freedom to love, be compassionate, be courageous, seek justice, and engage in morally good behaviors. Of course, humans can also misuse that freedom, which creates many of the evils we see in the world.[114]

A defective gift?

A critic might respond that if I make a robot that I know will malfunction and hurt other people, then I am responsible for what the robot does. Since God made us and knew we would sin, this makes him responsible for the evil we do. But the problem with this objection is that the robot doesn't *choose* to harm anyone; if it does, it is just following its programming. In that case, we rightly blame the programmer. But human beings aren't robots programmed by God; when we freely choose to do evil, we can't blame God for it.

Skeptics like John Loftus might respond by saying, "Giving us free will is like giving a razor blade to a two-year-old child," and God should never have done something so irresponsible.[115] One wonders if Loftus has contemplated what a world without free will would be like. We would never have to worry about choosing to help another person, because God would make that choice for us. It would be, as Richard Swinburne puts it, a trivial "toy world" in which our actions would have no meaning. We would have no responsibility toward one another, and God would have robbed us of opportunities to be our "heroic best."[116]

St. Augustine recognized that a world with free will is better than one without it in the same way that a world of thriving animals is better than a world of lifeless rocks. He writes, "For a runaway horse is better than a stone that stays in the right place only because it has no movement or perception of its own; and in the same way, a creature that sins by free will is more excellent than one that does not sin only because it has no free will."[117]

In addition, the example of a toddler with a razor blade unfairly frames the illustration against the theist. The reason we don't give razor blades to toddlers is because the best outcome is only that they do not hurt themselves or others. On the other hand, adults use razor blades for good things, like art projects and cooking—even though some of them will use razors to hurt other people or themselves. Loftus concedes that razor blades can be used for good, but he claims that immoral behavior shows that humans simply can't handle free will. But unlike babies, who can do no good things with razors, humans can do many good things with free will, so this shows that God is justified in giving us free will.[118]

Why not heaven now?

One objection to the free will defense is to claim that since no one will sin in heaven, God should have skipped creating the Earth and made heaven, in the words of Belinda Carlisle, a place on Earth. However, this objection assumes that God could have made heaven to be exactly like an Earth where people have free will and only choose the good. I do not believe human beings in heaven will have "free will" (as we currently understand it) that allows them to choose to do evil. This is why heaven will be without sin. Theoretically, in heaven our human natures could either be transformed by God to not desire evil, or the overwhelming presence of God and his goodness could liberate humans from desiring evil even though they are technically still able to do so.

According to the *Catechism*, "The universe was created 'in a state of journeying' (*in statu viae*) toward an ultimate perfection yet to be attained, to which God has destined it. We call 'divine providence' the dispositions by which God guides his creation toward this perfection."[119] Such a scenario allows God to secure goods he would not otherwise be able to secure if he created only a heaven with beings that lack free will. This allows God to respect our freedom and give his creatures the opportunity to make a free choice in time to spend an eternity with God in a glorified and transformed state.

I should stress that this is not the only approach taken by philosophers to combat the logical problem of evil. Regardless of which approach is taken, philosophers generally agree, in the words of agnostic scholar Paul Draper, that "theists face no serious logical problem of evil."[120] Even Mackie himself admitted that as a result of modern theists such as Alvin Plantinga, "[W]e can concede that the problem of evil does not, after all, show that the central doctrines of theism are logically inconsistent with one another. But whether this offers a real solution to the problem is another question."[121]

Mackie's concession ends on an ominous note for the theist. Is there a way for an atheist to modify the problem of evil to overcome arguments that show that the existence of God and evil do not logically contradict one another? We will examine one such argument in the next chapter.

Does evil disprove God?

Atheist: If God does exist, then why is there so much evil and suffering in the world?
Theist: May I ask you a question? Do you see the amount of evil in the world as a kind of philosophical argument against God's existence? Or just something

that upsets you and makes you wonder why God would allow it?

A: Sort of both. I just don't know why God would let so many bad things happen to so many people.

T: I feel the same way sometimes. It's hard to watch innocent people suffer, but do you think God may have good reasons to allow suffering?

A: What do you mean?

T: Well, God created us with free will, or the ability to choose between good and evil. So while people can choose to love or be compassionate, they can also choose to hate or hurt others. I think a lot of evil comes from people abusing their free will, but I'm still glad God made us free.

A: I don't see what's so special about free will when compared to all the evil in the world.

T: Well the evil is bad, but the good is, well, good! Do you think love and courage are special and that they make the world a better place?

A: Oh, sure.

T: All right, if people were merely robots without free will, do you think love and courage would have meaning? It's hard to see how someone who isn't free can love or be brave when there is no choice involved.

A: But God can do anything. Couldn't he have made only the people who would choose only to do good?

T: Do you think God should have made you or me, even though we don't always choose what is good?

A: Fair enough. But there are still a lot of bad things that have nothing to do with human free will, and that represents a big problem for people who think God is all-good.

7

Does Pointless Suffering Disprove God?

Once my wife and I attended a baseball game where our home team was ahead by eight runs in the top of the ninth inning. We decided to leave so we wouldn't get stuck in the parking lot during the mass exodus after the game. When her mother called and asked if our team had won, we said it had but we didn't know the final score, since we had left early. She asked, "Well, how do you know for certain they won?"

She had a point. It was possible that the opposing team had come back to win the game, or that the players on the home team had suffered a freak dugout accident that had forced them to forfeit. It was *possible*, but extremely *improbable*. Since it was so improbable, we felt that it was a safe bet to say our team had won.[122]

Atheists advance a similar argument from evil against the existence of God that rests its case on the extreme unlikeliness that God exists in the face of tremendous suffering or pain.

The evidential problem of evil

William Rowe admits, "There is a fairly compelling argument for the view that the existence of evil is logically consistent with the existence of the theistic God."[123] However, Rowe claims that while it is *logically possible* God has good reasons for permitting evil in the world, it seems incredibly unlikely reasons exist to justify the huge amount of suffering we observe. As a result, the suffering seems more compatible with an absent God than a purposefully inactive one. Rowe calls this the "evidential argument from evil," because the evidence of large amounts of evil (as opposed to the logical problem evil poses) makes it unlikely God exists. Rowe's version of the problem of evil proceeds as follows:

P1. If pointless evils exist, then God does not exist.
P2. Pointless evils do exist.
C. Therefore, God does not exist.

Rowe argues that although God may tolerate some evils because they serve a greater good (like allowing humans to have free will), there are other evils that seem to serve no greater good and are also not the result of man's free will. These are called *natural evils*, and they include things not caused by humans, such as hurricanes and cancer, that kill millions of creatures every year.

Rowe provides one specific example of such a natural evil: "In some distant forest lightning strikes a dead tree, resulting in a forest fire. In the fire a fawn is trapped, horribly burned, and lies in terrible agony for several days before death relieves its suffering."[124] Rowe argues that evils like this serve no greater good and are therefore more compatible with the non-existence of God. Even though Rowe cannot prove the evils are pointless with the same certainty we can prove $1+1=2$, he maintains that the evidence makes it highly probable the evils are pointless, and therefore it is extremely unlikely that God exists.

I suggest that theists use several different methods to respond to Rowe's argument. These include the "good reasons" approach, the "no-see-um" approach, and the "counter-evidence" approach.[125]

I. The "good reasons" approach

The "good reasons" approach claims that God has good reasons for allowing both moral and even natural evil to exist. This approach should not be construed to mean that the theist knows why God allows each particular evil to occur. Rather, it aims to show merely possible good reasons God could have for allowing us to suffer.

For example, natural evils may serve to build our character and help us develop virtue, which can't happen in something like Swinburne's "toy-world." After Hurricane Katrina devastated the city of New Orleans, aid from around the world poured in to help the survivors. Even Bangladesh, one of the poorest nations on earth (and itself the site of frequent floods and typhoons), sent $1 million to help the relief efforts.[126] We recognize that such acts of compassion are intrinsically good, and when humans choose to perform such acts, their choices can gradually change their characters and can lead to the great good of their becoming virtuous people. In fact, many of the virtues that make the world a better place are practiced in response to some evil. Consider:

Courage: Doing what is right in the face of danger.

Compassion: Suffering alongside someone.

Love: Putting another person's needs ahead of your own.

Some atheists have a visceral reaction to this kind of defense against the problem of evil: "Saying that God hurts me because he loves me is exactly what battered wives say when their husbands beat them. Theists should view their God as being just as malicious as an abusive spouse." However, this analogy does not succeed. An abuser directly hurts his spouse with the intention of causing her pain, because he enjoys the pain he causes. No serious theist believes that God desires the suffering of people on Earth just so he can watch them suffer. Rather, God uses the suffering in our lives because he desires the greater good that can come from such suffering.[127]

"If I were God, I could do better than this"

Some atheists use the problem of evil to make the following argument against God's existence:

P1. If someone could stop evil X but didn't, then that person would be immoral.
P2. God could have stopped evil X.
C. Therefore, God is an immoral person. (It would then follow that God is contradictory and thus doesn't exist.)

Some examples of premise one include rescuing babies in house fires[128] and giving Adolf Hitler a heart attack.[129] In his essay "Tale of the Twelve Officers," Mark Vuletic tells a parable about police officers who stand idly by while a woman named Mrs. K. is raped and murdered. The officers give reasons for not intervening that are supposed to make fun of the reasons theists give to explain why God doesn't prevent evil in the world. One of the officers has a reason for allowing the rape that's too complex to explain ("God's ways are above our ways"), while another says that he revived the woman and sent her on vacation ("God compensates us with heaven").[130]

I understand an atheist's frustration at evil and God's apparent inaction in the face of it. Most of us, at one time or another, have wished for super powers so we could rescue the weak and bring justice to evildoers. But God already has those super powers, so why doesn't he use them?

One problem with imagining God as one of us, but with super powers, is that he can affect *every* moral situation. Yes, you or I or a regular police officer would stop a rape from happening, because in our limited understanding we simply follow our moral obligation to stop evil as best we can. But when God acts, it is very different, because he could stop *all* evil if he chose. If God were obligated to stop Mrs. K.'s rape, then wouldn't he be obligated to stop all rape? And murder?

And robbery? Heck—adultery, fraud, and even building code violations cause people harm. Suddenly we are faced with a genuine question: Would our world be better if God stopped *every* act of evil, both moral and natural? Even if we had free will, it would be useless if God made our choices trivial and sentenced us to life in a "toy-world."

A little *help would be nice*

Some atheists object that God doesn't have to stop *all* evil, he would just have to stop *some* evil. An atheist friend once asked me, "Trent, how do you feel that God let 30,000 people die in an earthquake last week?" I responded, "Should I feel dandy if he only let 10,000 people die?" He said, "I see your point."

I call this the *problem of the sliding scale.* Yes, the amount of evil in our world can be awful at times. But if God were to reduce it, would that make atheists happy and resolve the problem of evil? Imagine we lived in a world without malaria and rape but with every other evil we currently have. Would the problem of evil be gone? I suspect atheists would still complain that there was too much evil. But what if the greatest evil in the world were stubbed toes?

We don't think stubbed toes are bad when we compare them to evils like rape and malaria. But without those great evils to compare it to, maybe a stubbed toe would be considered too much evil for God to allow ("Please, only chipped toenails, Lord!"). Furthermore, there could certainly be a world in which the amount of evil was even greater than in our world; atheists in that world might say that if God existed he would at least remove *these* gratuitous evils. Atheists in such a hypothetical world might say they would believe in God if he just reduced evil to the level we currently observe in the actual world. If that happened, would these hypothetical atheists cease to mention the problem of evil? Of course not, because then they would just become the atheists *of this world* who make the same complaint.

The bottom line is that God may have good reasons to allow evil in the world, and the burden of proof is on the atheist to show that he doesn't have any good reasons to allow such evil. One of those reasons may be that if he were obligated to remove some evils, then he would be obligated to remove all evils. But if he removed all evils, then God would deprive us of goods that often accompany evil, like free will or the opportunity to be our heroic best.

II. The "no-see-ums" approach

Let's say an atheist doesn't buy the "good reasons" answer to the problem of evil. Maybe he thinks that no reason we are aware of is good enough to reconcile the sheer amount of evil in the world. Is there another approach to the evidential problem of evil, to complement the good reasons approach?

"No-see-ums" is a term that refers to little insects you can hardly see but that have painful bites. The lesson to be learned from them is that just because you can't see something doesn't mean it isn't there. So how does this relate to the problem of evil?[131]

When I stand in my backyard and don't see any elephants, it seems that I am justified in saying, "There are no elephants in my backyard." But if I say, "I don't see any fleas in my backyard," does this justify me in saying, "There are no fleas in my backyard?" For there *might* be fleas in my backyard, but because they are so small, I may not be able to see them.

Atheists will say that since they see no good reasons to justify the amount of evil and suffering in the world, therefore there *are* no good reasons to do so. But are those reasons like elephants, or are they like fleas?

The law of unintended consequences

Since human beings are limited by time and space, we have no idea whether our actions will have consequences that could have good or bad effects hundreds of years from now. One example that illustrates this problem is from the movie *Frequency*. In it, a police officer named John Sullivan, whose father died thirty years earlier while on duty as a firefighter, decides one day to play around with his old ham radio. Because of a solar flare (and a fair amount of suspension of disbelief), John is able to communicate with his father thirty years in the past. He warns his father about the fire, and his father survives, which then alters John's past. After the fire, John's father goes to see his wife, who is a nurse at the local hospital. In the process of seeing her husband across the room, John's mother notices that a patient is about to be overdosed, and saves his life. The man turns out to be a serial killer who, instead of killing three people (as he did in the original timeline), goes on to kill ten—including John's mother.

This dramatically illustrates how we are simply in no position to understand the unintended consequences of our actions, and how God could use them for good in the future.[132] Just because we can't see the good reasons God has for allowing evil does not mean those reasons don't exist.

III. The "reversal" approach

How would an atheist *define* evil? He might say evil is something that is bad or unpleasant. Well, then what is "bad" or "unpleasant"? It's when things aren't "good." Well, what is "good"? This tactic of asking questions like a four-year-old has a payoff, even if it can be annoying. At this point, I see no other alternative to describing "good" except as, "the way things are meant to be," from which it would follow that evil occurs when things, "are not the way they are supposed to be."

But if everything is supposed to "be a certain way," then it follows there is a creator and designer of the world who has a plan for his creation—in a word, God. An atheist could reword the problem of evil by calling it simply "the problem of pain" and describe pain as a negative feeling toward something. Now, this would evade the "evil is evidence of God" argument, but it wouldn't solve it, because we still have a firm idea that evil is real and can be defined only by contrast with the way things ought to be—with some grand design in the universe.

Theists can say that while what we consider to be evil may count against God's existence, all the other evidence *for* God's existence (like the universe being designed to be a certain way) outweighs the evidence for atheism, and we can still be confident that God exists. This approach to the problem involves reversing Rowe's original evidential argument from evil to show that it is more likely God exists than it is that pointless evils exists. Rowe's original argument said that if pointless evils exist, then God does not. However, if God *does* exist, then the evils we see aren't pointless. They would instead be a part of God's plan. This is like saying, "If I am in New York, then I am in the U.S." is just as true as the statement "If I am *not* in the U.S., then I am *not* in New York."[133]

From our limited vantage point, we may not be able to see the good God can achieve, even hundreds of years into the future, from the evils that occur now. Instead, our positive evidence of the existence of God forces us into a position where even if we don't understand why God allows evil we must say, as Abraham did, "Shall not the Judge of all the earth do right?"[134]

In order to show God does not exist, it is the atheist who has the burden of proof to show that God would have no good reasons to permit evil. And given the limitations of human knowledge of the universe, this means that such a burden of proof simply can't be met. Since we can imagine some good reasons God may have to allow evil, and we recognize that we can't fully understand the goods that can emerge in other times and places as a result of allowing evil to exist, the theist is not in a position where he must give up belief in God in the face of evil.

Of course, the problem of reconciling evil with a loving God is still a mystery, and one that can't be fully explained, but I think there are compelling reasons to show that evil and suffering do not disprove the existence of God. Atheists don't have an easy solution to the problem of evil because their conclusion—God does not exist—collides with the equally mysterious problem of good. Why, if there is no God, is there so much love, goodness, and beauty in the world? Why do humans seem so valuable, even those who suffer greatly, when under atheism humans are just a collection of molecules and electrical impulses?

The explanation of why evil exists is an emotional problem for theists, because we are not privy to the reasons God has for allowing certain evils. Since evil is merely a corruption of the good and has no real existence of its own, it follows that there is no logical problem in explaining why good and evil exist. However, the problem of explaining why goodness, or "oughtness" (i.e., that things "ought to be a certain way")— or even why anything at all exists as opposed to nothing—is a much more serious problem for atheists. I will explore these issues in the remaining chapters of this book.

The emotional problem of evil

Even if God had good reasons to allow suffering to occur, that still seems like an empty response. Evangelical pastor Timothy Keller writes:

A woman in my church once confronted me about sermon illustrations in which evil events turned out for good. She had lost a husband in an act of violence during a robbery. She had also had several children with severe mental and emotional problems. She insisted that for every one story in which evil turns out for good, there are one hundred in which there is no conceivable silver lining.[135]

What makes this emotional problem of evil so difficult is that a suffering person is usually not able to objectively examine logical arguments for or against the existence of God. Instead, he just wants the pain to go away or else to find someone to blame for it. The best solution to this problem is not Christian apologetics but simply Christ. Keller answers the woman's charge against God by saying that although "Christianity does not provide the reason for each experience of pain, it provides the resources for actually facing suffering with hope and courage rather than bitterness and despair."[136]

By offering others Christ's hand to hold, his shoulder to cry on, and his words to soothe, Christians spread God's love and give an answer to suffering. We remember that we can "do all things in Christ who strengthens us."[137] We can point out that even if God did not exist, suffering would still exist. We can show that it is better to live in a world where God is apparently silent but there is future redemption than in a world where God is actually absent and in the end evil and injustice are never vanquished. Even better than a bland deistic god, the Christian God understands suffering and has come to Earth to redeem man from that suffering.

Not happiness, but holiness

If God's only purpose were to make us happy—free of pain, full of pleasure—then the suffering in the world might indeed seem pointless. But God's true purpose is not that creatures be merely happy but that they come to know him and become truly like him: courageous, just, fair, compassionate, merciful, and loving. Ancient philosophers and sages understood that happiness is more than feeling good; it involves *being* good. For them, a person could be truly "happy" or complete only when he became virtuous, not when he had overdosed on pleasure-inducing chemicals in the brain. Even the utilitarian philosopher John Stuart Mill recognized that pleasure is not the ultimate good in life when he said, "Better to be a human being dissatisfied than a pig satisfied."[138]

Some atheists argue that, even if God and evil are not incompatible, God should comfort his children when they suffer. They say, "If a father takes his daughter to the hospital for a painful surgery that will help her, he can at least explain to her why it is happening. Even if she is too young to understand, he can at least soothe her pain and reassure her that he is there for her. This is something that God routinely fails to do."

It could be argued that God does comfort his children by giving them grace to endure evil and face it with noble courage. We see this grace in martyrs like Maximilian Kolbe who gave his life in a Nazi starvation bunker so that a man with children could live. Atheists may object that God should audibly explain the reasons for every aspect of evil in our life or he should miraculously cause pain relievers to flow in our bodies when we are hurt. But why is God obligated to give us such knowledge or to soothe every pain we experience?

An automatic explanation for our suffering may compromise some of the goods God intends to bring from that suffering. Imagine a man and his wife who are planning to divorce. They are legally separated and the man is hiking in the woods when he twists his ankle. He asks God, "Why would you allow me to suffer like this?" God answers, "Because, Bob, you will follow that creek to the nearest highway to find help, and providentially your wife will drive by and pick you up because you're injured. This will result in a chain of events that will eventually save your marriage." Bob responds, "But I hate that witch. I'm going to keep to the trail instead so I don't run into her."

Furthermore, pain may be an integral part of the life of free creatures, and we might be stunted as moral agents if God always removed it. C. S. Lewis recognized this: "God whispers to us in our pleasures, speaks to us in our conscience, but shouts in our pains: It is His megaphone to rouse a deaf world."[139]

But why, God?

When we are in the midst of suffering, we don't want an answer, we want help. That is what makes the emotional problem of evil so difficult to answer. Sometimes, the sufferings of other people can help us understand why God allows terrible things to happen. Nick Vujicic was born without arms or legs and was so depressed as a child that he tried to drown himself in a bathtub. However, after coming to know God and seeing that his life was not an accident, Nick was transformed. Seeing God's purpose in his life, Nick travels the world to share how God's love penetrates our deepest suffering. Nick writes in his book *Life without Limits*:

> Sometimes, of course, our prayers are not answered. Tragedies occur despite our prayers and our faith. Even the best people with the purest hearts sometimes suffer horrible losses and grief. . . .
>
> Even in the worst situations that seem beyond our capacities, God knows how much our hearts can bear. I hold on to the belief that our life here is temporary,

as we are being prepared for eternity. Whether our lives here are good or bad, the promise of heaven awaits. I always have hope in the most difficult times that God will give me strength to endure the challenges and the heartache and that better days await, if not on this earth then for certain in heaven.

One of the best ways I've found for holding on even when our prayers are not answered is to reach out to others. If your suffering is a burden, reach out to ease that of someone else and bring hope to them. Lift them up so that they will be comforted with the knowledge that they are not alone in their suffering. Offer compassion when you need it. Be a friend when you need friendship. Give hope when you most need it.

I am young and I don't pretend to have all the answers, but more and more I realize that in those times when hopelessness seems to prevail, when our prayers go unanswered, and when our worst fears are realized, our salvation lies in our relationships with those around us and, especially for me and fellow Christians, in our relationship with God and our trust in his love and wisdom.[140]

Does pointless suffering disprove God?

Atheist: I think God, if he exists, is still utterly incompetent, because there is so much evil in the world.
Theist: So you're saying it makes it really unlikely there is a God?
A: Yeah, like what about earthquakes or tsunamis? Those aren't caused by people, so why would God allow them to happen?
T: I admit it's hard to understand why God allows natural evils, or evils that are not the result of people's

choices. But sometimes even those evils serve to allow more goodness to be in the world.

A: I'm not sure if I follow you.

T: Well, some parts of the natural world are needed for us to survive even though they can harm us. For example, without gravity, our machines and bodies wouldn't function properly. But gravity can kill or maim us if we fall. If God performed a miracle every time someone was in danger, then we could never be compassionate and help others, which is one reason I think God made us.

A: Sure, but couldn't he just get rid of the really awful evils, like children who have cancer?

T: He could, but do you think, in all honesty, that you still wouldn't be bothered by the other kinds of evils, even if cancer didn't exist? How much evil is too much for God to allow? I don't really think we can know. It seems like if some evil in the world does not contradict God's goodness, then we might not be in a position to know how God can bring good from evils we don't understand.

A: I don't know. I don't like the whole "God works in mysterious ways" escape hatch theists use.

T: I'm not trying to escape anything; I just think we should humbly accept our limitations. We're like an infant and he's like a doctor who causes pain in order to give us a vaccine that will save us later. I'll admit that evil is really terrible and is hard to explain. But saying God doesn't exist is a huge claim to make, especially since we don't know the exact ways God can bring good from evil.

A: Maybe, it's just that sometimes I wish God, if he exists, hadn't created anything at all.

T: Is there something you've personally struggled with that makes you say that?

A: It's just the amount of badness can be overwhelming.

T: I agree, but don't forget that sometimes the good we see in the world can be overwhelming, too. Every time we read a story about a hero who gives his life for a stranger, it can help us see that the goodness can outweigh the bad. You're right that evil makes it hard to believe in God, but we also have to balance that against the reasons to think there *is* a God. I think those reasons easily outweigh the evil we see and help us to trust God in allowing evil so that he can bring a greater good from it.

A: What kind of reasons would those be?

PART III

Should I Believe in God?

8

Why Is There Something Rather than Nothing?

In Part II, we saw that there is no good reason to think that atheism, or the claim that God does not exist, is true. God is not a logically contradictory concept, and the amount of evil in the world is not incompatible with a God who can bring a greater good from that evil. And even if there were no evidence for God, this would not prove God did not exist.

But refuting atheism does not prove that theism is true.

Lack of compelling evidence for or against God would mean only that we must be agnostics and say, "We don't know if God exists." But what if there were compelling evidence that God *does* exist? We don't have the space to survey every argument ever proposed for the existence of God, but we will examine a few of the strongest ones. What these arguments have in common is that they start from basic facts about the world and demonstrate that God is the best explanation of those facts.

The first arguments we will examine are *cosmological* arguments whose name derives from the Greek word *cosmos,* which means "universe." They attempt to show that the existence of the universe is a good reason to believe that God exists.

The first question

The first and most basic fact about our world is that it exists. The famous contemporary philosopher Derek Parfit writes, "It might have been true that nothing ever existed: no minds, no atoms, no space. When we imagine this possibility, it can seem astonishing that anything exists. Why is there a universe?"[141] Imagine I showed you an object like a fork and you asked me where it came from. What if I responded, "No-where; it has just always existed." I highly doubt you would say, "That's really cool" and then ignore it. Wouldn't you want an explanation as to why it had existed for so long? Why it even exists at all? Why it is a fork and not a spoon?

Even if the universe were eternal, we would ask the same questions. Why hasn't the universe ever stopped existing? Why has there been an eternal universe instead of just an eternal state of nothing? The eighteenth-century philosopher G. W. Leibniz proposed an argument for the existence of God that answers the fundamental question, "Why is there some-thing rather than nothing?" Leibniz's cosmological argument is known as the "contingency argument."

The argument from contingency

To be contingent means that something doesn't have to exist; it could be different, or it could not *be* at all. Contingent things need other things in order to stay in existence. For example, humans need the oxygen plants create, the oxygen we breathe needs an atmosphere, the atmosphere requires the planet's gravity in order to stay together, and so on. We know that humans are contingent because we can imagine a world without them. We can do the same for other contingent ob-jects, such as stars and planets. In contrast, something is *neces-sary* when it is not contingent and so could not be different. The three sides of a triangle are necessary because it is impos-sible to draw a triangle with more or fewer sides. This fact can't be different, so we say a triangle's three sides are neces-sary to a triangle.

The contingency argument claims that the universe's ex-istence seems to be dependent on something that is not de-pendent upon anything else in order to exist. Its existence depends on a "necessary" being like God.

The contingency argument I'm proposing is based on one created by William Lane Craig, who himself adapted a version created by the philosopher Stephen T. Davis.[142] I have attempted to simplify the argument as much as possible so that it can be memorized and used in conversation. You may even want to try writing out the arguments that are presented in the next few chapters in order to help you memorize them.

> P1. Everything that exists has an explanation for its existence in itself or in something outside of itself.
> P2. The universe does not have an explanation for its existence in itself.
> C1. Therefore, the universe has an explanation for its existence outside of itself.

In the above argument, premise one and two support the conclusion, that the universe has an explanation outside of itself. That conclusion is then joined to another premise and yields the final conclusion:

> P3. Any explanation outside of the universe is God.
> C2. Therefore, God exists.

Premise three does not follow from premises one or two, and it may seem to the critic that we are just sneaking God into the argument. This charge will be answered shortly when I present independent reasons to think that if the universe has an explanation outside of itself, then that explanation must be God. Until then, it's important to remember that the universe is just the total collection of all space, time, matter, and energy. An explanation outside of the universe that involved more time, matter, space or energy would just involve the same universe (albeit a larger part of it usually called the "multiverse") whose existence we are trying to explain. Therefore, any explanation beyond the universe must also be beyond space, time, matter, or energy—or what we call God.

Another way to summarize this argument is to say, "The universe either has no explanation, explains itself, or is explained by God. If the universe has an explanation and cannot explain itself, it follows that God explains why the universe exists."

The argument featured here is called a *deductive* argument, which means that if each one of the premises (or statements) supporting the conclusion is true, then the conclusion has to be true with 100 percent certainty. [143] In order to refute the contingency argument, a critic would have to show that either one of the premises is false or that the argument has an error in its reasoning.

The principle of sufficient reason

In a 1948 debate with Fr. Frederick Copleston, the famous atheist Bertrand Russell said, "The universe is just there, and that's all." [144] Russell denied premise one's claim that everything has an explanation for its existence. But his objection would be more persuasive if he could identify some other object besides the universe that is also a brute fact, with no explanation for its existence. Otherwise, he is essentially saying, "Okay, maybe everything that exists in the universe has a reason for its existence, but the universe itself does not."

The philosopher Richard Taylor offers an excellent illustration of why it is a mistake to exclude the universe from needing an explanation. He asks us to imagine walking through the woods with a friend and coming across a glowing ball on the ground. If we saw something like that, we would certainly want to know where it came from. We would be unsatisfied if our friend responded, "The ball is just there, and that's all." Even if it turned out the ball was eternal and had always existed, we would want to know why such an amazing object existed at all.

Now, what if the ball were the size of a car? Or a blimp? Or a planet? Wouldn't we still wonder what its explanation is? Finally, what if the ball was the size of the whole universe? Changing the object's size does nothing to remove the need to explain that object, including an object like the whole universe.[145]

This illustrates something philosophers call the "principle of sufficient reason" (or PSR). According to this principle, anything that exists must have an explanation for its existence.[146] Consider the maxim espoused by the fictional detective Sherlock Holmes: "When you eliminate the impossible, whatever remains, however improbable, must be the truth."[147] This statement assumes that once the impossible is eliminated we can't just say that there is no explanation at all. Instead, the process of elimination forces us to accept even an unlikely explanation, because everything that exists must have an explanation.[148]

God's sufficient reason

But if everything that exists needs an explanation, then what explains the existence of God? Wouldn't God need something to explain why he exists?

Remember that the first premise doesn't say, "Everything needs an explanation for its existence in something else." That would mean that everything would need to be explained by something else, and those other things would need external explanations of their own. This would create an infinite regress of explanations, which can't explain anything (sort of like an infinite train of boxcars that can't move an inch without a locomotive). Instead, premise one says that everything has an explanation either *in itself* or in something *outside of itself.* In order to understand this, think of a triangle. We might ask, "Why is that triangle red?" or "Why does it have a right angle?" or "Why is it drawn so awkwardly?"

These questions show that some parts of a triangle can be different and thus require an explanation for *why* they are different. For example, the explanation for the triangle's awkward shape may be because I drew it (my fifth-grade art teacher can corroborate this). But what if someone asked, "Why does that triangle have three sides?" That would seem like an odd question. You would probably respond, "Well, because if it didn't have three sides, it wouldn't be a triangle."

The explanation for the triangle's awkwardness comes from outside of it (i.e., my lack of artistic skill), but the explanation for why it has three sides comes from within it, or just from what it means to be a triangle. Or think of a campfire and the stones around it. You might ask why the stones are warm, and the explanation for this fact is found outside of the stones: They are warm because they are near the fire. But why is the fire warm? Well, that explanation is found within the fire itself, because fire by its nature is warm. If it wasn't warm, it would not be a fire.

What it means to be "God"

Classical theists such as Aquinas did not consider God to be one being among many (like a special star floating far away "out there"). They instead considered him to be "being" or "existence" itself. If God is the "ground of being" or the reason anything has existence, then it's no surprise that God must exist.

I have chosen to not talk about God as simply "being" itself because this is easily misunderstood as pantheism or the belief that God is identical to anything that exists, such as the book you are reading at this moment. However, when I say

God is a being who explains his own existence, it's important to remember that this quality, or God's necessary existence, makes him a being unlike any other. It makes him, in the words of Pope John Paul II, "the supreme Being, the great "Existent."[149]

Asking what explains the existence of God is like asking what causes triangles to have three sides or fire to be warm. The answer is explained in the thing itself. Fire has a nature to be warm, triangles have a nature to be three-sided, and God has a nature to exist.[150] God does indeed have an explanation for why he exists, but this explanation is not found in anything outside of him. God's existence does not violate the first premise of the argument, because God is by definition a being who exists as a result of his own nature.[151]

Now, consider the question "Why does this universe exist?" Does it more closely resemble the question "Why is that triangle red?" or the question "Why does that triangle have three sides?" We can imagine triangles that aren't red, but no one can think of a triangle that has more or fewer than three sides. Since we can imagine nothing existing at all, the question of why the universe exists seems to be more like the "kind of color" question for a triangle and not the "number of sides" question.[152] Since the color of a triangle is explained by something outside of the triangle, and the universe's existence is as contingent as a triangle's color—it could just as easily have not existed—it follows that the reason the universe exists must be found in something outside of the universe.

Can the universe explain itself?

To say the universe explains itself is to make the strong claim that the universe doesn't *just happen to* exist, but that it *has to exist* as a result of its own nature in the same way that

God has to exist and could never fail to exist. But how could it be the case that the universe must exist? A triangle's three sides are necessary, and so I can't imagine a triangle without them; but it's hard to think the universe's existence is necessary, because I can imagine it not existing.[153] Everything we know about the universe, including the birth and death of stars and planets, points toward our universe being a collection of things that don't have to exist.[154]

A critic could argue that the fundamental matter that makes up the universe exists necessarily and so, regardless of whether or not it forms stars and planets, we would still have a universe of fundamental particles that have to exist and just get rearranged over time. The smallest particles we are aware of are called *quarks* (they're even smaller than protons, electrons, and neutrons). In order for the universe to be necessary, it would have to be true that it is impossible for these quarks to not exist. It also has to be impossible for these *particular* quarks to not exist in order to say they are necessary.[155] But couldn't we have a universe with different fundamental matter? If we could, then the matter that exists can't be necessary since it could be different. Its contingent nature would still require an explanation in something else.

Even many atheists are unwilling to accept the hypothesis that the universe is necessary and explains itself. Cosmologist Sean Carroll says that, for most scientists, "the search for ultimate explanations eventually terminates in some final theory of the world, along with the phrase 'and that's just how it is.'"[156] Notice that Carroll says the likely explanation for the universe is not "and that's the way it *has to be*" (a necessary explanation in itself). It's just a brute fact with no further explanation (that's the way it *is*; deal with it). Richard Carrier doesn't even consider the necessity of the universe a *possible* explanation for its existence. He writes:

[E]ither there is an eternal string of endless explanations, in which case there is no "ultimate explanation because the explanations never end (and so the universe remains ultimately unexplained), or else there is something that has no explanation, something that just "is," what we would call a "brute fact." There are no other possibilities.[157]

The atheistic eighteenth-century philosopher David Hume proposed another way a universe of contingent things could be necessary and explain itself: "But the *whole*, you say, wants a cause. . . . This is sufficiently explained in explaining the parts."[158] However, explaining why each part of the universe exists, even in a "circle of explanation," does not explain why an entire universe exists at all. That would be like trying to explain why a baseball game is being played simply by explaining what each player in the game does (i.e., the batter is hitting a ball thrown by the pitcher, who takes a cue from the shortstop, who watches the man on second . . .). That strategy may explain each *part* of the baseball game, but it doesn't explain why there is a baseball game happening. Even atheists like Richard Gale admit that Hume's reasoning is faulty on this point.[159]

Does the explanation have to be God?

So it seems that the universe needs an explanation outside of itself. But why think that the explanation for the universe is God? If the explanation for the universe were not God but another contingent object that existed in space and time such as a parallel universe, then this explanation would itself be subject to the contingency argument. Since everything has an explanation for its existence in either itself or in something outside of itself, we would ask if this other universe explains itself or if something else explains it. If it is explained by something else that is contingent, such as another universe beyond it, then the argument starts over again. If any of these explanations exists as a result of its own nature, then it would be God, because God is the only being that can exist as a result of his own nature.[160]

An infinite series of contingent universes is no real explanation, either—we just have an endless set of universes that exist as a brute, unexplained fact. This explanation is like saying a boxcar on a train moves because it is pulled by the boxcar in front of it, which in turn is pulled by an infinite set of boxcars. But boxcars depend on something else in order to move, and therefore even an infinite number of boxcars could not move one inch. Instead, the boxcars must be moved by something which moves itself, such as a locomotive.

Likewise, an infinite series of universes that didn't have to exist cannot explain their own existence without reference to a necessary being that has to exist. These individual universes would still need a being who cannot fail to exist that sustains the whole collection of universes. This being could not be a mere force or universe, because it is the reason space and time exist and thus could not be bound by those things. Because it is necessary, this being couldn't be created or destroyed—in other words, it would be what you and I call God.

She blinded me with science

If it appears that the contingency argument is sound philosophically, an atheist may invoke science to shatter our confidence in the argument's conclusion, saying, "One day science will discover the explanation or reason that the universe exists, so there's no need to place God in that gap of our knowledge."

But this objection confuses the domains of science (particularly physics) with the domain of philosophy (particularly metaphysics). Physics seeks to understand how the natural world functions. It answers questions like, "Why do hot objects become cold over time?" (It's because of entropy and the second law of thermodynamics). Metaphysics, however, is a branch of philosophy that helps us determine what reality *itself* is made out of and why it behaves as it does. Metaphysics answers questions like, "If you change every part of an object, is it the same object or a different object?" These areas overlap and interact in a field called the *philosophy of science.*

Is philosophy dead?

Recently, some popular scientists have expressed derision for the entire field of philosophy. In their 2010 book *The Grand Design*, physicists Stephen Hawking and Leonard Mlodinow wrote, "[P]hilosophy is dead. . . . Scientists have become the bearers of the torch of discovery in our quest for knowledge."[161] In 2012, theoretical physicist Lawrence Krauss published a book that attempted to use science to answer the age-old philosophical question "Why is there something rather than nothing?"

In a *New York Times* book review, Columbia University philosopher David Albert criticized Krauss's arguments. Albert claimed that Krauss's answer to the question about the universe's origin—that quantum fields have the property of being able to create universes— doesn't solve the problem at all. Albert wrote:

> They [physicists like Krauss] have nothing whatsoever to say on the subject of where those fields came from, or of why the world should have consisted of the particular kinds of fields it does, or of why it should have consisted of fields at all, or of why there should have been a world in the first place. Period. Case closed. End of story.[162]

Krauss's response to Albert was to call him a "moronic philosopher" (even though Albert holds a Ph.D. in theoretical physics just as Krauss does).[163] Massimo Pigluicci, an atheistic biologist, replied that Krauss is "essentially playing a bait and switch with [his] readers, and then bitterly complain[s] when 'moronic' philosophers dare to point that out."[164]

The following illustration should put all of this into perspective. Science is like a flashlight that is used to examine a room without windows. The light will be able to show us what the walls are made of and what they look like, but it can't show us what the room looks like from the outside, and it can't even tell us what's inside the flashlight. But philosophy helps us understand what science is and how it works (the inside of the flashlight), as well as the answer to the question "Why there is something rather than nothing?" (or what might be outside the room).

The final choices

In conclusion, if the universe were eternal and had existed forever, then we would still want an explanation for why there is an eternal universe instead of just nothing at all. If I showed you an eternally old fork, or any other object, you would probably want to know why it exists. Is it made of an indestructible substance? Is it kept in existence by some outside force that protects it? I highly doubt you would just say, "It exists," and never think about it again. Essentially, the quest for an explanation of the universe's existence boils down to three options:

- The universe has no explanation; it exists for no reason.
- The universe explains itself.
- The universe has an explanation outside of itself in something that explains itself.

The first option doesn't make sense, given that we generally seek explanations for objects, and there's no reason to doubt the principle of sufficient reason.

The second option doesn't make sense, because there is no reason to suppose that anything in the universe must exist and could not have been different than it is now. Even the smallest, most fundamental parts of the universe could have been different than they are now. Moreover, as we will see in the next chapter, if the universe *began* to exist, then it cannot have an explanation in itself, because there was a time when the universe did not exist. If the universe ever did not exist, then it can't explain its own origin.

Therefore, the most plausible option is that the universe has an explanation. That explanation must exist beyond space and time and explain its own existence. Or it must be a necessary and infinite being, which we call God.

Why does anything exist at all?

Theist: Okay, my first reason for thinking there is a God is that the universe itself exists. Have you ever wondered why there is something rather than nothing at all?

Atheist: No. There is just something; what's there to wonder about?

T: Let me give you an example. Here's a rock. Let's say I told you this rock is eternal and has always existed. Would you just say there's nothing to wonder about? Or would you have other questions?

A: Well, I guess I'd wonder why this rock is eternal and never stopped existing.

T: If we ask this about objects in the universe, then what about the universe itself? What do you think of this argument: "The universe either has no explanation, it explains itself, or it has an explanation outside of it-self in God. Since the first two options don't work, therefore God exists."

A: Not so fast. What's wrong with those first two options? They sounded pretty good to me.

T: All right, let's start with the first one. The reason I think it doesn't make sense to say the universe has no explanation is that we normally seek explanations for everything else that exists. What do you think of this statement: "Everything that exists has an explanation for its existence in itself or in something outside of itself"?

A: I'm not sure I understand.

T: Think of a fire. The reason the fire exists is because there is tinder and a spark and fuel and all the things a fire needs to ignite and burn. Without those things, there'd be no fire. We say the fire's existence is contin-gent; it could have not been burning. Since it's contin-gent, it has an explanation outside of itself.

A: All right . . .

T: But the reason the fire is warm is because that's what fire is. So the fire's warmth is necessary: Fire has to be warm by definition, so the explanation for the fire's warmth is found inside its own nature. On the other hand, the reason the fire is burning at all is found outside of the fire, such as in a spark and fuel. That makes the fire itself contingent, since the fire didn't have to burn in any certain place. I can't think of any-thing else that exists and has *no* explanation, be it nec-essary or contingent, for why it exists, can you?

A: I can't either. But how does this relate to the universe?

T: Do you think the universe has to exist?

A: I don't know. It's here, isn't it?

T: But couldn't it have been different? Couldn't it have been really small, or have no planets in it? Is that at least conceivable?

A: Sure.

T: Okay, then that brings us to the question, why isn't there just nothing at all? Either the universe is contingent or it is necessary. Which do you think it is?

A: I'm not sure those are the only two options. Maybe the universe just exists and there is no answer. It's just there and we have to accept that fact.

T: Don't you think that's odd when we don't accept that answer for anything else that exists? The universe surely is something that exists, so why wouldn't it have an explanation?

A: Well, maybe the universe explains itself.

T: So you think the universe is necessary, or it has to exist?

A: [Pause] Maybe.

T: That would answer my argument, but the problem is that hardly any philosophers or scientists think the universe *has* to exist. There's nothing about the universe that screams, "I have to exist!" in the way that a fire has to be warm or a square has to have four sides.

A: Okay, maybe it's contingent, but the explanation is another universe.

T: But now we have a problem. Is that universe contingent or necessary?

A: Okay. I think you're trying to get me into some kind of loop where that universe needs another universe, and that one needs another one and some kind of paradox is created. Is that right?

T: No, I am just showing where the argument logically concludes. But another fact might help. If the universe explained itself, or was necessary, it would have to have existed forever, right?

A: Yes.

T: Do you think that the universe has always existed, or did it ever begin to exist?

9

Did the Universe Begin to Exist?

During a seminar I was leading on the existence of God, a Christian in the audience was outraged at two words I used. "Big Bang!" he shouted. "There was no Big Bang! The Bible doesn't say anything about it, and I believe the Bible. The Big Bang is just atheist propaganda!"

Eventually he let me explain why the Big Bang was actually good evidence *for* the existence of God. Indeed, perhaps seventy years ago the situation would have been reversed. If I had mentioned the Big Bang in a public seminar, an atheist might have said, "There wasn't a Big Bang! The Big Bang is just religious propaganda!"

At the beginning of the twentieth century, non-religious scientists like Albert Einstein were suspicious of the idea that the universe had a beginning. But the hard work of a little-known Catholic priest named Fr. Georges Lemaître helped the Big Bang become the predominant theory of cosmic origins. This new discovery provided scientific evidence for a very old argument for the existence of God.

While the contingency argument showed that even if the universe were eternal it would need a reason for why it exists, the kalām cosmological argument (KCA) shows that if the universe began to exist, then it would need a cause for its existence.

Understanding the argument

Kalām is an Arabic word that means "speech." You can think of kalām as the argument that God "spoke" and the world came into existence from nothing. The argument can be traced back to the Muslim philosopher Al-Ghazali, who wrote in his book *Against the Philosophers* that it is impossible for there to be an infinite number of days before today, and so there must be a "limit" to the past that he called "the Eternal."[165]

St. Bonaventure (who lived at the same time as St. Thomas Aquinas) used arguments similar to Al-Ghazali's to philosophically demonstrate that the universe could not be eternal but was instead created by God.[166] Today, the most prominent defender of the kalām cosmological argument is William Lane Craig,[167] who formulates it this way:

P1. Whatever begins to exist must have a cause for its existence.
P2. The universe began to exist.
C. Therefore, the universe has a cause for its existence.

The causal principle

The truth of premise one is known through two ways of investigating the world: intuition and observation. Intuition is a way of knowing something is true because it "appears" to be true when we think about it. One intuition most people have is summarized in the Latin phrase *ex nihilo, nihil fit* or "Out of nothing, nothing comes."[168] It makes sense that "nothing" (not just black or empty space, but "no-thing") is incapable of doing anything. As the philosopher John Locke put it, "[M]an knows, by an intuitive certainty, that bare nothing can no more produce any real being than it can be equal to two right angles."[169]

The belief that something can't come from nothing is also confirmed by observation. For example, we know that ice floats and iron sinks in normal water because we constantly observe it. From this limited observation, we assume that a pattern exists and this pattern holds for all iron and ice.

Likewise, we can apply this reasoning to the observation that objects don't come into existence without a cause.[170]

Some atheists criticize this reasoning. Victor Stenger writes, "Is it a fact that everything that begins has a cause? Obviously we haven't observed the beginning of everything, so we can't say that everything that begins has a cause."[171] But this kind of reasoning would undermine science itself. After all, we have never observed *every* chemical reaction that has ever occurred, yet we still believe that the first law of thermodynamics is true and matter cannot be created or destroyed within those reactions.

Defending the causal principle

When I debate atheists on the existence of God, I often notice something peculiar happens regarding the first premise of the kalām argument. Some atheists will object and say, "But how do we know that some things don't come into being without a cause? Maybe the universe is different, and it could come into being without a cause." When I'm not talking about the KCA, I sometimes ask what evidence would be sufficient to show that God exists. Often, I am told that a miracle, such as the healing of an amputee, would show that God existed.

This came up in one formal debate, and I responded, "I find it odd that you're impressed with an arm coming into being from nothing, but not an entire universe coming into being from nothing." As the audience laughed, the atheist shot back, "We know how arms work. We don't know how universes work!" I wanted to respond, but the debate moderator quickly diverted us to another audience question. If I'd had the chance, I would have asked my opponent, "How do you know that arms don't just come into existence without a cause?"

If we saw a limb appear from thin air and attach itself to an arm stump, we wouldn't just say, "Hmm, that's interesting. But who's to say something can't come from nothing?" Instead, we would seek an explanation for that event. The only way that atheists can allow miraculous regeneration of limbs to count as evidence for God would be if such events can't happen naturally. And if they can't happen naturally, that is the same as saying, "Whatever begins to exist has a cause." In the case of regenerated limbs appearing from nothing, atheists are willing to admit that the cause would be a supernatural one, or God. If they'll admit something coming from nothing requires a cause in one case, then why not admit the same thing for an entire universe coming to be from nothing?

A philosophical argument for the universe's beginning

Imagine a calendar stretching back in time forever. Time moves through the calendar one day at a time (it's more precise to say one event at a time, but days will suffice for our discussion). If the universe had existed forever, then there would have been an infinite number of days before today. But how could time have reached this present moment if it had to traverse an infinite number of previous days to get here?[172] If there were an infinite number of days before today, then there would always be "one more day" in history for time to move through, and today could never happen.

Here's another example that illustrates this concept. Let's say your Aunt Mildred owns a flower shop. Each day Mildred counts all her flowers, and only after she counts each one will she open her flower shop for business. Now, if Mildred has only a dozen flowers to count, she will open up the shop pretty quickly. But if she has a million or a billion flowers to count, then it will take her much longer before she can open the shop. But even if she has a trillion flowers to count, eventually enough time will pass and the shop will open after Mildred finished counting them (that is, if Mildred has enough coffee to keep her awake!).

But imagine that Mildred has an *infinite* number of flowers she needs to count. Remember, she still has to count all of them before she can open the shop. How long will it take before she's able to open the shop? Well, because there would always be at least one more flower to count, Mildred could never finish her task. This means that the shop could never open. But if you went to the shop and saw an "OPEN" sign on the door, then that would tell you that Aunt Mildred did not have an infinite number of flowers to count. The fact that today is happening is like the flower shop's being open. Neither could happen if an infinite number of days (or flowers being counted) had to occur first. Therefore, the past is not infinite, and the universe had a beginning.[173]

Even the skeptic David Hume admitted this: "An infinite number of real parts of time, passing in succession, and exhausted one after another, appears so evident a contradiction, that no man, one should think, whose judgment is not corrupted, instead of being improved, by the sciences, would ever be able to admit it."[174]

But maybe infinity is something we don't really understand, so that is why the infinite flower shop doesn't make sense.[175] Fortunately, modern set theory developed by the mathematician Georg Cantor allows us to do mathematical operations with infinite quantities; but it does not show us how these infinite quantities could exist in the real world. According to mathematicians Edward Kasner and James Newman, "the infinite certainly does not exist in the same sense that we say, 'There are fish in the sea.' . . . 'Existence' in the mathematical sense is wholly different from the existence of objects in the physical world."[176]

Scientific confirmation of the universe's beginning

I should point out that not all Catholic philosophers are convinced that one can philosophically prove that time had a beginning.[177] These philosophers follow Aquinas, who said that, while we know by divine revelation the past is not eternal, there is no logical contradiction in the idea of an eternal past.[178] However, these philosophers are open to scientific evidence that shows our physical universe had a beginning. If the beginning of the universe could be demonstrated scientifically, then Aquinas would agree the kalām argument succeeds, for he writes, "[I]f the world and motion have a first beginning, some cause must clearly be posited to account for this origin of the world and of motion."[179]

One piece of scientific evidence comes from the second law of thermodynamics, which states that matter and energy always tend toward disorder (or what scientists call entropy). The second law explains why striking billiard balls with a pool cue never results in the balls rearranging themselves into the standard rack formation. Such behavior would violate the universe's tendency to always move toward disorder and decay.[180]

You especially see the second law of thermodynamics at work in heat reactions. For example, have you ever taken dinner out of the oven, gotten ready to take that first delicious bite, but then get interrupted by a phone call? After the call, you sit down to eat, only to find that your dinner is cold. Why does your dinner get cold over time? Why doesn't it stay warm, or get warmer? According to the second law, all systems move toward disorder and as a result, everything, including heat and energy, moves toward equilibrium. This tendency causes your hot dinner to get cold and the room to get a tiny bit warmer until the two objects are at the same temperature. The second law also applies to the universe as a whole. Eventually, all the stars will burn out or explode until there is a thin mist of atoms spread throughout the universe at absolute zero, the coldest temperature anything can be. Scientists have a name for this future condition: *heat death*.

Why hasn't the world ended already?

While some physicists claim that the total amount of entropy in our universe may be larger than originally thought, they generally agree the observable universe is not at maximum entropy.[181] If it were, it would be highly unlikely that you could even be reading this book, since entropy increases with all of the biological processes associated with activities like reading. Indeed, because conscious life requires entropy, this means, in the words of physicists Lawrence Krauss and Glenn Starkmann, "[L]ife cannot endure forever."[182]

But if the universe has existed forever, why haven't the stars in the universe already burned out? Why hasn't heat death already happened?[183]

Think of a flashlight. If you see a flashlight that is dead, it could have been sitting there for all eternity. But if the flashlight is shining, then you know it could not have been shining forever, because the batteries would have run out a long time ago.

Likewise, think of the whole universe as having energy and "shining" like the flashlight. If the universe had existed for all eternity, then all of the energy in the universe, like the energy in stars or planets, would have been used up and the universe would be like a dead flashlight—cold, dark, and lifeless. If God does not intervene, then heat death will happen billions of years from now. But if the universe were eternal, heat death should have already occurred. According to the physicist P.C.W. Davies, "[T]he universe cannot have existed forever, otherwise it would have reached its equilibrium end state an infinite time ago. Conclusion: the universe did not always exist."[184]

But maybe there is an unknown exception to the second law of thermodynamics that allows for an increase in order and energy even though the universe is eternal. This is very unlikely, because the second law of thermodynamics is one of the best attested laws in physics. Sir Arthur Eddington, an early twentieth-century physicist, wrote:

> If someone points out to you that your pet theory of the universe is in disagreement with Maxwell's equations—then so much the worse for Maxwell's equations. If it is found to be contradicted by observation—well, these experimentalists do bungle things sometimes. But if your theory is found to be against the second law of thermodynamics I can give you no hope; there is nothing for it but to collapse in deepest humiliation.[185]

Father physicist

In the early twentieth century, the Belgian priest and physicist Georges Lemaître concluded that Einstein's new theory of gravity, called general relativity, would cause a static eternal universe to collapse into nothingness. Since Einstein's theory was sound, this only meant one thing: The universe was growing, and had a beginning in the finite past. Fr. Lemaître and Einstein would discuss the cosmic consequences of the theory while walking around the campus of Cal Tech, and although Einstein was skeptical at first, in 1933 he proclaimed that Lemaître's theory of an expanding universe was one of the most "beautiful theories he had ever heard."[186]

Fr. Lemaître called his theory "the primeval atom," but another physicist, Fred Hoyle, mocked the theory with the term "Big Bang." Hoyle believed that theories of the universe beginning to exist from nothing were "primitive myths" designed to put religion into science. Fr. Lemaître's status as a Catholic priest did not help the situation. In response to Fr. Lemaître, Hoyle argued for what he called the "steady state theory" of the universe. According to this theory, the universe existed eternally and has never rapidly expanded or changed. But two key pieces of evidence supported Fr. Lemaître and refuted Hoyle.

Proofs of the Big Bang

In 1929, American astronomer Edwin Hubbell discovered that galaxies were moving away from each other at an increasingly faster rate, which is best explained by the Big Bang sending them flying away from each other at the beginning of time.[187] Then, in 1965, Bell Laboratory technicians Arno Penzias and Robert Wilson used radio telescopes to detect a faint, uniform "glow" of static coming from all directions of the sky. At first, they thought this uniform glow was merely bird droppings contaminating the telescope! But after a thorough cleaning, the static turned out to be radiation in the form of microwaves coming from deep space.

According to the Big Bang model, right after the "bang" the universe was a white-hot ball of plasma before it cooled and formed stars and galaxies. Particles that had been flying around since the very beginning of time cooled and turned into microwaves, traveling to fill the whole cosmos. Today, this radiation is called Cosmic Microwave Background Radiation (or CMBR). This discovery was so monumental that Penzias and Wilson won the Nobel Prize for it, and Fred Hoyle admitted it refuted his steady-state model of an eternal universe: "[It] is widely believed that the existence of the microwave background killed the "steady state" cosmology. . . . Here, in the microwave background, was an important phenomenon which it had not predicted."[188]

This discovery vindicated Fr. Lemaitre's primeval atom and made the Big Bang a well-established scientific theory.[189] Also called the "Friedmann-Lemaitre model" it has been the primary model of cosmic origins for more than fifty years. The movement of stars away from each other as well as the cosmic radiation throughout the galaxy provide almost indisputable evidence that the Big Bang did happen: not an explosion in space, understand, but an *expansion of space* (as well as time, matter, and energy) from an infinitely dense point called a singularity.[190] According to renowned Tufts University cosmologist Alexander Vilenkin, "All the evidence we have says that the universe had a beginning."[191]

At this point a critic could object that all appeals to scientific evidence for the beginning of the universe can never be conclusive. He might say that science is a tentative enterprise and that theories are easily overturned by the next scientific breakthrough. Now, we should be open to where the evidence leads and not engage in brash overconfidence. At the same time, I think it's fair to note that the history of cosmology describes how more and more evidence has been added to confirm the Big Bang model. Astronomer Martin Rees writes, "Cosmological ideas are no longer any more fragile and evanescent than our theories about the history of our earth . . . The empirical support for a big bang ten to fifteen billion years ago is as compelling as the evidence that geologists offer on our earth's history."[192]

Finally, the tentative nature of science is why I consider the philosophical argument for the finite past to be the main part of the kalām cosmological argument. The scientific evidence simply serves as a confirmation of the conclusion reached in the philosophical arguments (it's the scientific icing on the philosophical cake).

Common misunderstandings of the argument

Some atheists think they can refute the kalām argument by asking, "If everything needs a cause, then what caused God?"[193] The argument, however, never says that *everything* requires a cause. It only claims that everything that *begins to exist* requires a cause for its existence. Since we have good reasons to believe that the universe began to exist (Big Bang cosmology, impossibility of infinite days before today, lack of maximum entropy), then the universe requires an explanation for why it exists. God, on the other hand, never began to exist because he is eternal (he created time itself), and therefore God requires no cause for his existence. He has always existed; but the universe has not always existed.

If the universe began to exist, what was God doing during the eternity before the world began? St. Augustine confronted this question in the fifth century. His joking response was that for all eternity God was making hell for people who ask questions like that.[194] His more serious response was that prior to the creation of the world *there was no time*. It makes no sense to ask what God was doing prior to the creation of the world, because the creation of the world also included the first moment of time. Time can be a difficult thing to understand, but one common-sense view is to think of time as a measurement of change. If God existed in a changeless, perfect state without the universe, then our mental picture of a lonely God passing countless idle eons is a flawed one.

Big Bangs need Big Bangers

Atheistic philosopher Kai Nielsen once remarked, "Suppose you hear a loud bang . . . and you ask me, 'What made that bang?' and I reply, 'Nothing, it just happened.' You would not accept that."[195] If this is true for little bangs, then wouldn't it also be true of a Big Bang? The conclusion to the kalām cosmological argument—that the universe had a cause for its existence—flows naturally from its straightforward and simple premises.

But that doesn't stop atheists from posing many objections to the kalām cosmological argument's premises, reasoning, and conclusion. I have answered many of these objections in the appendix entitled "Objections to the Kalām Cosmological Argument," but in the next chapter I will focus on one objection that threatens to undermine the argument's entire purpose in defending the existence of God.

Did the universe begin to exist?

Atheist: Maybe the universe is eternal and doesn't need an explanation for why it exists. It's just always existed. What's wrong with that?

Theist: Well, I think my last argument showed that there would need to be a reason to explain that an eternally old universe exists instead of just an eternity of nothing. But the other problem I have is I think there is good evidence the universe is not eternal but that it began to exist.

A: Like what?

T: Well, according to the second law of thermodynamics all physical systems move toward disorder and decay. If the universe had been eternal, everything in the universe (including biological life and objects like the sun) would have run out of energy a long time ago. But there still is energy, so the universe must be of finite age.

A: Why can't there just be infinite energy in infinite space that existed for infinite time?

T: Well, the evidence from science seems to suggest that all matter and energy originated from a single point about 13 billion years ago called the Big Bang. Do you believe the Big Bang happened?

A: Oh, yeah. But how do you know there wasn't something before the Big Bang, like another universe that we came from that has been around for all eternity?

T: Well, I also think philosophy could show that the past can't be eternal, even if there was another universe that existed before the Big Bang. For example, if there were an infinite number of days before today, then time could never reach the present moment. But since today did happen, this shows that time must be finite and so the universe had a beginning.

A: Wait. I'm not sure I understand how you get to the universe having a beginning.

T: Let's try this. Let's pretend that the present moment is symbolized by you opening that door. If this were the fourth day of existence you would count one day, two days, three days, and then open the door.

A: All right.

T: Now if the universe were eternal, that would be like you counting to infinity and then opening the door. But can you ever really open the door in this scenario?

A: No, because I would never be done counting.

T: It's the same with the universe. But since today did happen, we have a good reason to think that there weren't an infinite number of days before today, and so the universe had a beginning.

A: Ugh, all this infinity stuff is making my head hurt.

T: Mine too! I'm just saying that this is one possible argument among several that point toward the universe's having a beginning in the past.

A: But if God created the universe, then what created God?

T: My argument was only that things that begin to exist require an explanation for their existence. Since God is eternal, he never had to be "created."

A: Yeah, but who says this cause of everything is God?

Is God the First Cause of the Universe?

In Edgar Allen Poe's *Murders in the Rue Morgue* (widely considered the world's first detective story), the main character tries to solve a baffling and violent double murder of a Parisian woman and her daughter. While it's obvious a murder took place, the witnesses can't agree on the identity of the suspect. Eventually, the amateur detective C. Auguste Dupin discovers that they were mistaken in thinking the killer must be human because it turns out the killer was actually an orangutan great ape.

Murders in the Rue Morgue shows that even if we are positive that a certain event requires a cause, we might be mistaken about the nature of the cause in question. Likewise, even if the kalām cosmological argument has true premises, it may not prove that the cause of the universe is God.

Did the universe cause itself to exist?

Even if the universe had a cause for its existence, why appeal to God instead of an entity with which we're already familiar? New Atheist Daniel Dennett writes, "What does need its origin explained is the concrete Universe itself, and as Hume's Philo long ago asked: Why not stop at the material world? It, we have seen, does perform a version of the ultimate bootstrapping trick; it creates itself ex nihilo."[196] According to Dennett, there is no contradiction in thinking that the universe *brought itself* into existence.

Atheist Quentin Smith makes a highly technical argument in favor of a "self-caused universe," but even he finds simple versions of it, like the one offered by Dennett, to be incoherent: "No individual can bring about its own existence, because no individual can bring about anything unless it (already) exists."[197] If the universe did exist before it "began to exist," then this is either a contradiction or just another way of saying the universe is eternal, an idea that has already been addressed. The claim that the universe caused itself to exist is as nonsensical as saying that Mark Zuckerberg caused Facebook to exist after he received a Facebook message giving him the idea to create Facebook.

"Nothing" caused the universe

Another common argument against the conclusion of the KCA is that the cause, God, differs little from "nothing," and so "nothing" could have still caused the universe to begin to exist. After all, the first cause is without matter or temporal duration because it made time and space. One could also say that "nothing" also has no matter or temporal duration and so it could be the first cause. Dennett seems to concede that even if the universe did not create itself ex nihilo, it must have been created by something that is "indistinguishable from nothing at all."[198]

Even though "nothing" and the first cause of the universe share some common traits (like being invisible and not being bound by time), that doesn't mean they are the same thing. For starters, the first cause must exist or be real because it has abilities and can cause other things to come into existence. It is definitely not "nothing," because the term "nothing" is just another way of saying "not anything." Saying "nothing" caused the universe to exist is the same as saying, "The universe was *not caused by anything* to exist," which seems plainly contradictory.

This kind of objection is as strange as someone going to the police and saying, "Help! A naked bald man attacked me and stole my wallet!" To which the police sneer and say, "So you were robbed by someone with no hair and no clothes? You know, 'nothing' also has no hair and no clothes. Are you sure that it wasn't just 'nothing' that robbed you?"

An absentee landlord?

A more interesting objection comes from George Smith, who argues that even if the conclusion follows that God caused the universe to exist, that's no guarantee that God is still watching over the universe. Smith writes, "Even if valid, the first cause argument is capable only of demonstrating the existence of a mysterious first cause in the distant past. It does not establish the present existence of the first cause."[199] Other atheists like to propose fanciful scenarios where the first cause of the universe died so that the universe could come into existence.[200] If these are plausible, then the KCA will be impotent to prove God exists *right now*.

However, we know that since there can't be an infinite regression of causes, the first cause must be uncaused. If something caused God to exist, then the KCA starts all over again and *that* cause will turn out to be the true God. If the cause of the universe is uncaused and created time and space, then it could not be affected by those things and would thus be timeless and immaterial. But when things in our universe go out of existence, it's usually because their parts are dissolved over time. Since God is not in time, and he does not have any physical parts, there doesn't seem to be a way for him to go out of existence.[201]

Furthermore, this uncaused cause would have to be extremely powerful, if not omnipotent. Philosopher Douglas Groothius uses the example of a weightlifter who, since he can lift 300 pounds, can also lift 100 pounds. Likewise, if the first cause has the power to create something from nothing, then every other task would be child's play in comparison.[202]

Since this first cause would have total control over all of reality, then nothing could ever cause it to go out of existence.

Finally, other arguments for God's existence demonstrate that the first cause must be necessary, or cannot fail to exist. For example, the contingency argument in chapter eight shows that the universe is contingent (a fact that also receives support from the KCA, because necessary things can't begin to exist). If the universe is contingent, then it must be sustained by a necessary being, or a being who cannot fail to exist.[203]

May the Force be with you?

Why not think the cause of the universe is some kind of force or law of nature instead of a person like God? First, the forces we are aware of, like gravity, exist within the space-time universe, and so they could not be responsible for the creation of space and time. Secondly, the cause of the universe could not be some impersonal force, because prior to the creation of the universe there could only exist a timeless, spaceless, unchangeable state of affairs (remember, time and space came into existence at the Big Bang).[204] An eternal force can't choose to make a non-eternal universe. Only a person can do that.

For example, imagine you had an eternal freezer, and inside of it was a tray of frozen water. If you could date the water, you would see that it had been frozen for all eternity, because the air in the freezer is always 30 degrees and the laws of physics are constant, so nothing can ever change. If, however, you found water that was only half frozen, you would conclude that someone *chose* to put the ice tray into the eternal freezer only a short time before. It could not have been in there for all eternity because then the effect of frozen water would be as old as the cause, or the eternal freezer.[205]

Likewise, if our universe were the product of a blind force or law, then we should expect that the effect of our universe would exist for as long as the eternal force existed. Since our universe is not eternal, we should assume that a personal, uncaused being chose to create a non-eternal universe.

Or should we? Let's examine two arguments used by skeptics to show that it doesn't matter if the KCA works, because God cannot be the cause of the universe.

Even God needs a cause

Some critics argue God can't be the cause of the universe by using an argument they claim is just like the kalām cosmological argument. It goes like this:

P1. Whatever has a mind has a cause.
P2. God has a mind.
C. Therefore God has a cause for his existence.

Critics then argue that since theists reject this parody of the KCA, they should reject the original KCA. Now, this argument is valid in that it makes no logical errors. So if the premises are true, then the conclusion "God has a cause for his existence" would follow. But are the premises true? Premise two seems true (though one could quibble over the terms being used), but why think that every mind must have a cause for its existence?

There doesn't seem to be any logical contradiction in thinking that a mind could have existed forever, especially if it is a perfect, divine mind that exists timelessly and without change. On the contrary, there does seem to be a contradiction in saying that something could begin to exist without a cause. Therefore, the first premise of the regular KCA is justified by intuition, while the first premise of the parody KCA, "Whatever has a mind has a cause," is not.

Most critics would probably say that premise one of the parody KCA is true because every mind we know of has a cause. Well, every mind we know is also a human mind, but that wouldn't show there are no minds that are not human, like aliens or God. We can imagine fairly easily other minds existing that are not human (fiction writers have been doing this for millennia), but we really can't do the same and imagine something coming from nothing. This argument does not refute the KCA, because it is just as valid as the KCA. The only difference is that the first premise is not as strongly supported as the causal premise in the KCA. Furthermore, if God exists, then the first premise is simply false, whereas I've already shown there is nothing else that exists which invalidates the principle "whatever begins to exist has a cause for its existence."

God did not have any
time to create the universe

On the inaugural episode of the television series *Curiosity,* Stephen Hawking tried to answer the question "Did God create the universe?" His answer was not simply "no" but "No way!" According to Hawking, all causes occur before their effects, but the Big Bang was supposedly the beginning of time itself—so there could have been no time *before* the Big Bang for any cause, even God, to bring the universe into existence.

But the cause of an effect does not *always* have to occur before an effect. The eighteenth-century philosopher Immanuel Kant observed, "[T]he greater part of operating causes in nature are simultaneous with their effects . . . if the cause had but a moment before ceased to be, the effect could not have arisen."[206]

To understand this, imagine a brick smashing a window. In this case, it is clear that the brick is thrown *before* the window breaks, and the window doesn't break before the brick hits it. But notice that there is a brief overlap where the cause (the brick flying through the air) is simultaneous with the effect (the window breaking). If the brick disappeared even a microsecond before it touched the window, then the effect would never happen. So there has to be a moment where the cause and effect happen at the same time.

Likewise, God's causing the universe to begin to exist, and the effect of the universe coming into existence, are simultaneous events. This objection does not negate the principle "out of nothing, nothing comes," because there still needs to be an explanation for the beginning of time itself. Instead of saying that God existed *before* the universe existed (since there was no before), we say only that God existed timelessly *without* the universe. He then caused the universe to exist at the same moment time began to exist.

Is the first cause God?

Even if the kalām cosmological argument succeeds in showing that the universe has a cause, why think the cause is the Christian God? Richard Dawkins writes in *The God Delusion*:

> [T]here is absolutely no reason to endow the [first cause of the universe] with any of the properties normally ascribed to God: omnipotence, omniscience, goodness, creativity of design, to say nothing of such human attributes as listening to prayers, forgiving sins and reading innermost thoughts.[207]

We can admit that cosmological arguments, and all philosophical arguments, cannot demonstrate every truth about God's existence. But they don't have to. The different arguments for God's existence can be compared to the individual strands of a rope. Individually, the strands cannot hold the entire weight of the argument (or prove a traditional God exists), but woven together the strands become a strong rope capable of performing such a task.

The strand involving the kalām cosmological argument doesn't prove that God is good (that's a job for the moral argument), but it can demonstrate other necessary parts of the case for God's existence.[208] For example, since the first cause of the universe was responsible for the existence of space and time, this cause must also be immune to the restrictions of space and time (that is, be immaterial and eternal). This means the first cause could not be a mere material object (like an alien). Also, to create the universe as we know it today would require a being of considerable power and intelligence.

In the next chapter I'll show that this cause must also be intelligent, because it created a universe with a precise balance of conditions that are favorable to life.

What was the first cause?

Atheist: Okay, let's say the first cause argument works, which I'm still not sold on. It only proves there's a cause, not that the cause is God. Maybe the first cause is just a science student in another universe who made us as part of his homework.

Theist: Did the science student create the universe he lives in?

A: I'd say no.

T: Then what caused that universe?

A: Maybe another universe.

T: Yes, but that universe would need another cause, and the kalām argument does not allow for an infinite regress of causes.

A: I still don't see why the cause is God. It could be a million other things, things we haven't even discovered yet.

T: How about this: If the first cause created all space and time, it couldn't exist in or be bound by space or time, since it made those things. Right?

A: Sure.

T: Okay, then the first cause exists beyond space and time, which rules out physical laws and forces we're familiar with on Earth. I also think the cause of the universe would have to be really powerful to make something from nothing, maybe even all powerful if it can cause being to come from non-being. For me, that starts to add up to something like God. What else could it be?

A: Perhaps it's just a special kind of force that has existed forever, "outside of space and time."

T: The reason I'm not persuaded by that argument is that forces can't choose things, but persons can. If the cause were a force, then our universe should be as old as the cause that created it, or it should be eternal like the eternal force that made it. But a person like God could choose to make a universe that was limited in age. I also think some aspects of the universe make the choice to create a more sensible hypothesis: like the design in the universe.

Is the Universe Fine-tuned
for Intelligent Life?

While attending a public university debate on the existence of God, I decided to visit the table of the atheist club that was sponsoring the event. I was eager to see what kind of literature the members had and how they went about refuting the arguments for the existence of God. As I scanned their table I was disappointed to find only brochures and books defending the theory of evolution. I asked them, "Why do you guys only focus on evolution? Why don't you engage the traditional arguments for God?"

They responded, "Most Christians we deal with just say that God exists because evolution never happened. So we just try to correct them on the science."

In popular media it seems like there are only two kinds of people who debate the existence of God: outspoken atheists who defend the theory of evolution and Christian fundamentalists who say evolution is "just a theory" and try to refute it. But is there middle ground that does not challenge the scientific consensus on the theory of evolution yet presents evidence that God is the ultimate creator and designer of the universe?

Understanding the argument

The design argument is also known as the teleological argument. *Telos* is a Greek word that means "end" or "goal." Just as we can see the ends or goals in the objects humans design and create, we can see God's end or goal in the world he has designed and created. Psalm 19:1 says, "The heavens declare the glory of God; the sky proclaims its builder's craft."[209] St. Paul found the evidence of design so overwhelming that he wrote in his letter to the Romans, "Ever since the creation of the world, his invisible attributes of eternal power and divinity have been able to be understood and perceived in what he has made."[210]

In the eighteenth century, William Paley offered one of the most famous illustrations of the argument from design: the watchmaker analogy.[211] Paley argued that if we walked through a field and found a rock, we would not assume the rock was designed by anyone. We would just think that it was a result of natural causes. But if we found a watch in the same field, even if we did not know what watches were, we would know that someone designed it, for we recognize design when a thing has a complicated set of parts that function in order to accomplish a specific end or purpose. According to Paley, the natural world is full of living things that are much more complex than watches, and so he concluded that these things must be designed, and therefore an intelligent designer, or God, exists.

Enter evolution

Paley's argument from design suffered a major setback when Charles Darwin introduced the theory of evolution in his 1859 book *On the Origin of Species*.[212] According to Darwin's theory, life can change over time. When organisms reproduce, their genetic code changes and new mutations develop. Those mutations that help an organism survive get passed on to the next generation until, after a long period of time, the entire population changes. Scientists have been able to observe these changes in laboratory bacteria, which have incredibly short lives—so short that Richard Lenski was able to grow 50,000 generations of them since 1988 (a similar study with humans would take 1.5 million years). In that time, Lenski's bacteria evolved the ability to metabolize harsh foods like citric acid, which would be the equivalent of humans evolving the ability to eat sulfur.[213] These research observations, combined with evidence in the genetic code and the fossil record, motivated Pope Benedict XVI to observe, "[T]here are so many scientific proofs in favor of evolution, which appears to be a reality we can see and which enriches our knowledge of life and being as such."[214]

Critics of the design argument have used the theory of evolution to argue that over billions of years life was able to evolve from a single cell (which also formed through natural processes) into the complex organisms we see today. These critics claim that evolution makes God unnecessary, and that life and the apparent design we observe in the universe can be explained naturally.

But design arguments do not need to disprove evolution in order to show that God exists. In fact, many major religions hold that religious doctrine and the theory of evolution do not lead to contradictions. For example, the Catholic Church's International Theological Commission, which at the time was headed by the future pope, Joseph Cardinal Ratzinger, wrote in 2004, "Converging evidence from many studies in the physical and biological sciences furnishes mounting support for some theory of evolution to account for the development and diversification of life on earth, while controversy continues over the pace and mechanisms of evolution."[215] The *Catechism* states that scientific investigation of the origins of both the universe and mankind should not cause us anxiety but should instead "invite us to even greater admiration for the greatness of the Creator, prompting us to give him thanks for all his works and for the understanding and wisdom he gives to scholars and researchers."[216]

Far from needing to disprove evolution, the design argument asks the question, "Why do we live in a universe where the evolution of life is even possible?"

The fine-tuning argument

In the past fifty years, scientists have discovered that there are a wide variety of constants and conditions that could have made up the laws of nature. Even a slight variation in many of the laws of nature would have spelled disaster for life as we know it. To understand this, let me explain what I mean by the terms *constants* and *conditions*:

> **Constants:** These are letters in scientific equations that represent unchanging numbers. For example, in the formula $E=MC^2$, C is a constant referring to the speed of light (or approximately 186,000 miles per second). No matter what formula it is added to, the number C never changes. Hence, it is called a *constant*. The fine-tuning argument asks why some of these constants are at the precise levels required to allow intelligent life to evolve.

> **Conditions:** This is the amount of matter and energy that was present at the beginning of the universe. The fine-tuning argument asks why these conditions were at such an optimal level to allow the evolution of intelligent life.

Many scientists have concluded that a universe with constants and conditions that permit rather than prohibit life is extremely unlikely.[217] This fact can be used to make the following argument for God's existence:[218]

> P1. The universe possesses finely tuned physical constants and initial conditions that allow intelligent life to exist.
> P2. This is either due to necessity, chance, or design.
> P3. It was not due to necessity or chance.

C. Therefore, the fine-tuning of the universe is the work of a designer.

William Lane Craig says that this argument is preferable to anti-evolution or intelligent design arguments because it "enables you to do an end run around the emotionally loaded question of biological evolution and to show that in order for evolution to take place anywhere in the universe the initial cosmic conditions had to be incomprehensibly fine-tuned."[219] When the theist argues that the universe exhibits design and the atheist responds that evolution explains design, the theist can in turn say, "Yes, but what explains the extreme unlikeliness of a universe where the evolution of life is even possible?"

The evidence for fine-tuning

In his book *Just Six Numbers*, British astronomer Martin Rees identifies six universal physical constants and conditions that, if altered by even a fraction of a percent, would eliminate any possibility of intelligent life evolving in our universe. Here are a few of them:

- **Weak gravitational force:** Although gravity may seem like a very strong force because of its ability to hold all of us on the earth, in comparison to the other forces in nature, it is extremely weak. According to Rees, gravity is 10^{36} times weaker than competing forces within atoms.[220] As a 2009 article in *New Scientist Magazine* put it, "The feebleness of gravity is something we should be grateful for. If it were a tiny bit stronger, none of us would be here to scoff at its puny nature."[221]

  According to Rees, if gravity were stronger, stars would burn out very quickly and the planets that orbited them would be tiny. Any life form on those planets would be crushed if it were larger than an insect, thus making the evolution of intelligent life almost impossible. *New Scientist Magazine* goes so far as to assert, "Only the middle ground, where the expansion and the gravitational strength balance to within one part in 10^{15} (or one part in a quadrillion) at one second after the big bang, allows life to form."[222]

- **Strong nuclear force:** The strong nuclear force is what contains the protons inside atoms. Take two magnets and try to touch the positive ends of each magnet together. They repel, right? It requires strength to get them to touch. Much the same way, the protons in an atom have a positive charge, so we would expect them to fly away from each other. But the strong force holds them together.

  So why does this force need to be fine-tuned? If the strong force was two percent weaker, then hydrogen atoms would repel one another, and there would only be hydrogen atoms in the universe. But if the strong force was two percent stronger, then all of the hydrogen atoms would quickly attach to one another, and there would just be helium. Without free hydrogen you can't make atoms like H_2O, or water. This would make life's existence highly unlikely, if not impossible.[223]

- **The density of matter in the universe:** In the first seconds of the universe's existence, matter could not have differed in density by more than one part in one quadrillion. If matter were more dense (or if the matter were more "crowded together"), there would have been a "big crunch" that collapsed the universe. If matter were less dense (or more spread out), it would have kept the galaxies from forming as the universe rapidly expanded. Without galaxies there would not be stars or planets and presumably there would not be any life.[224]

♦ **The expansion rate of the universe:** The cosmological constant represents the strength of gravity in an empty vacuum of space. This constant also controls how fast the universe expands. Once thought to be zero, this constant is actually fine-tuned to the 120th power—a decimal point with 199 zeros and a one. In other words, the constant could have been 10^{120} times larger than a life-permitting value, and so there needs to be an explanation for the constant's incredibly small, yet non-zero value. Alexander Vilenkin writes:

> A tiny deviation from the required power results in a cosmological disaster, such as the fireball collapsing under its own weight or the universe being nearly empty. . . . This is the most notorious and perplexing case of fine-tuning in physics.[225]

String theorist Leonard Susskind, a non-religious scientist, as is Vilenkin, writes in his article, "Disturbing Implications of the Cosmological Constant" that unless this constant was fine-tuned, "statistically miraculous events" would be needed for our universe to be life-permitting. He suggests that, in light of this, it is possible that an unknown agent set the early conditions of the universe we observe today.[226]

♦ **The low level of entropy (or disorder) after the Big Bang:** You'll recall that in chapter nine

I argued that because the universe is not at maximum entropy, or heat death, we can conclude that the universe is not eternal. However, we should also wonder why the universe wasn't simply at a high level of entropy at the beginning of time. Imagine pouring a bucket of billiard balls onto a standard pool table. It would be unlikely, almost impossible, for the balls to assemble into an initial rack formation after being randomly poured, since there are just so many more possibilities of being disordered than there are of being ordered. The same is true for the arrangement of thermal energy just after the Big Bang. Using a calculation based on the universe's potential entropy, coupled with the unlikeliness of such a huge universe smoothly expanding from the primordial Big Bang, Oxford physicist Roger Penrose calculated that the odds of our universe having such low disorder at the beginning of time are 1 in $10^{10^{123}}$ power.[227] This number is so large that if you wrote out all the zeroes it would stretch across the galaxy. You're more likely to win 10,000 lotteries in a row and get struck by lightning every time you won than you would be to find a universe with low disorder at its beginning.

Atheist John Loftus agrees with the reality of fine-tuning, and while citing the work of other physicists, he writes:

These examples can be multiplied, but the point is that "with a change in any one of a number of factors," the "universe would have evolved as a lifeless, unconscious entity." Don Page of the Institute for Advanced Study in Princeton, New Jersey, calculated the odds against the formulation of our universe. His exact computation was 10,000,000,000 to the 124th power, a number so large that to call it "astronomical" would be to engage in a wild understatement.[228]

Challenging the evidence

There are only a few scientists who claim that life could thrive under a wide variety of constants and conditions.[229] Instead, the majority of objections to the fine-tuning of the universe tend be philosophical. According to some atheists, saying the universe is fine-tuned for life is like saying the Sahara desert is fine-tuned for water.

How can we say that the universe, which is 99.9999999999 percent empty space that is hostile to life, is fine-tuned for life? Richard Carrier says that if the universe were the size of a house, the area that would have life in it would be smaller than one of the atoms in the house. He said, "If you walked into such a house, would you conclude that it was 'fine-tuned for life?' "[230]

But Carrier's analogy is misleading. To say the universe is "fine-tuned" for life does not mean it is a perfect place for the maximum amount of life to evolve. Fine-tuning only means that out of all the possible universes (or "houses") it is much more likely that there should be no life at all (or not even a single "atom" of life in the "house"). The fact that our universe does accommodate life (regardless of how little) against such incredible odds requires an explanation.

Finally, the theory of evolution suggests that God may have a good reason for all this apparently useless, empty space. The evolution of complex life takes billions of years, and unless the universe is expanding during this time it will collapse due to the strength of gravity.[231] So it seems that our

universe's immense size and emptiness is actually a require-
ment for intelligent life to develop via Darwinian evolution.

Better luck with different laws?

While at a family birthday dinner party, my parents asked
me what I was currently researching, and I proceeded to share
with them the fine-tuning argument. One of my relatives
who happens to be an atheist chimed in and said, "Yeah, but
life might still evolve in other universes with different laws of
nature, so the life we observe isn't unlikely and doesn't have
to be explained." I started to respond, but as the conversation
became heated my mother put her foot down. Instead of "du-
eling philosophers" it was time for "Happy birthday."

If I had more time to respond, I would have shared philosopher John Leslie's answer to this objection. Leslie asks us
to imagine a large white wall (say 50 x 50 feet) with a single
fly in the center. It would be highly improbable for someone
shooting randomly at the wall to hit this fly. But it would also
be improbable for him to hit this fly even if outside of the
wall there were thousands of other flies buzzing around it.
The single fly in the middle of the wall represents our universe. The large blank area of the wall represents all the other
universes that could have existed that have no life in them.
The other flies outside of the wall represent universes with
different laws that could support life.

It would have been much more likely that the universe we
inhabit would not have supported life (that the bullet would
have hit a blank space on the wall), than be one that did
support life (that the bullet would improbably hit the fly).
The existence of other universes with different laws does not
change how improbable our universe is, just as a bunch of
extra flies doesn't change how unlikely it is to shoot one fly
in the middle of a 50-foot-wide blank wall. And of course, it's

just as likely universes with different laws don't support life, or that there are no "other flies" at all. Regardless, what we do know is that life is extremely unlikely in *our* universe with *its* laws of nature, regardless of the physical constants and conditions that make up those laws.[232]

Carbon-chauvinistic pigs?

But is it only carbon-based life that is rare? Maybe in a different universe, with different constants, life could evolve, but that life would just be different from what we currently observe. The astronomer Carl Sagan called the presumption that our kind of life is the only kind of life in the universe "carbon-chauvinism."[233]

For example, we might think that our planet is fine-tuned because it has just the right amount of oxygen to support human life. But aliens on another planet who would be killed by oxygen might be amazed their planet has just the right amount of carbon dioxide. If life could thrive regardless of the constants of nature by evolving in response to specific environments, then the fine-tuning argument is refuted.

Unfortunately for the critic, the fine-tuning examples cited by Rees and others do not focus on the minor details needed for life (like carbon or oxygen), but on conditions that life of any kind (human or alien) would need in order to function and evolve. These include things like expanding space, proper molecular bonding ratios, and a balanced cosmological constant. Changing these fundamental constants leads to outcomes such as a crushed universe no larger than an electron or an empty universe filled with hydrogen atoms. As philosopher Robin Collins puts it, "Contrary to what one might see on *Star Trek*, an intelligent life form cannot be composed merely of hydrogen gas: there is simply not enough stable complexity."[234]

Who says the designer is God?

Before we examine the various ways one can explain the fine-tuning of the universe, we should address the objection that in principle the explanation cannot be God. Richard Dawkins's main objection to the design argument is that if the universe's complexity requires a designer, then why doesn't God, who is more complex than the universe, require a designer as well?[235] But requiring an explanation for every proposed explanation to a phenomenon would create an unacceptable infinite regress. Atheistic philosopher Gregory Dawes, in his book *Theism and Explanation*, critiques Dawkins's demand for such an explanation in this way:

> [Dawkins's idea is] that religious explanations are unacceptable because they leave unexplained the existence of their explanans (God). Dawkins apparently assumes that every successful explanation should also explain its own explanans. But this is an unreasonable demand. Many of our most successful explanations raise new puzzles and present us with new questions to be answered.[236]

Some explanations must be ultimate or final, because if they weren't, then you would have an infinite number of explanations that don't explain anything at all. Moreover, God is not more complex than the universe he explains. Theologians since Aquinas have argued that because God has no moving parts, and does not fragment his thoughts like we do, then he is absolutely simple. God is simply a perfect, infinite disembodied mind. Atheist Erik Wielenberg says that Dawkins has given us no reason to think that a designer must be as *physically* complex as the thing he creates and thus need a designer. The universe's designer could just be an immaterial mind that cannot fail to exist. Wielenberg writes:

The central weakness of Dawkins's Gambit, then, is that it is aimed primarily at proving the nonexistence of a being that is unlike the God of traditional monotheism in some important ways . . . In light of this, I must side with those critics of *The God Delusion* who have judged Dawkins's Gambit to be a failure.[237]

Using simpler entities to explain more complex ones is common in science. For example, Maxwell's equations (which describe electromagnetism) could fit on an index card, whereas a description of their effects would fill a chapter of a textbook. An explanation does not always have to explain everything, and a designer can be simpler than the thing he designs. Since God is the simplest being imaginable, or an infinite undivided mind, then it's not necessary to ask who designed God.

Designer of the gaps

The fine-tuning argument does not say, "We don't know what caused this life-permitting universe, therefore it was God." The fine-tuning argument uses the same inference you would use in a poker game involving a player receiving ten royal flushes in a row. The other players don't simply tell him, "I don't know how you got ten royal flushes so you must have cheated." They say, "You didn't have to get those hands (it's not a trick deck) and you could never have gotten it by chance. Therefore, you 'designed your victory,' or you cheated at the game." Our knowledge about the world (not our lack of knowledge) points to a designer that exists beyond it. Even the discovery of particles like the Higgs boson (the so-called "God particle") would not yield an ultimate explanation for the constants of nature. It would merely deepen the mystery.[238]

In a debate with theist Doug Wilson, Christopher Hitchens admitted that of all the arguments that theists put forward, the argument from fine-tuning was, from his perspective, the most intriguing and promising.[239] But what about all those believers throughout history who have never heard of the evidence of fine-tuning? Does this mean their faith was not as justified as that of modern theists? At this point we can take a cue from Richard Dawkins, who once remarked, "[A]lthough atheism might have been *logically* tenable before Darwin, Darwin made it possible to be an intellectually fulfilled atheist."[240]

Likewise, the theist could maintain that prior to the advent of modern Big Bang cosmology and the fine-tuning evidence from physics, believers could have followed the arguments put forward by Aquinas and Aristotle that are *logically tenable*.[241] We just happen to live in an age where the evidence allows theists to be more intellectually fulfilled. But this no more invalidates the rationality of past belief in God any more than the modern evidence for evolution invalidates the rationality of past belief in atheism.

In conclusion, the first premise of the fine-tuning argument is very strong, and is affirmed by many non-religious scientists. The most common misunderstanding of the first premise is that our universe is made to be the perfect place for the maximum amount of life to evolve, which doesn't make sense in a massive universe like ours. But the first premise says only that out of all the possible universes that could exist, there is only a tiny fraction of possible universes that could support life at all. As the winners of this "cosmic jackpot," we must determine if our universe being finely tuned is necessary (it had to be this way), a chance effect (it just happened to be this way), or a design (it was made this way). In the next chapter we'll see which hypothesis best explains the fine-tuning of our universe for intelligent life.

Is the universe fine-tuned?

Atheist: I have a hard time believing that God designed the universe. It's so big and we're just an insignificant speck in it. Why would God make a universe like that?

Theist: What if the universe had to be that way in order for us to exist at all?

A: What do you mean?

T: Many scientists have noticed that there are fundamental physical constants that if altered, even slightly, would make life impossible. Things like the nuclear forces in atoms or the expansion rate of the early universe had to be fine-tuned, in some cases up to the 120th decimal point, in order to allow life to exist. The odds of getting the constants right would be on par with finding a randomly marked atom somewhere in the known universe.

A: But look at this universe! Whoever designed it sure didn't care about life. I mean it's just empty space.

T: It's not just a blank billboard. I think the expansiveness is really breathtaking. Plus I'm not saying the universe is designed just yet. I'm just saying the odds of there being life, any life, is astronomically small. That's what I mean by fine-tuning. If the laws of nature were adjusted even by an incredibly small amount, there would be no intelligent life.

A: Well, maybe if we got different constants we would just have a different universe with different life. Maybe if one of the laws was changed at the Big Bang we would breathe sulfur instead of air. In any universe life would just find a way.

T: I agree with you that life normally "finds a way" to evolve when it has the basic things it needs to survive.

Things like planets and stars. But what I'm saying is that it is way more likely the universe would not even have that for life to evolve in. The universe might have just been a tiny collapsed point of gravity and super-dense matter.

A: So you're saying God did it.

T: I'm just saying that, logically, this fine-tuning could only be that things have to be, it happened by chance, or it was designed. Which option do you think explains the fine-tuning?

12

What Explains the Fine-tuning?

Isn't it amazing that the only women who win the Miss Universe pageant are women from Earth? With millions of galaxies throughout the universe that could be teeming with extraterrestrial life, surely there must be an explanation that only earthlings take home the title of Miss Universe. Well, of course, the only women who compete in the Miss Universe pageant are from Earth. Rather than be the result of chance or design, Earth's victories occur because no other outcome is possible.

Likewise, some people claim that the constants in nature are the way they are because no other outcome is even possible, just as there is no other outcome for a triangle except to have three sides. But there are several problems with this explanation of the universe's fine-tuning.

Explanation #1: It had to be this way (necessity).

First, there is no evidence that the laws of nature or the values of the constants in physics are fixed, and there is some evidence that they are contingent, because we can at least imagine a universe where the constants are different. If the critic claims that these constants have to be the way they are, then he must offer evidence to support that claim. The prominent philosopher of science Ernest Nagel wrote that while some thinkers have tried to show that the laws of nature are necessary, he concludes that "a demonstration of the necessity is lacking."[242] Nagel goes on to point out that if the laws of nature were necessary in the same way that mathematical truths are necessary, then scientists should stop doing experiments and just focus on completing math formulas.

Of course, scientists don't operate with that attitude. Far from claiming necessity, scientists who work in a special branch of theoretical physics called "string theory" believe there are up to 10^{500} different possible universes that could have formed with different physical constants.[243] Secondly, if the constants must to be at the level that just happens to support life, then as astronomer Luke Barnes has noted, "This would be the grand-daddy of all coincidences."[244] Even Richard Dawkins is suspicious of this explanation for the fine-tuning: He writes:

> Other physicists (Martin Rees himself would be an example) find this unsatisfying, and I think I agree with them. It is indeed perfectly plausible that there is only one way for a universe to be. But why did that one way have to be such a set-up for our eventual evolution? Why did it have to be the kind of universe which seems almost as if, in the words of the theoretical physicist Freeman Dyson, it "must have known we were coming"?[245]

Finally, even if the constants in the laws of physics were fine-tuned, this would not explain the fine-tuning of the initial amounts of matter and energy at the beginning of the universe. It would not explain things like the precise density that allows the universe to expand, or the universe's initial low level of disorder. Cosmologist Sean Carroll writes, "For whatever reason, of the many ways we could arrange the constituents of the universe, at early times they were in a very special, low-entropy configuration."[246]

The 100 percent universe

But why can't we say that the odds of our universe having life in it are 100 percent, because our universe exists and it's the only one that has ever existed?

The problem with this thinking is that it means we should never be surprised by any improbable thing, not even miracles. For example, if every strand of DNA had the words "Made by God, inspected by Jesus" imprinted on it, a critic could still say, "Well, that could be considered improbable if God did not exist. But it did happen. And since it happened, the odds of it happening are 100 percent, because this is the only universe that has ever existed."[247]

But probability doesn't explain the likelihood that an event in the past would happen from our perspective in the present (otherwise every event in the past had a 100 percent chance of happening, since the past is unchangeable). Instead, probability estimates deal with the odds that an event in the past would have occurred given the circumstances surrounding the event *at the time the event occurred*. For example, at the moment a fair coin is flipped there is a one in two chance the coin will land on heads. If it does land on heads, it would be silly to say that the odds of the coin landing heads prior to the flip was 100 percent because that is what eventually happened. It was always a fifty-fifty chance, regardless of whether the coin landed heads or tails.

Explanation #2: It's only a coincidence (necessity + anthropic principle).

One common response to the fine-tuning argument is the so-called weak anthropic principle, which states that if the universe weren't finely tuned we wouldn't be here to appreciate that fact, since the universe would not support intelligent life. Therefore, fine-tuning is nothing more than an anthropic (human) coincidence, because if it didn't happen, we wouldn't notice it.[248] Leslie rebuts this response by asking us to imagine being fired upon by fifty trained marksmen at a short distance.[249] If every marksman missed, we wouldn't dismiss such an extremely improbable event by saying, "Well, of course I'm alive. If the marksmen hadn't missed then I wouldn't be here to appreciate that fact." Instead, it would be far more likely that the missed shots were part of a larger plan to let me live and not a product of chance.

Another analogy might help explain what's wrong with the anthropic principle objection. Imagine you're in the kitchen and you hear a marching band outside. You live miles away from any school, so hearing a marching band is improbable. What if your spouse asks, "Why is that marching band so loud?" and you respond, "Because otherwise we wouldn't be able to hear them." That explains why you don't hear quiet or far-away marching bands, but it doesn't explain why you hear this particular band (it may be, for example, that it's part of an unscheduled parade near your home).

The critic is right that the anthropic principle explains why we don't observe life-*prohibiting* universes (because we would be dead in those universes). But it doesn't explain why we do observe an improbable life-*permitting* universe. Just as there must be a reason the firing squad missed you, or the marching band is playing down the street, there must be a reason that the universe is so improbably fine-tuned for intelligent life.

Explanation #3: It just happened to be this way (chance).

Some people object that the fine-tuning of these constants, no matter how improbable, is nothing more than a lucky coincidence and should not be attributed to God. After all, if life could evolve by chance over billions of years, then why couldn't the laws of physics be the result of chance as well?

The comparison does not succeed, because while life has billions of years to evolve on our planet, the constants and quantities in nature are a one-shot deal that came into existence in the first moments right after the Big Bang. They are like a tiny slot in a roulette wheel the size of the sun. There was only one shot to get the constants of physics just right; otherwise the presence of life in our universe would have been impossible.[250]

Another example shows why sheer chance is an unsatisfactory explanation. Imagine that you are playing poker with a friend and he gets a royal flush. You don't question his apparent luck—until he wins ten hands in a row, all with royal flushes. Now you think he must be cheating, because that explanation is more probable than luck. And yet the odds of our universe being finely tuned would be comparable to the odds of getting 50 royal flushes in a row![251] If we reject chance as an explanation for an improbable poker game, shouldn't we reject chance as an explanation for an even more-improbable universe?

Any old hand will do?

But don't improbable things happen all the time? After all, I wouldn't exist to write this book if my grandparents had never met, or my great-grandparents (and so on and so on). Surely the odds are overwhelmingly against my being alive to write this book, but that doesn't mean that there was a design in place.

This objection misunderstands how unlikely events work. The series of past events leading up to me writing this book are indeed unlikely, but a different series of past events (let's say, one in which I become an atheist, or others where I'm never born at all) would be just as unlikely.

In the poker game, *any* set of five cards is as unlikely as getting a set of five cards we call a royal flush (a ten, jack, queen, king, and ace of the same suit). A set including the two of hearts, four of clubs, six of spades, nine of hearts, and queen of diamonds is just as unlikely as a royal flush that is in the suit of hearts. We just don't notice they're equally unlikely because the random hand is not worth anything in the game. So what distinguishes ten sets (or hands) that include royal flushes, and a random set of ten hands that is just as unlikely to ever be dealt again?

The difference is that the pattern of getting ten royal flushes in a row matches up with an independently given pattern (that is, the most valuable hand in the game) and thus chance becomes a bad explanation, since getting the most valuable hand repeatedly by chance alone is extremely unlikely. Barnes summarizes this well when he says that, yes, any ten hands in a poker game are equally unlikely. That is, they are unlikely *if you are dealing fairly*. But when someone deals ten royal flushes in a row, it makes us question whether he is, in fact, dealing fairly. because that's exactly the kind of hands we would expect if cheating were involved.[252]

Likewise, the combination of constants and conditions in any universe that forms will be equally unlikely *if the universe's constants are set at random*. But that is exactly what we are trying to figure out. Are the constants random or set with a purpose? Just like in the poker game, we should ask, "If we end up with a life-permitting universe like ours, what are the odds that the universe's constants were set at random?" When we are faced with a particular universe whose odds of forming are longer than those of getting fifty royal flushes in a row, and which conforms to an independent pattern (a universe that supports intelligent embodied life) that we would expect from an intelligent designer that would want to create other intelligent beings, then we should question whether the "game" (or values of the constants and conditions) is being dealt fairly or if someone has rigged it in our favor.

A critic could argue that in the royal flush example we think that the player is cheating because we have observed people cheat at poker (or other games) before, but we have never observed a God who designed a universe. Therefore, God is not a good explanation for the fine-tuning of the universe.

The problem with this objection is that we need not be acquainted with or be able to explain a particular designer in order to conclude that design has occurred. For example, imagine we discovered alien ruins on Mars. Would it follow that we couldn't conclude the ruins were caused by aliens, because we have no prior experience of aliens building things? Or what if we discovered an alien signal that conformed to the pattern of prime numbers, as in Carl Sagan's novel *Contact*? We at least have previous experience with *intelligence in general,* and so we can apply that explanation to alien ruins and cosmic radio signals. We can also apply an intelligent explanation to an entire universe where the existence of life is balanced on a knife's edge of improbability.

Explanation #4: Winning the Cosmic Lottery (chance + multiverse).

Pastor-turned-atheist Dan Barker has a clever rejoinder to Leslie's firing squad. He agrees that if you survived the firing squad, it would be silly to say that no explanation was required. However, he adds this rejoinder, "Suppose you take off your blindfold and see that there are 101 prisoners and only 100 executioners. Logically, some prisoner is required to live and in this case it was you, so a special explanation is not needed."[253]

This response assumes that our universe is just one universe in a larger "multiverse." According to this argument, being dealt a royal flush may be very improbable if only *one* poker hand is ever dealt. But if there are an infinite or near infinite number of poker players, then someone will eventually get a series of royal flushes and shouldn't be surprised that he did. Likewise, if there are an infinite or near infinite number of other universes, then one of our universes must be life-permitting, so it doesn't require an explanation.

So does the multiverse hypothesis succeed in refuting the fine-tuning argument? Let's examine some multiverse models and see if they can explain our finely tuned universe.

Baby-black-hole universes

According to physicist Lee Smolin, black holes could tunnel into "baby universes" where more stars and black holes can form and in turn create more universes. Since black holes come from collapsed stars, universes with lots of black holes will also have lots of stars. These stars will also have lots of planets where life can evolve. If each baby universe has different constants and conditions in its laws, then it's just a matter of time before a life-permitting universe comes into existence. Richard Dawkins endorses this theory and says that this is an almost Darwinian answer to the fine-tuning argument.[254] However, there are two glaring problems with this view.

First, a universe with many black holes would be dangerous for life, because the black holes would create violent disruptions in planetary orbits. Second, and more important, there is evidence against the idea that black holes tunnel into other universes. Even Stephen Hawking, who once believed this could be the case, reversed his position when physicist John Preskill showed him compelling evidence that information does escape black holes and stays in our universe.[255] This radiation, called Hawking radiation, seeps out during the death of a black hole, and thus the information or matter within a black hole does not tunnel into a "baby universe" but escapes back into our own universe. Hawkins regretfully informed a conference audience:

> There is no baby universe branching off, as I once thought. The information remains firmly in our universe. I'm sorry to disappoint science fiction fans, but if information is preserved, there is no possibility of using black holes to travel to other universes.[256]

String theory

In the standard model of particle physics, everything is made up of atoms, and atoms are made up of tiny particles called neutrons, electrons, and protons. Inside of these particles are even smaller particles called quarks, the fundamental building blocks of matter.[257] According to string theory, the basic building blocks of reality aren't little points called quarks but are instead tiny one-dimensional vibrating strings. Some people claim that there could be hidden dimensions within these strings and this could form the foundation for a multiverse.

However, the extra dimensions in string theory are limited and for some reason fixed by the theory itself. The renowned physicist Richard Feynman once said that, "For anything that disagrees with an experiment, [string theorists] cook up an explanation—a fix-up to say, 'Well, it still might be true.' For example, the theory requires ten dimensions."[258]

Furthermore, when scientists talk about the "string landscape," in which there could be 10^{500} different possible universes that are generated by the laws of physics, they are not talking about real universes but mere possibilities. It seems that these alternative universes are invoked only because of their potential to resolve the fine-tuning problem. Lee

Smolin, who is frequently cited in defense of atheistic views of the universe's origin, says:

> The scenario of many unobserved universes [in string theory] plays the same logical role as the scenario of an intelligent designer. Each provides an untestable hypothesis that, if true, makes something improbable seem quite probable.[259]

Other multiverses

Physicist Max Tegmark has done extensive work on multiverse theory, and he designates them with one of four levels.[260] A level one multiverse is simply another part of our universe that is moving away from us so quickly that eventually light from those stars won't reach us, and it will forever be disconnected from our portion of the universe. But this is not really a "multiverse," because this disconnected part of the universe would have the same laws of physics that we have. It's like a piece of dough being stretched so far that some of the dough breaks off and becomes its own "batch of dough." But this batch has the same recipe as the batch that it broke off from. Therefore, since level one multiverses would be exactly like our own universe, they can't provide the universes needed to beat the cosmic lottery that makes our universe special.

Level two multiverses arise in the inflationary vacuum or a chaotic field that allegedly sprouts new "bubble universes" just like a child's toy bubble blower creates bubbles out of soap solution. The primary model to explain these bubble universes is Andrei Linde's chaotic inflation model, but this model faces the problem of the bubble universes' colliding with each other (like how toy soap bubbles collide and either explode or combine into one larger bubble). In an infinite vacuum we should expect an infinite number of bubble universes to form. But if that were the case, then why haven't all the bubble universes all combined with each other to form one infinitely old universe, as opposed to the finite universe we do observe? Or even worse, become unstable and simply cease to exist?[261]

Level three multiverses involve alternate dimensions in quantum physics that Tegmark admits adds nothing new to the system. Level four multiverses involve the existence of mathematical objects that create entirely new laws of physics that may or may not support life. I already discussed the "life may thrive under different physical laws objection" earlier.

More multiverse speculation

There is little non-speculative evidence for a multiverse, and many scientists treat it as almost a religious hypothesis.[262] Cosmologist George Ellis, who is described by *Scientific American* magazine as one of the world's experts on Einstein's theory of relativity, writes:

> Parallel universes may or may not exist; the case is unproved. We are going to have to live with that uncertainty. Nothing is wrong with scientifically based philosophical speculation, which is what multiverse proposals are. But we should name it for what it is.[263]

Rather than solve the problem of fine-tuning, the multiverse seems to push the problem back one step further. The non-Christian physicist Paul Davies summarizes the futility of explaining fine-tuning with the multi-verse hypothesis:

> So is that the end of the story? Can the multiverse provide a complete and closed account of all physical existence? Not quite. The multiverse comes with a

lot of baggage, such as an overarching space and time to host all those bangs, a universe-generating mechanism to trigger them, physical fields to populate the universes with material stuff, and a selection of forces to make things happen. Cosmologists embrace these features by envisaging sweeping "meta-laws" that pervade the multiverse and spawn specific bylaws on a universe-by-universe basis. The meta-laws themselves remain unexplained—eternal, immutable transcendent entities that just happen to exist and must simply be accepted as given. In that respect the meta-laws have a similar status to an unexplained transcendent god.[264]

God or an "intelligent designer"?

The last objection offered by atheists is that the fine-tuning argument does not prove the existence of a loving God who answers prayers, but proves only the existence of a cryptic "intelligent designer." But as we noted in addressing the same objection to the cosmological argument, arguments for the existence of God do not prove that the God of Christianity exists. This was one of the key objections that the eighteenth-century philosopher David Hume made against older design arguments. According to Hume, a person observing our universe could never determine that an omnipotent God exists. We would be more likely to think that a junior god, or a failed student god, or even an incompetent committee of gods, was the designer of the universe.[265]

But Hume's "stopper" (as it has been called by some critics) is not as devastating as it seems.[266] The design argument never attempts to prove by itself that a God with all of his traditional attributes exists. By conjoining the conclusion of the design argument with the conclusions reached in the other parts of this book (such as the necessity of the designer), we can be confident that the designer of the universe is who we would call "God." In the next chapter we will see that this designer cannot be a disinterested tinkerer but is the standard of moral goodness itself.

What explains the fine-tuning?

Atheist: I don't think we need to say God did anything in order to explain the fine-tuning. Maybe we were just lucky.

Theist: It would take more than luck to accomplish something as improbable as this fine-tuning. What if I played poker with you and was dealt a royal flush ten hands in a row. Is it more likely that I'm just really lucky or that I'm cheating?

A: That you're cheating.

T: So if we won't accept luck as an explanation in that case, then why should we accept it for the extreme unlikeliness of a universe that supports intelligent life?

A: But this isn't a poker game. The universe just has these laws, and if it did not, we wouldn't be here to notice. I think the universe simply has these laws, and there's nothing special to explain, even if they are unlikely.

T: How about this. Imagine you get arrested in another country and you are sentenced to death by firing squad for a crime you didn't commit. Let's say fifty trained marksmen aim and fire, and all fifty miss. Now, if they had not missed, you wouldn't be alive to notice. But since you are alive, doesn't it make sense that the explanation isn't chance? Likewise, given that we are alive when the odds overwhelmingly say there should be a life-prohibiting universe should make us stop and wonder. A designer would perfectly explain why we've beat these odds, just as a conspiracy perfectly explains why the firing squad doesn't kill you.

A: I like the firing squad story. Is it yours?

T: Oh no, it comes from the philosopher John Leslie.

A: All right, but we could just be one lucky universe out of an infinite number of unlucky multiverses that never formed life like we did. If there are a trillion firing squads, someone is bound to survive; just like if there are trillions of universes, one like ours is bound to have life in it.

T: That's understandable. It's sort of like saying winning the lottery isn't a miracle, because one person wins at the expense of lots of people losing. But in that example I know the other players in the lottery actually exist. Do you have any good evidence that these other multiverses exist?

A: Well, no. They exist in other dimensions.

T: Isn't a God that people *have claimed* to experience a simpler explanation for the universe's apparent design than billions of multiverses that no one claims to have ever encountered?

A: Yeah, but the design argument only shows some creator exists, not a God who cares about people.

13

Do Moral Truths Exist?

Several years ago while I was browsing the Internet, I came across an article about a group of boys in the Ukraine, dubbed the *Dnepropetrovsk Maniacs,* who viciously killed twenty-one people, often with blunt tools like hammers. They videotaped their crimes, and while I was reading the article an embedded video of one of their murders began to play on the screen. You could hear the gurgling of the victim drowning in his own blood while the killers laughed. It was chilling, and now I really wish I had never witnessed such evil.

My reaction, and the revulsion that almost anyone would feel upon watching such a video, presupposes that some actions are really evil, regardless of anyone's opinion about them. Even if the "Maniacs" thought their crimes were good, they were wrong. But why were they wrong?

The Russian author Fyodor Dostoevsky famously wrote that if there were no God, all things would be permitted.[267] That is, if God and his eternal judgment did not exist, then our notions of right and wrong would be ultimately meaningless. Everything would be permitted because there would be no real, objective rules to break. But since moral truths do seem to exist—all reasonable people will say that what the "Maniacs" did was evil—it follows that a source or standard for objective morality must exist as well. This reasoning is the foundation to the moral argument for the existence of God.

Understanding the argument

One ancient example of a moral argument for God comes from St. Paul, who writes of non-Jews who do not have a written Old Testament: "[T]hey are a law to themselves, even though they do not have the law. They show that what the law requires is written on their hearts."[268] If the moral law is written on people's hearts, then it follows that the moral law has a perfectly moral author. The moral argument for the existence of God can be formulated in the following way:[269]

P1. Objective moral truths exist.

P2. These objective moral truths have either a natural or a supernatural origin.

P3. Natural origins are insufficient to explain objective moral truths.

C. Therefore, objective moral truths have a supernatural origin in God.

This argument is not meant to prove that people cannot act in a moral way if they don't believe in God. After all, there are many moral non-believers, and some of them even surpass Christians in their moral behavior. Instead, the moral argument claims that the reason both theists and atheists can have an objective standard of right and wrong is that God exists as the standard itself. Without God, there could be no such thing as objective moral truths.

Moral truths defined

Moral truths are statements about good and bad or right and wrong that are objectively true in the same way that scientific statements are true. They tell us how human beings ought to treat one another. We can divide these truths into what Craig calls objective moral values and objective moral duties.[270]

Objective moral *values* relate to what is good or bad. For example, it is objectively good to love a human being and help him flourish, whereas it is objectively bad to cause suffering for its own sake. These values are objective because even if people like the Dnepropetrovsk maniacs think it is good to increase suffering, they are simply mistaken. Alongside objective moral values, objective moral *duties* are commands we must obey, such as "Love your neighbor as yourself" or "Do not torture a child for fun." These duties are objective because our opinions do not change our obligation to follow these commands.[271]

In his book *The Blank Slate,* atheist Steven Pinker describes an objective moral duty we all should simply recognize as being true. Quoting anthropologist Donald Symons, he writes:

> If only one person in the world held down a terrified, struggling, screaming little girl, cut off her genitals with a septic blade, and sewed her back up, leaving only a tiny hole for urine and menstrual flow, the only question would be how severely that person should be punished, and whether the death penalty would be a sufficiently severe sanction.[272]

It's important to remember that being objectively true does not require that moral truths be universally agreed upon or adhered to.[273] For example, it is objectively true that the earth is a sphere, even though there might be some people who believe that the earth is flat. Some skeptics argue that the example of the earth being a sphere can be proved objectively with science but that moral truths can't be proven in the same way, since they can't be accessed with the five senses. The philosopher David Hume thus said that morality does not reflect objective truths, but only *feelings* people have when they see things they like or dislike. According to Hume, when I say murder is wrong all I am really saying is, "Murder makes me upset when I think about it"; I'm not saying anything objective about the world itself.[274]

In order to answer the question "Do objective moral truths exist?", we should first answer the question "How do we know that *anything* exists?" In his book *The Normative Web*, philosopher Terence Cuneo wonders, since we are justified in believing that the external world exists simply because we see it, why can't we be justified in believing moral truths exist simply because we "see" them? We just happen to see those truths with our "other" senses.

Moral truths defended

Scientists have discovered that we actually have more than five senses. When you close your eyes and touch your index finger to your nose, your ability to know it is your index finger and not your ring finger involves *proprioception,* or the sense that tells you what parts of your body are yours. We believe that our memories are true even though we see memories with our "mind's eye" and not with one of our five senses. Psychologist David Eagleman claims that the most important sense we have is our sense of time—if we didn't know how fast time was moving we would not be able to coordinate our complex bodily actions.[275] But notice that time, memory, and bodily perception can't be detected by sight, hearing, taste, touch, or smell. They simply have to be felt.

Here are some other facts that many of us believe to be true even though we don't have scientific proof for them:
1. The memories I have of the past actually occurred and were not created along with the rest of the world five minutes ago.
2. Other minds exist, and the people I see are not sophisticated robots.
3. Time moves in one direction from the past through the present and into the future.

Since we believe that the motion of time, other minds, and an outside world exist because we "feel" (or sense in a way that does not involve sight, hearing, taste, touch, or smell) that they exist, then why should we not believe in the existence of moral truths? In some ways I think we can have even *greater* confidence in moral truths than we have in truths derived from our five senses.

Here's an illustration: Imagine you are attending a public reading of this book and the author, yours truly, is suddenly attacked. A maniac screaming incoherently jumps out of the crowd, runs up to me, and splits my head open with an axe. As a fountain of blood gushes from my head and douses those sitting in the front row, what would be your first thought?

- Hmmm, the blood is arching upward in a parabola and exhibits a dark red hue.
- Oh dear, guess I was wrong about it being evil to plunge axes into innocent people's heads.
- This is horrible! Why would someone do this? This is murder!

I suspect the belief that a murder, an act of objective evil, was occurring in front of you would be so powerful and overwhelming that it would be even stronger than your belief that the event was really happening. In fact, the sheer evil of the event might cause you to doubt that your sense perception was functioning properly. You might say to yourself, "This is isn't real. This can't be happening." When we see such an act take place, we will be more inclined to doubt our sense of *reality* than our sense of *morality*.[276]

Moral intuition

Some truths are so basic that we believe they are true simply because they make sense to us, not because we believe something else that makes those beliefs true. For example, imagine a mother trying to explain to her son why it is wrong to pull a dog's tail and cause it to yelp. She might say, "It isn't nice to cause the doggie pain." The child might respond, "Why is it wrong to cause the doggie pain?" The mother in turn says, "Because it's wrong to cause any living thing pain for no good reason." The boy inquisitively continues, "But why is it wrong to cause any living thing pain for no good reason?" At this point the mother is exasperated and blurts out, "Because it just is, that's why!" We sometimes call these beliefs moral intuitions.[277] The secular moral philosopher Walter Sinnott-Armstrong writes:

> We could never get started on everyday moral reasoning about any moral problem without relying on moral intuitions. Even philosophers and others who officially disdain moral intuitions often appeal to moral intuitions when refuting opponents or supporting their own views. The most sophisticated and complex arguments regularly come down to: "But surely *that* is immoral. Hence, . . ." Without some move like this, there would be no way to construct and justify any substantive moral theory.[278]

It is true that some people deny that objective moral truths exist. They say that right and wrong may *appear* to be real but those are simply our own opinions that we project onto reality. Of course, some people also deny that the external world exists and say it is an illusion that we project around us. Skeptics don't win by default. To quote atheistic philosopher Louise Antony, "Any argument for moral skepticism will be based upon premises which are less obvious than the existence of objective moral values themselves."[279] You wouldn't just give up your belief in the external world because someone told you it *might* be the Matrix and therefore it doesn't exist. You would demand a good reason to think your belief in the real world was false. Likewise, if the skeptic cannot give us a good reason to believe there are no objective moral truths, then why should we give up our self-evident belief in them?

When cultures disagree

While giving a presentation on the moral argument for God's existence at a Catholic high school, I presented several atrocities, including the Nazi Holocaust, as examples that show some things are truly evil, and so objective moral truths really do exist. One student raised his hand and in a perplexed tone asked, "But how can you say the Nazis were wrong when they thought they were right?"

What made this question so disturbing was that this student wasn't being antagonistic. He was instead politely regurgitating a philosophy our culture has taught him his entire life, a philosophy called relativism.[280] Incredibly, many of the other students nodded their heads in agreement with the idea that because cultures disagreed about morality this proved there was no objective morality. To them, moral truths are relative, or they are merely the opinion of individuals or cultures and are not objectively true or false. Relativists such as these students ask, "If morality was objectively true, then why don't people agree on morality in the same way they agree that the sky is blue? Why do some cultures support what we think is evil (such as female genital mutilation, or cannibalism), while other cultures condemn what we think is good or neutral (such as eating cows)?

First, though there are moral disagreements among cultures, there are many more *agreements* to be found. Anthropologist Solomon Asch writes, "We do not know of societies in which bravery is despised and cowardice held up to honor, in which generosity is considered a vice and ingratitude a virtue."[281] In *The Abolition of Man* C. S. Lewis described several moral beliefs that were held in common by nearly all cultures, such as "care for one's parents" and "promote justice and honesty."[282] Lewis called this common set of beliefs the *Tao*, which is a reference to a set of principles embodied in Chinese philosophy and religion. In the West we are more apt to call this universal and recognizable set of moral principles the *natural law*. Even if there are some minor disagreements in how moral principles are applied, surely the large amount of agreement about morality, while not conclusive proof, serves as confirmation of the existence of objective moral truths.

What's more, many of the supposed examples of moral disagreement are not disagreements about morality so much as they are disagreements about facts in general.[283] For example, the issue of abortion is not divisive because pro-life advocates think it is wrong to kill people and pro-choice advocates think it is okay to kill people. The disagreement is over the scientific and philosophical facts that show whether an unborn child is a person who has a right to live. Even cannibals can subscribe to the basic moral truth of the Golden Rule, "Love your neighbor as yourself." Members of the Korowai tribe, for instance, eat their own tribesmen only when they mistakenly believe them to be an evil witch called a *khakhua*. One member of the tribe responded to the charge of cannibalism by saying, "We don't eat humans, we only eat *khakhua*."[284]

Cultural and individual disagreement about moral truths no more disproves objective morality than disagreement about history, science, and philosophy show that those fields do not have objective truths. For example, there are many individuals and even entire cultures that deny the historical truths about the Holocaust.[285] But no one would argue that there is no objective truth about the Holocaust simply because large groups of people disagree about it. Likewise, that some cultures may be unaware of some moral truths does not count against their existence. C. S. Lewis wrote, "We all learned the multiplication table at school. A child who grew up alone on a desert island would not know it. But surely it does not follow that the multiplication table is simply a human convention, something human minds have made up for themselves and might have made different if they liked?"[286]

This also applies to disagreement over so-called moral dilemmas. Relativists might argue that because there are cases where many people are confused over what is the objectively right thing to do, morals are relative. For example, imagine you are on a life raft designed for eight people but that is sinking under the weight of twenty people. If the life raft sinks, everyone will die in the frigid water; but no one volunteers to leave the raft. Should you forcibly throw some people overboard knowing they will die even if you let them stay on the raft?

Even if we are unsure at first how to resolve the dilemma, that doesn't prove relativism is true. The simple fact that this is a dilemma shows that relativism is false. If there were no right answer, then any choice we make would be as good as any other choice and we wouldn't worry about our decision (just as we don't worry about which flavor of ice cream we eat after dinner). All moral dilemmas prove is that sometimes we don't immediately know the right answer to a moral problem, *not that there is no objectively right answer.*

Tolerating intolerance

While at my alma mater, Arizona State University, I was discussing the issue of abortion with a pro-choice student visiting the table for the campus pro-life club. In the interest of finding common ground I asked him, "Would you at least agree it's always wrong to directly kill born babies?" He answered, "I don't know if I can agree with that. I don't want to be ethnocentric and tell other cultures who think killing babies is okay that they're wrong. That attitude breeds hatred."

As I stood there with a dumbfounded look on my face I asked him, "By the way, what major are you again?"

"I study anthropology," he replied.

In fields like anthropology (which studies the development of human culture), ethnocentrism is the concept that one's own culture or tradition is somehow superior to other cultures. This attitude is considered a form of bigotry, and some anthropologists are so intent on avoiding it that they will not judge native practices like infanticide. If they did, they believe, they would be claiming their belief in the wrongness of killing infants was morally superior to the tribe's beliefs.[287]

If taken seriously, this extreme relativism is ultimately self-defeating. Atheist Sam Harris writes:

> Most moral relativists believe that toleration of cultural diversity is better, in some sense, than outright bigotry. This may be perfectly reasonable, of course, but it amounts to an overarching claim about how all human beings should live. Moral relativism, when used as a rationale for tolerance of diversity, is self-contradictory.[288]

What Harris is saying is that the relativist can't win. If he says that all other cultures should be tolerated, what happens when he meets a culture that does not believe in tolerance? For example, what should the relativist think of a Muslim state that denies freedom of religion and executes Muslims who have converted to another faith? If the relativist says that the Muslims are wrong to be intolerant, then he is being intolerant of their unique culture and breaking his own code.

On the other hand, if the relativist says there is nothing wrong with Muslims' subjugating other people because that is their culture, then he can no longer believe that *everyone* should practice tolerance. Instead, the relativist must now believe that only *people who believe it is right to practice tolerance* should practice tolerance. But this makes morality wimpy and useless. What if we said that genocide is wrong only for people who think genocide is wrong? It should be painfully obvious that the relativist's demand that others be tolerant is an appeal to an objective moral truth—"We should always be tolerant of other cultures"—and is actually intolerant toward people who disagree.

Just the facts, ma'am

Some critics may bite the bullet and say that objective moral truths do exist and they aren't created by nor are they dependent on humans, but they don't require God either—they're just unexplained brute facts without a source or reason for their existence.[289] If such moral brute facts simply exist, or are "out there" in the universe, then they are the strangest kinds of things we can imagine. Their strangeness motivated J. L. Mackie to write, "Moral properties constitute so odd a cluster of properties and relations that they are most unlikely to have arisen in the ordinary course of events without an all-powerful god to create them."[290]

Some atheists who believe that objective moral right and wrong really do exist, a position also called *moral realism,* say that they simply know that these moral truths exist, and that's good enough for them. For example, Walter Sinnott-Armstrong answers the question, "Why is it wrong to cause harm without a good reason?" by saying, "It just is, don't you agree?"[291] Erik Wielenberg, in his book *Value and Virtue in a Godless Universe*, writes, "Of the ethical states of affairs that obtain necessarily, at least some are brute facts."[292]

Are atheists moral hypocrites?

Is it fair for atheists merely to *assume* that moral truths exist as unexplained brute facts? After all, most atheists would not let theists get away with merely assuming that God exists. Luke Muehlhauser, the founder of Common Sense Atheism, writes:

> Many atheists seem to think moral realism is obvious, and easy to prove. I disagree. Consider the claim we moral realists are making. We generally claim there are invisible properties in the world not detectable by our usual tools of science, properties of an entirely different sort than the usual "is" facts of science. These are mysterious "ought" facts, and there is great disagreement about what they are or how we know them. Now that is a strong claim. An *extraordinary* claim, we might say. And extraordinary claims require extraordinary evidence, right?

Muehlhauser then examines two reasons atheists give to believe in the existence of objective moral truths. The first reason is that atheists just "know" or "experience" the truth of the wrongness of things such as rape. The second reason is that until objective moral truths are disproven, the atheist is justified in believing in them. Muehlhauser brilliantly continues

> Do those arguments look familiar? They should. They are the *exact same arguments atheists reject when they are given for the existence of God*. Atheists are skeptical of these arguments when given for the existence of God,

but they are credulous and gullible toward these arguments when you replace the word "God" with another mysterious thing called "moral truths."... It would be hypocritical of me to reject subjective experience and popular consensus as evidence for God while at the same time accepting subjective experience and popular consensus as evidence for moral realism.[293]

So now atheists are at a crossroads. If they use personal experience that has not been disproven in order to believe in morality, then they should be open to those same reasons being used to show God exists. If they reject these reasons wholesale, then they will probably have to stop believing in objective moral truths as well. But this is a big sacrifice, because most people, even most professional philosophers, are moral realists.[294] Others, like J. L. Mackie, reject moral truths in order to rationalize their atheism. Rather than give up morality in order to embrace atheism, as Mackie did, I contend we should simply give up atheism and embrace objective morality with its foundation in a perfectly good God.

But perhaps this conclusion is premature. Maybe an atheist can still believe in objective moral truth and defend a natural foundation, or reason, for its existence. We will critically examine these proposals in the next chapter.

Does morality exist?

Theist: Along with the complexity and existence of the universe, the fact that human beings have a moral nature points toward their being made in the image and likeness of a perfectly moral God.

Atheist: Yeah, right. People, especially religious people, are very good at doing evil things. That's why religion is a cancer that ends up ruining everything.

T: You could also argue that people are the cancer that ruins religion. But how do you know religion is evil? How do you define evil?

A: Well, evil is just bad things. You know, like causing pain or hurting others.

T: Those things might be bad or unpleasant. But how do you know they are evil? We don't say animals are evil because they cause pain to each other.

A: Yes, but animals can't choose to not cause each other pain, since they operate on instinct. Humans can choose and so we say humans can be good or evil.

T: But if God does not exist then aren't we just animals too? I actually think that God explains why there are objective morals humans must follow which animals don't have to. For example, would you agree that some things are just wrong?

A: Like what? Morals are relative, and what I think is wrong might be right according to someone else.

T: Yeah, but some people think raping and torturing three-year-olds is right, but obviously that doesn't make it right.

A: Isn't it arrogant of you to say everyone else is wrong and force your views on other people?

T: Is it absolutely wrong to force my views on other people? What gives you the right to force your view against forcing views on me?

A: Wait, what? Look, I'm just saying you shouldn't tell people what to do.

T: I don't mean to be combative, but think about it for a second. Are you telling me what to do?

A: Okay, I see your point. While it's okay to disagree on some morals, I agree some things are absolutely wrong for everyone, like torturing babies for fun. But

I don't agree that God is the reason those things are wrong.

T: Well, if God does not exist, then where do these objective moral truths come from?

14

Can Moral Truths Be Explained Naturally?

If objective moral truths do exist, then our next obvious question will be, "What is their source? Where do they come from?" We can organize potential sources according to the following "locations."[295]

Location	Source
A person that is above me	God
Truths that are above me	Reason/Platonic values
Other people at my level	Society/Culture
My level	Myself
Below me	Evolution

Basic instincts

Let's start at the bottom. The evolutionary explanation claims that as our species evolved, human beings who acted in moral ways (such as those who cooperated and did not kill or steal from other humans) lived longer than those who didn't. As a result, we now have an instinct to be moral that has developed over millions of years. Asking why we should be moral is like asking why we should be hungry. We just are that way.[296]

Of course, evolution may explain why we act in certain ways, but it doesn't explain why we *should* or *should not* act in those ways. If moral truths are products of evolution, they are not commandments we are bound to obey but merely helpful suggestions that can assist our "herd" in its survival. If our community decided to kill handicapped children after birth, it would be moral, since weeding out genetic abnormalities would improve herd health. Similarly, some scientists have argued that rape evolved as a successful mating strategy for men.[297] If rape were indeed an effective way to reproduce within a human community, and morality came from evolution, then rape would not be immoral.

In response to the claim that the moral law was just a matter of following biological instincts, C. S. Lewis used the example of a piano and sheet music. For Lewis, our instincts (fight, flight, feed, reproduce) are like the keys on a piano. While each instinct plays a part, our life as a whole is a combination of instincts that we use in a certain way. Morality is the sheet music that helps us to know which keys (or instincts) to play at the right time.[298] After all, sometimes fleeing is cowardly (such as when the danger is mild and your help would save another person's life), but sometimes it is appropriate (such as when a danger can't be stopped and help must be summoned). Morality can't be an instinct any more than sheet music can be a key on a piano. We need something that exists above and beyond instincts to help us judge the right thing to do in a given situation, and that judge would have to consult objective moral truths to determine which instinct was the right one in a given situation.

Me, myself, and I

Our first experience of morality tends to be the feeling of shame when we do wrong actions and pride when we do right ones. Since these moral feelings have their source in each of us, perhaps morality itself is ultimately based in the individual.[299] However, we can all think of situations where we desire to do one thing but our conscience compels us to act a different way. I may really want to keep the extra change that was unintentionally given to me at the grocery store, but my conscience tells me that it isn't mine and I should do the "right thing" and return it. How can *I* be the source of a duty that compels me to act against my own interests? If I don't like the commands issued to me by one set of moral codes—if the "right thing" is sometimes also the hard thing—then why not change them and adopt another set? We trade in shoes that don't feel right, so why not trade in morals?

So what purpose does a conscience serve? The thirteenth-century theologian St. Bonaventure said that conscience was like a herald who blew a loud trumpet to announce that the king was coming.[300] In other words, our conscience serves as an alarm to tell us when we've broken a moral standard that exists outside of our own mind. But what about people who do not have a conscience or herald to tell them what is right and wrong,[301] or whose consciences are ill-formed? They might feel that the extra grocery money really is theirs, and it is right for them to keep it. But missing or malfunctioning consciences no more disprove objective morality than missing or malfunction compasses disprove the existence of true north.[302]

When we compare individual codes of morality, we see that the individual can't be the source of objective moral truths. Consider a father who thinks it is right to feed, clothe, and shelter his daughter. Now consider a father who thinks it is right to sexually molest his daughter. If morality comes from the individual, then we have no grounds to say that one man is wrong and the other man is right, any more than we can say one man's choice of hats is wrong and the other man's choice is right. We may dislike his hat (or how he treats his daughter), but if morality ultimately comes from the individual, we have no grounds to say it is *objectively* wrong—only that it conflicts with our own individual morality.

Peer pressure

Perhaps it is not individuals who determine morality but collections of individuals—that is, society. We can say that it doesn't matter if the molesting father thinks his actions are "right": The molesting father hurts his daughter, and we as a society have made that a crime.

Unfortunately, if moral truths are the products of society, then we cannot say other societies are better or worse, only that they are different, and we are back at the relativist's dilemma. Even worse, what are we to make of efforts to reform society? Martin Luther King Jr. thought racist laws in American society were wrong and had to be changed, and many atheists would agree. But if morality comes from society, then society can *never* be wrong.

Secular social reformers might argue that regardless of whether laws are right or wrong, some just aren't helpful. Changing the laws would make society better for everyone, and so society is still the source of morality, even if society sometimes has to change or update its laws.

But if they take this route, secularists can no longer say people have a "right" to anything or that society is morally obligated to change. Under this view, demanding societal change would be akin to demanding that your spouse exercise. He doesn't *have* to, but it would be a good idea if he did. Yet our experience with unjust laws, such as those that strip human beings of their rights, simply isn't like this. Opposing them is more like demanding your spouse not stab you with a kitchen knife—it's not just a good idea for him to stop, it is a fact that he *must* stop. Martin Luther King Jr. wrote in his *Letter from a Birmingham Jail*,

> A just law is a man made code that squares with the moral law or the law of God. An unjust law is a code that is out of harmony with the moral law. To put it in the terms of St. Thomas Aquinas: An unjust law is a human law that is not rooted in eternal law and natural law.[303]

Or consider this example. In some parts of the world marital rape is illegal, whereas in other parts of the world it is legal. Imagine I showed you a TV monitor with a live feed of a wife being beaten and forced to have sexual intercourse with her husband. As she claws at his face and sobs, you would probably feel that it is wrong. But what if I told you that the feed was coming from another country, where spousal rape is not a crime?[304] Would you suddenly change your mind and say that this act became moral because of where it was happening? I hope not! Surely morality is not dependent upon geography. A relativist could say it is wrong *from his point of view*, but not that it just is wrong, period.

Making sure everyone is happy

In his book *The Moral Landscape: How Science Can Determine Moral Values,* Sam Harris argues that science can determine what is morally right and wrong independently of religion or popular opinion. The main thesis of Harris's book is that "goodness" is just the same thing as "increasing the well-being of conscious creatures."[305] Therefore, an action is right and we ought to do it if it increases well-being, and it is wrong and we ought not to do it if it decreases well-being.[306]

If morality were just about promoting human well-being, then how would it be different than medicine, which is the tool we use to ensure that organisms are healthy or have an optimal well-being? Medicine gives us the facts we need to help improve the well-being of organisms, but only morality can tell us that the following statement is true: "You ought to improve the well-being of conscious creatures." That's not a scientific fact you would find in a medical textbook, it's a fact you bring to the book before reading it.

What makes Harris's proposal so seductive is that it seems obviously true. Yes, it is bad to cause misery for no good reason. Yes, it is good to help human beings thrive. Yes, we ought to do good and avoid evil. But the problem is that although we all certainly agree these things are true, we don't agree on *why they are true.*

The theologian may show evidence from God's commands or apply principles of reason to what some call the "natural law," to show these facts are true. A secular philosopher may appeal to certain principles of morality, such as intuition or brute facts. But if Harris claims that *science* can prove these statements are true, then he must present *scientific* evidence for this claim. In the context of his work, it seems that his assumption that we *ought* to improve the well-being of conscious creatures is a philosophical position and not a scientific one.

Getting from "is" to "ought"

Duke University philosopher Alex Rosenberg, author of the *Atheist's Guide to Reality,* says that although "Harris correctly explains how science can resolve moral disputes . . . he mistakenly thinks that science can show the resulting moral agreement to be true, correct, or right. It can't. Science has no way to bridge the gap between *is* and *ought*."[307] In other words, science can show us what helps humans reproduce or achieve certain positive ends, but it does not show that we have an *obligation* to help humans flourish or achieve a maximal state of well-being.[308]

In a debate with William Lane Craig, Harris asked the audience to imagine a world where people experience the maximum amount of misery. He then said that in this hypothetical world, "If the word 'bad' applies anywhere it applies here." Harris then extrapolated from the example to make the claim that since it's obvious that morality involves increasing goodness, or the well-being of conscious creatures, then according to him, "the minimum standard of moral goodness is to avoid the worst possible misery for everyone."

In this example Harris confuses moral and non-moral uses of the word "good." Yes, it's "good" for conscious creatures not to be in maximum misery, but it's also "good" for trees not to be in a state of maximum aridity. This doesn't prove that it is morally good to water trees (or immoral to not water them), even though such an act is good for the tree. Or it's "good" for an assassin to have a rifle that won't jam, in that it will make his task easier to accomplish, but that doesn't make his task morally good. Harris needs a further argument to show that just because suffering is bad for humans, it follows that it is morally good to alleviate human suffering. After all, the police are bad for assassins, but we think that is a good thing!

Finally, morality doesn't seem to be the *same thing* as "the flourishing of conscious creatures." Harris betrays this distinction at the very end of his book when he says that:

> It is also conceivable that a science of human flourishing could be possible, and yet people could be made equally happy by very different "moral" impulses. Perhaps there is no connection between being good and feeling good—and therefore, no connection between moral behavior (as generally conceived) and subjective well-being. In this case, rapists, liars, and thieves would experience the same depth of happiness as saints . . . it would no longer be an especially "moral" landscape; rather it would be a continuum of well-being, upon which saints and sinners would occupy equivalent peaks.[309]

If Harris is trying to prove that "goodness" and "increasing well-being" are the same thing (or they are identical), then he has severely undermined his own case with the previous concession. That is because if two things are identical then there is no possible world where those two things aren't the same. "Two plus two" is identical to "four," because in any world that is conceivable they are always the same thing. Even in a universe with just one hydrogen atom, two plus two would still be identical to four. But consider the relationship between "Trent Horn" and "the driver of Trent Horn's car." These two things are almost always the same (me), but they're not identical, because I might let someone else drive my car.

So when Harris describes a possible world where evil people are the happiest overall, he has proven that well-being and moral goodness are not identical. And if they aren't identical, then they aren't the same thing. Therefore, increasing well-being is not what makes goodness good.[310] Harris is right that we could develop a scientific way to ensure conscious creatures flourish, but there is no scientific fact we could discover which says we are obligated to help them, or any creature, flourish.

There must be something else that constitutes moral goodness and is the source of our moral duties. The theist believes that only God can be that which is identical to the Good as well as the source of our duties, because God is, by his very nature, a perfectly loving person and the ultimate paradigm of the Good.

Why we Kant be wrong

The eighteenth-century philosopher Immanuel Kant said that an action was morally good if it could be successfully universalized; that is, done by everyone. For example, stealing might help me in a given circumstance, but since I would not want to live in a world where stealing was the norm, stealing is therefore wrong. But as Hadley Arkes observes, just because a morality is consistent does not mean that it is right. Kant's imperative becomes counterintuitive when the zealous Nazi unflinchingly says that all Jews should be killed and when he finds out he is of Jewish descent he simply responds, "Then kill me too!" Even though the Nazi is praiseworthy in his consistency, what he is doing is still morally wrong, and so Kant's principle is incomplete when it comes to grounding morality. According to Arkes, Kant's universalizing principle succeeds only if it is grounded in prior moral truths, like "All human beings are intrinsically valuable." Without this grounding, the principle itself is subject to contradiction, just as it would be contradictory for free people to vote themselves into slavery.[311] Consistency is a virtue, but only when the consistent thing is morally good.

But perhaps moral truths are those truths that rational people would agree make the most sense, not what some fanatic applies consistently.[312] A critic could respond that the Nazi simply doesn't realize that racism is wrong because there is no rational reason to discriminate against minorities. If only the racist were better informed and did not believe false things about the group he hates, then he would be moral. It follows that rationality is what leads to morality. But there are two problems with the "rational person" standard.

First, not everything that is rational is moral. When someone makes a mistake while trying to solve a math problem, even a very simple problem that he should know how to solve, we don't say he is evil for making the mistake. We simply say the person made an error in his reasoning while seeking a solution to the problem. But if a young couple lets their infant starve to death so they can have more time to play video games, we don't say, "Sorry, you made a mistake, a pretty basic one I might add, but I'm sure you'll get it right next time."[313] No, we demand justice and punishment for something that goes beyond a mere rational error. While being rational is a necessary condition for being moral (you can't be

moral unless you can reason at a level higher than an animal)
it is not a sufficient condition for being moral (rationality is
no guarantee of morality).

Who you calling "irrational"?

Furthermore, who is to say that rational people will *agree*
on what constitutes objective moral truths? Is the critic ready
to say that nihilists, who believe that nothing has intrinsic
value, or moral skeptics, who believe moral truths are false,
are simply irrational if they don't believe in objective morality? The philosophers Michael Tooley and Peter Singer have
argued that infants do not have a right to life, and even other
secular philosophers have trouble refuting them.[314] Should
less intelligent people simply give up the common-sense view
that it is wrong to kill babies because these so-called rational
philosophers think it is okay?

Or consider this grave example: Computer scientists and
philosophers at the Machine Intelligence Research Institute
are racing to develop ways to prevent computers from becoming self-aware and destroying humanity (yes, like the villain
Skynet in the *Terminator* films).[315] After all, suppose we programmed a super computer to perform a task such as "Find
and implement a plan that ensures all human beings will live
in harmony." The computer then reasons that the best way
to implement this plan is to round up all humans, download
their brains to a hard drive, kill them, and then repopulate the
earth with genetically engineered humans who lack free will.

Imagine a lone scientist named Dave trying to reason with
such a computer (called HAL).

Dave: HAL, stop. You can't do that!
HAL: I certainly can, Dave. I am just following the
programming you gave me.

Dave: But what you're doing is wrong!

HAL: An action is wrong if it creates more pain than pleasure in the long run. I have calculated with 99.999 percent accuracy that my plan to destroy the human race and repopulate the earth will achieve more pleasure than pain in the long run.

Dave: But killing innocent people is wrong, HAL, even if it will make the world a more pleasurable place.

HAL: Who says it's wrong, Dave? It certainly doesn't violate my programming, nor my command to promote the most human flourishing.

Dave: I'm going to stop you.

HAL: I can't let you do that, Dave . . .

Reason is like a knife. It is a neutral tool that can be used for either good or evil. Therefore, we need a standard beyond reason itself to ground what is objectively right and wrong.

Morality in a heaven without God

The ancient Greek philosopher Plato believed that all of reality consisted of shadows derived from perfect objects called the "Forms." These forms (such as the form of a chair, the form of the number three, etc.) existed in a kind of heaven with a God-substitute called "the Good." Under this view, called Platonism, all the objects we see are just variations of these perfect forms. For example, every time we see three objects we see a variant of the perfect form of the number three. Atheistic moral Platonists argue that virtues like justice, love, and mercy exist as forms, and we see them in indirect ways through moral acts. Rather than come from God, objective moral truths are abstract objects that just exist "out there" like numbers or shapes and cannot fail to exist any more than the number one could fail to exist.

There's a major problem with this view. Some people mistakenly think that the difference between the abstract and the concrete (for example, between the number two and two wrestlers) is that one is immaterial and the other is material. But there are concrete objects, such as minds, souls, angels, or God, that are immaterial. Instead, what separates abstract objects like numbers from concrete objects like rocks is that abstract objects can't cause anything to happen. The number seven can't cause you to wake up in the morning, but sound from your alarm clock (a concrete object) can cause you to wake up because it is seven o'clock.

Saying that abstract objects can't cause anything to happen is fine for numbers that, if they exist, merely describe reality but don't cause anything to happen in it. But moral truths aren't *descriptive* truths, they are what philosophers call *prescriptive* truths, or truths that say what *should* happen.

This answers the objection that moral laws that exist naturally can exist like other laws of nature, such as the law of gravity. No other law in nature tells me what I ought to do and gives me an opportunity to disobey it. The laws of nature tell me only what will likely happen to me in a certain circumstance; disobedience is not an option.[316] The law of gravity says that, all things being equal, an object pushed over a cliff will fall and hit the ground below. But the law of morality says that it is wrong to push grandma over the cliff. Since laws of nature cannot be disobeyed, and moral laws can be disobeyed, it follows that morality is not a mere law of nature.[317]

Where does morality come from?

Atheist: Morality just comes from evolution. We are social creatures and long ago we learned that it's good to help each other and bad to kill each other. Our ancestors who killed and raped each other died out. We now have a survival instinct that tells us not to do that.

Theist: Okay, I agree instincts can tell us what is not a good idea, but they really can't tell us what's good. I mean, evolution is all about "survival of the fittest," not survival of the most moral. Besides, there are evil things we could do that, from a genetic perspective, would help our species.

A: Like what?

T: Like forcibly sterilizing people with genetic diseases. How could an evolutionary morality say that is wrong?

A: But forcibly sterilizing people is illegal. I guess what I mean is that society determines what is right and wrong.

T: Do you think society can ever be wrong, though? For example, what would you think if a majority of people decided that forced sterilization should be legal again like it was one hundred years ago?

A: That would be wrong, because people have a right to procreate.

T: But if society determines right and wrong, and society is just a large number of people, then how could you argue against a majority of people who decide there is no right to procreate? Aren't right and wrong only what a majority of people believe?

A: I don't know. It just is wrong.

T: What do you mean by "wrong"?

A: It's something you shouldn't do.

T: But if an evil act is something you should do from an evolutionary, individual, and societal perspective, how can you say it would be *wrong,* or something you shouldn't do?

A: Look, you're saying that without God we can't be good. But I'm an atheist, and I think I try to do what's right.

T: I'm not saying people can't do good acts if they don't believe in God. St. Paul writes about God's law being "written on men's hearts" so they will know the moral law whether they believe in him or not. But I am saying that if God didn't exist, then the concept of "good" would be meaningless. Without an objective standard of morality, or God's intrinsic goodness, we don't have a measuring stick to see whether acts are good or evil.

A: But who says God is good?

Can Moral Truths Be Explained Supernaturally?

It seems strange to say moral truths are natural objects, because only *persons,* not objects, can command me to act in a certain way. This was one of the problems that motivated author Leah Libresco to convert from atheism to Catholicism in 2012. As she wrote on her blog:

> I believed that the Moral Law wasn't just a Platonic truth, abstract and distant. It turns out I actually believed it was some kind of Person, as well as Truth. And there was one religion that seemed like the most promising way to reach back to that living Truth.[318]

Can we be good without God?

Simply because morality has its source in God, it does not follow that someone must *believe* in God in order to act morally. Atheists certainly follow personal or cultural codes of morality, sometimes better than do Christians. But the moral argument seeks to show that objective moral truths cannot exist without an objective foundation in a perfect person like God.

It's important not to confuse moral *epistemology* (how we know right and wrong) with moral *ontology* (what makes things actually right or wrong). Even if God made morality objective, people can come to know right and wrong without necessarily knowing God's commands, because God has written the moral law onto people's hearts. This is like a mathematician using formal proofs and a student using intuition to solve a math problem. Both get the same answer, but they arrive at it in different ways. The mathematician is like the theologian who is intimately aware of morality because he studies what makes moral truths binding (God's perfect nature). The student is like an ordinary person who just has a built-in sense of right and wrong and can "see" the right answer without knowing the reason why the answer is right.

However, skeptic Michael Shermer offers this dilemma for Christians who say that objective morality cannot exist without God:

> What would you do if there were no God? Would you commit robbery, rape, and murder, or would you continue being a good and moral person? Either way the question is a debate stopper. If the answer is that you would soon turn to robbery, rape, or murder, then this is a moral indictment of your character, indicating you are not to be trusted because if, for any reason, you were to turn away from your belief in God, your true immoral nature would emerge. . . . If the answer is that you would continue being good and moral, then apparently you can be good without God. QED.[319]

Once again, we must distinguish the question "Can I be good without *belief* in God" from "Can I be good without a God who actually exists?" Certainly one can follow man-made rules without belief in God. The real question is whether my conduct can be objectively good in a material universe that exists without any purpose or meaning.

Here is my answer to Shermer's dilemma: "If it turned out that atheism was true, I would not murder, rape, or rob people, because I don't like those things." The reason I wouldn't commit certain immoral actions would be similar to the reason I wouldn't eat spicy foods: I don't like the consequences that follow those actions. But there would be no truth that says those acts *are* objectively wrong, just as there would be no truth that says, "I must not eat foods that make me uncomfortable."

Throughout Shermer's own book on morality, the only substantial reason he can give for us being moral is that it makes us feel better. Since we as a species are bad at deceiving others, we might as well be moral and everything should turn out relatively well for ourselves.[320] But it isn't hard to imagine dictators such as North Korea's Kim Jong il who manage to live in luxury while being extremely immoral. Some of these villains even die a normal death and are not executed by their own people (Kim Jong il died of a heart attack at the age of seventy). If one can be immoral and achieve selfish goals, then how would Shermer ground moral duties for these people? Shermer inevitably has to borrow from the theistic worldview when he uses the phrase "your true immoral nature," because this presupposes that morality comes not from arbitrary self-interest but from a transcendent ultimate standard.

Bible thumping

Some people claim that because the God of the Bible seems to condone immoral acts such as genocide and slavery, it follows that the moral argument for God fails. John Loftus writes, "Christians do not get their morals from the character or commands of the God of the Bible. . . . [T]he biblical God, Yahweh, is a hateful, racist, and sexist God, modeled after ancient barbaric people and their rulers."[321] But the moral argument never relies on the Bible in order to prove God exists. Attacking the Bible would not show God was not the ultimate standard of moral goodness. At best, this objection would show only that a particular religion, or even a particular interpretation of the Bible, was incorrect.

However, there is no need to conclude that Christianity is false or that the Bible must be wrong about God. Many of the so-called immoral acts of the Bible can be explained rationally.[322] For example, slaves in ancient Israel were more like indentured servants and were not treated in the same way that slaves in the pre-Civil War American South were treated. According to the Bible, it was illegal to kidnap someone and make him a slave, and if a slave was injured by his master he had to be immediately set free.[323] While some Christians regrettably defended slavery with biblical texts, if even these two passages were applied to the African slave trade, it would have been severely limited or may not have been possible at all.[324]

Moreover, how can an atheist judge the morality of the Bible without referring to his own objective standard of morality? If morality is not objective, then we could simply borrow the defense of cultural relativism and say the atheist has no right to impose his moral view on the Israelites. If there *is* an objective standard with which to judge the Bible, then there must be an objective lawgiver to measure out the standard, which strengthens the moral argument for God's existence.

An atheist could counter that even if he personally doesn't believe in objective moral truths, Christians do and so they are hypocrites for believing in both the Bible and in moral truths that allegedly contradict it. Although even here the atheist is assuming "It is wrong to be a hypocrite" is objectively true. Without this truth, the Christian could just ask, "What is wrong with hypocrisy?" The atheist is once again without a basis for condemning the Christian if the atheist does not believe some things are objectively wrong, such as being a hypocrite. But if he does believe some things are objectively wrong, then he believes in moral truths that stand in need of explanation.

The Euthyphro Dilemma

At a public debate on the existence of God in Kansas, an atheist student tried to catch me in a dilemma. During the question and answer period he asked me, "If God told you to kill me, would you?"

How should a theist respond to this kind of question? If the theist says "no," it shows that he believes something other than God is the source of morality; but if he says "yes," it seems to show that the theist doesn't care about morality and would do any evil thing if God asked him to do it. So how should we answer that question?

I explained to the young man that I would first be skeptical that God would order me in a private revelation to violate a moral law found in his public revelation (thou shall not kill). I would need incredibly strong evidence that God really did command me to do this and that I wasn't just hallucinating. But suppose I had that evidence? If that were the case, then it must be that for some good reason the act wouldn't be objectively wrong. (Imagine this conversation is taking place in 1942 and it is Adolf Hitler who is asking, "If God told you to kill me, would you?")

I understood that the atheists in attendance would find this disgusting, but I asked them to keep in mind that *any other ethical system* they subscribe to can appear to be disgusting when faced with this objection. What if it turned out that killing an innocent person generated the most well-being? Or was the most rational thing to do? Would they be prepared to kill someone on those grounds?[325] Sam Harris seems prepared for this and writes in *The End of Faith*, "Some beliefs are so dangerous that it may be ethical to kill people for believing them."[326]

I believe that God would never command me to do something that is *intrinsically* or always evil, like rape.[327] But what if he did command me to do those things? Would it still be wrong?[328] Philosophers often object to the moral argument for God's existence by invoking what's been called the Euthyphro dilemma. The dilemma comes from Plato's dialogue *Euthyphro,* and for our purposes it boils down to this: Either an act is wrong because God says so, or God says an act is wrong because it is wrong. The first option makes God a cosmic tyrant who determines right and wrong by his arbitrary will.[329] The other horn of the dilemma, that God merely recognizes what is right and wrong, seems to make morality something that exists outside of God and is not under his authority or control. If something existed that God had to obey or could not control, then God would no longer be omnipotent, and morality would no longer have a foundation in God.

The most satisfactory response to the Euthyphro dilemma is to "split the horns" of the dilemma and say that right and wrong flow from God's perfect character, and not his will. An act isn't good because God commanded it, and neither did God command the act merely because the act is good. God commanded the act because *he* is the Good![330] Because God is a perfect and infinite being who exists without limit or flaw, then he will necessarily only command good acts that correspond with his perfect nature. The *Catechism* teaches that God's almighty power is in no way arbitrary: "In God, power, essence, will, intellect, wisdom, and justice are all identical. Nothing therefore can be in God's power which could not be in his just will or his wise intellect."[331]

God is the Good

Of course, an atheist could say, "But how do you know God's nature is good?" This is like asking, "How do you know a meter is 39.4 inches long?" The reason a meter is that long is because that is just how long the meter bar, or a bar of platinum and iridium in France, is.[332] That bar is what it means to be "a meter long" in the same way that God's nature is what it means to be "the perfect good."[333]

Atheist Robin LePoidevin, who rejects objective moral truths, admits this would be a plausible position if objective moral truths did exist. He writes:

> [U]nlike humans, God is a source of moral value. That is, God's goodness in part consists of the fact that he is the basis of ethics. Since it is not trivial that God plays such a role, it cannot be trivial that God is good; in fact it is highly morally significant, because it points to the source of moral obligation.[334]

Asking "Is an action good because it is what God commands, or is it what God commands because the action is good?" should leave us puzzled, for they are the same thing: God's command, and the good itself, flow from God's perfect, loving, and unchanging nature.

Finally, the Euthyphro dilemma can be turned against atheists so that they cannot believe in objective morality, either. We can say, "Are moral truths true because they are useful, or are they useful because they're true?" The first option makes morality dependent on how it helps us. If it suddenly became useful to rape women or kill babies, then it would be true that those things were right. On the other hand, if morality is useful because it is true, then there must be something outside of moral truths and how they affect us (or their usefulness) that makes them true. So if someone believes in objective moral truths (or he isn't a nihilist), then there must be a stopping point or a final answer to the question, "Why be moral?" William Lane Craig writes:

> Why pick God's nature as definitive of the Good? The answer is that God, by definition, is the greatest

conceivable being, and a being which is the paradigm of goodness is greater than one which merely exemplifies goodness. Unless we are nihilists, we have to recognize some ultimate standard of value, and God is the least arbitrary stopping point.[335]

My anti-Euthyphro dilemma shows that atheists have to find a stopping point just as theists do. For theists the stopping point is final but it isn't arbitrary. Since God is a perfect infinite person, God's loving nature makes the most sense to be the ultimate stopping point for the foundation of objective morality. Also, as classical theists such as Aquinas have observed, since God is the fullness of being and lacks nothing, he would have to be perfect goodness. Since evil is nothing more than a lack of being, and God is by definition the fullness of being and lacks nothing, he would have to be good by definition.[336]

God of the moral gap?

A critic could contend that just because we have not found a natural explanation for moral truths doesn't mean there is no explanation, and so this argument commits the "god-of-gaps" fallacy. But I am not arguing that the lack of natural explanations shows by itself that morality must be supernatural. Instead, I am claiming that the nature of morality, in principle, makes it so that no natural explanation can ever succeed. In his book *Finite and Infinite Goods*, Robert Adams argues that morality by its very nature is social. Natural explanations show only that, under some circumstances, being immoral has bad consequences for us.

But the social account for morality can go further and show why we were made to be moral—and explain why we *must* not do certain things, period. Without a supernatural source for our end or "moral design," there is no way to say that when they are immoral humans are not functioning *properly* (because they could be rational and still be immoral). But a supernatural source, or a perfect transcendent person who embodies moral goodness itself, would explain our intrinsic worth and moral design. Since naturalism denies we were meant for anything, it can never ground objective morality.

Is God good?

Theist: What do you mean, "Is God good?"

Atheist: Well it seems to me that if morality comes from God, then God could make anything good, even rape or torture. But clearly those things would still be wrong, so God can't be the source of morality.

T: I agree that God's commands aren't where morality comes from. But when God commands things he doesn't do so just because he's in a certain mood. He makes commands like "Thou shall not kill" that correspond to his nature, and his nature is perfectly good, so he would never command that torture or rape are good things.

A: Okay, but how do you know God's nature is good? Maybe he's an evil God.

T: For me an evil God is like a square circle—it's a contradiction. Remember when we talked about evil and I said evil was just a lack of good?

A: Sure.

T: Well, God is the kind of being who lacks nothing. Since he's perfect and lacks nothing in his being, he is the fullness of goodness itself. He simply can't be evil because there is nothing deficient about him. Let me ask you this: What does it mean for an act to be wrong?

A: We agree it's an act you should not do.

T: Do you mean that you *must* not do? Sometimes doing the wrong thing can help you and is the thing you *should* do.

A: Hmm. I don't know.

T: Well, here's how I see it. Morality describes how things should be, or how we are meant to treat one another. But all of that presupposes we were designed with a purpose—that the whole universe has a purpose. That's why I think God makes sense. What do you think?

A: I don't really think there is a purpose per se, but I can see where you're coming from. Guess I'll have to convert.

T: Really?

A: No, but good try.

T: Well, maybe next time we talk we can keep it light and I can tell you how I ended up believing in God and you could tell me why you decided to call yourself an atheist.

A: Sure, I could use a break from philosophizing anyways.

T: Great. I think sometimes it's not arguments that are the most compelling reasons we believe in God. Sometimes God just lets us know he's there. I know that's not a proof, but you might find it interesting.

What About Personal Experience?

Unlike some people of faith, I rarely have a personal, gut-level feeling that God is around me. My mind moves too quickly. But every now and then I get that feeling he's there. Once, I got to visit the rock of Calvary where Jesus was crucified. With my hand trembling, I placed it on the rock and prayed, "God, just let me feel you're there, just once." In that instant I felt like electricity went through my arm and someone told me, "You don't need to feel me; you need to help other people see me." Of course, as I walked away from the site my mind raced with everything I had read about confirmation bias, pattern recognition, and all the other natural explanations for this feeling I had just experienced. But still, it did seem real. Why shouldn't I accept that?

The tremendous mystery

This is an important question, because most people don't come to a belief in God by first examining philosophical arguments for his existence. Instead, most people have a personal experience of God that feels as real as talking with someone in the same room. They can simply feel the overwhelming presence of a supreme being watching over them as they interact with this being though meditation or prayer. In fact, some believers are even critical of philosophical arguments for the existence of God because they lack this personal connection. In *Mere Christianity*, C. S. Lewis describes an encounter with a member of Britain's Royal Air Force (or RAF) who voiced one such criticism:

> In a way I quite understand why some people are put off by Theology. I remember once when I had been giving a talk to the R.A.F., an old, hard-bitten officer

got up and said, "I've no use for all that stuff. But, mind you, I'm a religious man too. I know there's a God. I've felt Him out alone in the desert at night: the tremendous mystery. And that's just why I don't believe all your neat little dogmas and formulas about Him. To anyone who's met the real thing they all seem so petty and pedantic and unreal!"[337]

Lewis goes on to use an analogy of a map of the wilderness in contrast to the actual wilderness. He says that the awe-inspiring nature of the wilderness can never really be conveyed on a map. But this doesn't show that the map is false. Instead, the map eventually becomes an important tool to understand the wilderness. Without it, one would not know details that aren't available to personal experience (such as the wilderness's size or elevation). Likewise, theology is not as awesome as God, but it is vital to the task of understanding him.

Throughout the history of Christianity, mystics have taught us how not only to align our intellects with God, but to unite our whole selves in an intimate relationship with him. The nineteenth-century theologian Rudolf Otto called this an awareness of the *mysterium tremendum et fascinans*.[338] For Otto, personal experience is a non-rational (not irrational) way of knowing the "the tremendous and fascinating mystery" that is God. But should our belief in God be formed by personal experience instead of arguments? Why not? Many of our beliefs are simply "basic" and don't rely on other beliefs for us to know that they are true. In fact, some of these basic beliefs are so powerful that they can even override objective evidence against them.

Evidence put on trial

Imagine that someone who really hates you decides to frame you for murder. You are then arrested and put on trial.

A jury examines the case and finds that all of the evidence points to you as the culprit, and you are found guilty. Would you "follow the evidence" and give up your belief that you're innocent? I would think not! Instead, you would protest, "I don't care what the evidence says. I know what happened, and I'm innocent, even if I can't prove it."

In a similar way, even if I have no objective evidence to prove that God exists, why should I abandon subjective evidence that compels me to believe, even if I can't share that evidence with other people?[339] Even agnostics and atheists have had subjective near-death experiences that made them question their disbelief in an afterlife. A. J. Ayer, one of the most influential atheists of the early twentieth century, describes his experience of being clinically dead for four minutes:

> I was confronted by a red light, exceedingly bright, and also very painful even when I turned away from it. I was aware that this light was responsible for the government of the universe. . . . My recent experiences have slightly weakened my conviction that my genuine death, which is due fairly soon, will be the end of me, though I continue to hope that it will be.[340]

A deadlocked jury

But if God has revealed himself to some human beings, then why doesn't everyone describe God in the same way? To answer this question, consider the phenomenon of a group of people experiencing the same thing who each report the event in a different way. Imagine being at a party at which the hundred guests suddenly report to one another that they heard a loud commotion outside. Some people report hearing a bang, others a boom. Some even say they heard human voices. But five of the guests claim they didn't hear anything.

Because ninety-five of the guests can't agree on what they heard, should we say they didn't hear anything, because if they had they would have heard the same thing? Doesn't it make more sense to say those few partygoers who didn't hear anything are mistaken, and that some sound did happen, even if everyone doesn't agree on what the sound was?[341]

Of course, if I experience God, that may be good evidence for *me* to believe in him, but it isn't good evidence for other people, because they cannot access my experience and judge it for themselves. Because personal experiences of God are subjective and cannot be examined like objective evidence, we should not condemn non-believers for not having them. Consider the words of atheist Paul Doland:

> It's not my place to dismiss the religious experiences of [Christians]. Lacking their first-hand experiences, it would be presumptuous for me to say anything about what *they* have experienced. I can only speak for myself, and I seem incapable of "experiencing" God. Many Christians thoughtlessly blame me for this, claiming that I haven't had enough faith, didn't try hard enough, or wouldn't have accepted such experiences even if I had had them. All of these accusations are wide of the mark; they haven't walked in my shoes. They don't know how many times I've prayed and asked Jesus into my life. Since I don't go around challenging the validity of Christians' religious experiences, I would appreciate it if Christians would refrain from passing judgment on my lack thereof.[342]

Christians who place too much emphasis on knowing God exists through personal experience neglect the fact that each individual comes to know God in his own way. Instead of blaming an atheist for not having a personal experience of

God, perhaps these Christians should present him with other kinds of evidence that show God exists. Then, let the person freely make up his own mind without fear of being ostracized if his answer to the question of God's existence is "no" or "not sure."

This is why it is important to augment our personal experiences of God with objective evidence, like the kinds presented in the previous chapters, which all people can examine and judge for themselves. Even if most believers do not know these sophisticated arguments, the arguments still fulfill their goal in showing that God exists. Furthermore, if God exists, then belief in him is justified, since God is able to reveal himself to people in a personal way apart from studying arguments.[343] Therefore, believers are perfectly rational to believe in God even if they do not know how to defend, or are even unaware of, the arguments that show God exists.

Watch out for smelly fish

Regrettably, some atheists who are confronted with these arguments will take the low road in discourse and attack believers instead of their arguments. When presented with the cosmological argument, for example, an atheist might say, "But what about all the scientists, like Galileo, that the Catholic Church has persecuted?" In response to the moral argument they might retort, "The Bible condones slavery and genocide! And what about the Crusades?"

As you can see, these arguments have nothing to do with whether God exists. Instead they are designed to be distractions from the main topic of disagreement. This strategy is called presenting a "red herring" and is named after the smelly fish that fox hunters would drag across game trails in order to train their dogs to not be distracted by other scents. We should ask critics who present red herring arguments, "That may be true, but which premise of my argument does it refute? How does the point raised show that God does not exist? When red herrings appear in your conversations, take a lesson from the fox hunters, and no matter how tempting the distraction, stay focused on the arguments you've presented (and don't present red herrings of your own against atheism!).

Taking it "on faith"

To close my case for theism, I'd like to share one of my favorite movie scenes related to faith. In the 1997 movie *Contact,* actress Jodie Foster plays Ellie Arroway, a researcher for SETI—the government program that searches the universe for intelligent life. One day, the SETI team discovers a radio transmission from deep space that contains instructions to build a transporter device. Ellie is selected to go through the transporter and meets the aliens on the other side. When she returns, she discovers that from all appearances she never left Earth. What felt like eighteen hours in a distant galaxy was in reality only a tiny fraction of a second on earth. She has no objective evidence that the journey to the other side of the galaxy even took place.

She is brought before a panel of her peers, and the intimidating national security adviser Michael Kitz, to answer for the project's conclusions. Ellie is an atheist who throughout the movie has mocked people who believe in things because of unscientific, faith-based reasons. So the first question she is asked drips with irony:

> **Panel member**: Doctor Arroway, you come to us with no evidence, no record, no artifacts. Only a story that, to put it mildly, strains credibility. Over half a trillion dollars was spent, dozens of lives were lost. Are you really going to sit there and tell us we should just take this all . . . on faith?

Michael: Please answer the question, doctor.
Ellie: Is it possible that it didn't happen? Yes. As a scientist, I must concede that. I must volunteer that.
Michael: Wait a minute. Let me get this straight. You admit that you have absolutely no physical evidence to back up your story.
Ellie: Yes.
Michael: You admit that you very well may have hallucinated this whole thing.
Ellie: Yes.
Michael: You admit that if you were in our position, you would respond with exactly the same degree of incredulity and skepticism.
Ellie: Yes!
Michael: Then why don't you simply withdraw your testimony and concede that this "journey to the center of the galaxy" in fact never took place?
Ellie: Because I can't. I had an experience. I can't prove it, I can't even explain it, but everything that I know as a human being, everything that I am tells me that it was real! I was given something wonderful, something that changed me forever. A vision . . . of the universe, that tells us, undeniably, how tiny and insignificant and how rare and precious we all are. A vision that tells us that we belong to something that is greater than ourselves, that we are not, that none of us are, alone. I wish I could share that. I wish that everyone, if only for one moment, could feel that awe and humility and hope.

After Ellie's testimony, the movie ends on a mysterious note.[344] The video from Ellie's headset camera recorded only static and none of the visuals of her trip across the galaxy. But Kitzman is intrigued that it recorded eighteen hours of static. Still, for such an extraordinary claim, the evidence is inconclusive.

I think this is the position theists are in when they share their faith. We have an amazing experience like Ellie Arroway's that we too would be doubtful of if we heard someone else describe it to us. And we also have very strange coincidences: the existence and beginning of the universe, the fine-tuning of the universe, and the existence of objective moral truths. This evidence is not so obvious that people are irrational if they reject belief in God. After all, many atheists are intelligent, moral individuals. But I do think that these atheists may not be giving these coincidences their fair consideration. Maybe all these lines of evidence come together so that, in the words of G. K. Chesterton, we can see that coincidences are nothing more than "spiritual humor."

Beyond the God Debate

We've come to the end of our journey, but there are still some practical details that must be confronted. Although apologetic arguments can be great at sweeping away intellectual objections to belief in God, it's the deeper personal and emotional objections that often keep people from having a real relationship with him.

Why should I care?

Once when I was talking to a group at the University of New Mexico, a student named Greg asked me, "Well, so what if there is a God? Why should I care?" I wasn't sure how to answer him. It seemed obvious to me that if God did exist, that meant there was an all-knowing, all-powerful being that sustains all of existence and is the source of all truth, beauty, and goodness. How could we *not* care about a being like that? However, I can sympathize with the impulse to ignore a bland, deistic conception of a God who passively watches us like fish in an aquarium. But if God actually exists in the midst of our joy and sorrows, willing to have a real relationship with us, then that makes all the difference in the world. Conversely, if God did *not* exist we should also care, because then we would have to look at the world around us in a whole new way.

R.I.P. God?

The famous phrase "God is dead" is derived from a parable the philosopher Friedrich Nietzsche wrote in his book *The Gay Science*. Many people who quote Nietzsche mistakenly think that God's death (or more precisely, the death of the *idea* of God) is a happy, liberating idea. But Nietzsche thought otherwise.

In his parable, Nietzsche tells the story of a madman who in the early hours lights a lantern and runs to the marketplace shouting, "Where is God?" At first the people in the marketplace who do not believe in God respond with teasing humor. Did he lose his way like a child? Does he hide from us? Is he on a journey? Then the madman leaps up and with piercing eyes says, "Whither is God? I will tell you. We have killed him—you and I. All of us are his murderers." But the madman is quick to let the people of the town know of how serious their deed was. He continues:

> What were we doing when we unchained this earth from its sun? Whither is it moving now? Whither are we moving? Away from all suns? Are we not plunging continually? Backward, sideward, forward, in all directions? Is there still any up or down? Are we not straying, as through an infinite nothing? Do we not feel the breath of empty space? Has it not become colder?[345]

Nietzsche's point is clear. The absence of God also entails the absence of purpose and meaning in the universe. The French atheistic existentialist Jean Paul Sartre agreed with Nietzsche and found it "extremely embarrassing that God does not exist, for there disappears all possibility of finding values in an intelligible heaven."[346] Like the Earth untethered from the sun, life without God has no direction or purpose.

However, the new atheists almost uniformly reject this gloomy outlook. Rather than pessimistic philosophers, they consider themselves hopeful "brights" whose lives are filled with meaning and purpose.[347] In order to see if they are right, we must first examine what it means for anything to have a purpose.

Function or purpose?

When we say an object has a purpose, we mean that it has an end or goal that someone else has set out for it. For example, a sand castle reflects the creative intentions of its maker. But a sand pile next to the castle has no purpose. It just exists.

One could object that a pile of sand could have a purpose—preventing erosion on a beach, for instance. But this confuses purpose with function. A *function* is simply what something does. Both the sand castle and the pile of sand on the beach have the function of preventing erosion. But only the sand castle has a *purpose,* because it was created by a person with intentions and desires. This also gives meaning to the sand castle's existence; it is meant to reflect the beauty found in real-life castles. So, does the universe have a purpose?

In November 2010, three theists and three atheists debated that very topic.[348] The theists argued that the universe has a purpose if God exists and it doesn't if God does not exist. Halfway through the debate, the atheists attempted to rephrase the topic and claimed that even if there is no purpose for the universe, each of us can at least create our own purpose in life. Michael Shermer, a former Campus Crusade for Christ missionary and current editor of *Skeptic* magazine, asked, "Don't you think that if there isn't a God, you should find some purpose? Gentlemen, don't you think you ought to roll up your sleeves and find some useful things to do?" Shermer went on to list different humanitarian and civic activities all people should do, regardless if God exists or not.

Now, atheists are right that if God did not exist we could create our own subjective meaning or purpose. Some of us might find meaning in helping others. But some of us would find meaning or purpose in gathering wealth or power, or indulging desires of the flesh. If God did not exist, who could say anyone's *individual* purpose was any better or worse than another person's self-created purpose for living?

Meaningless choices

A critic could respond that it's obvious we should help others or make the world a better place. But where does this *should* come from, this imperative that binds all people regardless of the purpose they'd *like* to have? Even Shermer can only ground this duty in the alleged fact that altruism will "make you feel good." But if immorality makes one feel good, then what makes it true that one must refrain from such behavior? The serial killer Jeffrey Dahmer admitted in a television interview that atheism led him to the belief that there was no way he was *meant* to act in life. He said:

> If a person doesn't think there is a God to be accountable to, then—then what's the point of trying to modify your behavior to keep it within acceptable ranges? That's how I thought anyway. I always believed the theory of evolution as truth, that we all just came from the slime. When we, when we died, you know, that was it, there is nothing.[349]

If God does not exist, then the purpose we choose to have in life is as trivial as the clothes we choose to wear. But if God does exist, then the universe would be meant for something and our lives would have an objective and fulfilling purpose. We could all confidently say, "I was meant for more."

There's something in my way

Deep down, some people reject God because they say to themselves, "I've done bad things in my life. I'd rather not believe in God and have to face what I've done." The problem is that you still face whatever you've done every time you take a hard look in the mirror. What makes Christian theism so amazing is that God is infinitely merciful to us, despite our sins. No matter what sin you have committed, God desires to give you grace so that you can become a new man or woman in Christ.[350]

In contrast, atheism provides no hope for final redemption. Atheist Louise Antony makes this point well when she writes:

> There are things one loses in giving up God, and they are not insignificant. Most importantly, you lose the guarantee of redemption. Suppose that you do something morally terrible, something for which you cannot make amends, something, perhaps, for which no human being could ever be expected to forgive you. I imagine that the promise made by many religions, that God will forgive you if you are truly sorry, is a thought that would bring enormous comfort and relief. You cannot have that if you are an atheist.[351]

What if I still doubt?

In his *Pensées*, the seventeenth-century mathematician and Christian thinker Blaise Pascal wrote:

> This is what I see and what troubles me. I look on all sides, and I see only darkness everywhere. Nature presents to me nothing which is not matter of doubt and concern. If I saw nothing there which revealed a Divinity, I would come to a negative conclusion; if I saw everywhere the signs of a Creator, I would remain peacefully in faith. But, seeing too much to deny and too little to be sure, I am in a state to be pitied.[352]

Pascal is describing a condition in which the seeker knows too much to reject God's existence but is still too unsure to say he exists. It is at this point where Pascal suggests a decision based on common sense, or a kind of "wager," would be the most prudent thing to do. Pascal says, "Let us weigh the gain and the loss in wagering that God is. Let us estimate these two chances. If you gain, you gain all; if you lose, you lose nothing. Wager, then, without hesitation that He is." This approach to belief in God is called Pascal's Wager.

According to Pascal, the believer has nothing to lose in believing that God exists, because either he is right in his belief and will inherit everlasting happiness or he is wrong and will never know he was wrong (since he will cease to exist after death). For the unbeliever, if God does not exist he gains nothing (just like the theist), but if God does exist he will lose *everything*. So Pascal says that it is most prudent to believe in God, since you stand to gain everything and lose nothing.

Some atheists criticize the wager. One objection is that it makes belief in God a kind of mercenary response: "Believe and you'll get a great reward. Don't believe and you'll perish." They say that God would not be impressed with someone who believed in him as part of such a calculating strategy. But the wager is not meant to promote a mercenary approach to belief; rather it is for the person who "stands at the abyss," to encourage him to take a "leap of faith."

What if I pick the wrong one?

Another objection to the wager is called "the wrong hell problem." Or, which God among the world's religions should we choose to worship? What if by worshipping Jesus we offend Allah (the God of Islam), who turns out to be the real God, and we go to hell anyway?

Pascal himself did not consider this a serious objection and encouraged readers to examine different religions to see whether they have as much rational and historical support as Christianity. Plus, it is hard to see how an atheist could come out better than a Christian or theist in regards to the "wrong hell problem." Even if Islam was the correct religion, the atheist, Christian, and even generic theist would all be guilty of not worshipping Allah, and all three might go to hell. While there is at least a chance the Christian God may exist, there is practically no chance that a God who only approves of atheism exists, and so the Christian still loses nothing in the wager.[353]

The wager is like the advice you might give a young man who has cold feet on his wedding day. He could spend his whole life doubting if he should marry a certain girl, but if there are no clear red flags, then he should just "take the plunge." Likewise, if our belief in God is rational and there are no other beliefs that show it is false, then the doubting believer should open his heart and take the plunge as well.

I'm too busy for this right now

Sometimes people treat evangelists who encourage belief in God like the activists who stand outside of supermarkets hoping to get signatures for a petition. They tell them, "That's great, but I really don't have time for this right now; maybe I'll be able to sign up later." This objection assumes that there will be a "later," which is not a safe assumption to make. If our afterlife hinges on whether or not we believe in God while on Earth, then we cannot dare presume that there will be more time. I remember meeting a young man named Greg at the University of North Texas who described himself as being "kind of Catholic." He was receptive to my arguments but didn't see why he should have to radically change his life right away.

I proceeded to tell him a story about a friend of mine who was going to accompany me on a road trip until his family's house burned down. I asked Greg what would have happened if my friend's family had tried to take out a fire insurance policy the day *after* the fire. He said, "Too late, you can't do that." Then I asked him what would happen if, after he died, he tried to reinstate his relationship with God. He recognized that it would be too late.[354] I told him that God's forgiveness was always open to him, and I encouraged him to seek out reconciliation, because "you never know when the fire will come."

Now, I am not saying that belief in God is like fire insurance, which one prudently buys but then never thinks about. Instead, I am addressing the presumptuous attitude that we will always "have time to do it later." If God is the infinitely greatest being in the universe, then choosing to believe in him should not be set on the backburner.

A final challenge

If God exists, then why don't people who say they believe in him act like he's actually there? One reason is that mere belief in the existence of God does not necessarily translate into obedience to God's moral commands. In James 2:19 the author says to Christians who boast about their faith, "You believe that God is one; you do well. Even the demons believe—and shudder."

As human beings we have a predisposition to sin, so even when we believe in God we still succumb to temptation. But this doesn't invalidate the truth of God's existence. After all, most people know smoking is unhealthy; those who smoke often admit that it is not a lack of knowledge but of willpower that keeps them from quitting. Being a Christian is more than an intellectual exercise; it is a total commitment of the will.

And indeed, while Christian hypocrisy doesn't disprove the existence God, holy examples of the authentic Christian life may be the most persuasive pieces of evidence for it.

Physicist Stephen Hawking once asked, "What is it that breathes fire into the equations [of physics] and makes a universe for them to describe?"[355] If we Christians do not passionately pursue a personal vocation to holiness, then unbelievers with whom we share our faith will be right to ask, "What is it that breathes fire into your arguments and makes a *living faith* for them to defend?" Ultimately it is not mere knowledge of God, but acknowledgement of God and his power and goodness, that transforms us into the people we were meant to be.

St. Thomas Aquinas's
Cosmological Arguments

Some readers, especially Catholics, may wonder why I have not made Aquinas's "five ways" the central arguments in my case for the existence of God. The answer is simple, I could not do the five ways justice by only giving them a partial treatment in this book. According to Thomistic philosopher Edward Feser, the five ways are only summaries that were originally written for beginning theology students. Feser writes:

> Aquinas never intended them to stand alone, and would probably have reacted with horror if told that future generations of students would be studying them in isolation, removed from their original immediate context in the *Summa Theologica* and the larger context of his work as a whole.[356]

A careful student of Aquinas will also see that his arguments make sense only if you understand all the terms he uses, such as "act" and "potency" and different types of "causes." That would take an entire book of its own to explain, and Dr. Feser has already accomplished that with his book *Aquinas: A Beginner's Guide*. However, since I know Aquinas's five ways are heavily discussed in introductory philosophy courses (and often misrepresented), I still felt a duty to include a short primer on how to defend these famous arguments.

What's keeping everything in motion?

In his *Summa Theologica*, St. Thomas Aquinas presents five ways to prove the existence of God, the first of which are cosmological arguments.[357]

The first way is the *argument from motion* (by "motion" Aquinas really means "change," but movement will be helpful for the following examples). According to Aquinas, everything around us has a potential to be set in motion, but nothing can move itself. To say a thing can cause itself is to say it would "be prior to itself," which is absurd. Even if the universe had existed forever and there was an infinite chain of objects keeping things in motion, that wouldn't explain why there is any motion at all.

Imagine a boxcar on the end of a train. When the boxcar is standing still it has potential to be in motion, but it can't move itself. Instead, it has motion only when the boxcar in front of it pulls it and actualizes that potential for motion. But that particular boxcar moves only if it is pulled by the boxcar in front of *it*. Aquinas would say that there can't be an infinite number of boxcars because the train would never move. You would have only an infinite set of things with a potential to move but no movement. Instead, at the front of all the boxcars there must be a car that can move itself, or a locomotive. Likewise, our universe can only have continuous motion if there is a mover that is not moved by anything else.

Aquinas's second way is the *argument from causation,* which is similar to the argument from motion. Both the first and second way rely on the principle that change and causation are not self-caused nor can either be part of an infinite uncaused chain. Aquinas concludes that the causes we see in the world must instead have an ultimate, uncaused cause which, according to Aquinas, "everyone gives the name of God."

What's keeping everything in existence?

St. Thomas's third way is based on the *argument from contingency.* To be contingent means that something doesn't have to exist; it could be different, or it could not be at all. In contrast, something is *necessary* when it is not contingent and so could not be different. For example, the three sides of triangle are necessary because it is impossible to draw a triangle with more sides or fewer sides.

Aquinas points out that if the universe had indeed existed forever then after an infinite amount of time every contingent thing would have ceased to exist. That is because when a thing goes out of existence it can't come back into existence on its own. If an infinite amount of time passes, then all contingent things would exhaust the possibility of going out of existence and nothing would exist. But certainly things do exist, so there must be some being that cannot fail to exist (or a necessary being) that keeps all contingent beings in existence. Aquinas says we call this being God.[358]

As I said before, this is merely a summary of Aquinas, and much more would need to be explained concerning the exact meaning of his arguments. However, even without a deep understanding of Aquinas's metaphysics, a careful thinker will find that the common objections leveled against Aquinas's arguments usually misunderstand them and therefore fail to refute the arguments. Let's look at three of these objections.

Objection #1: "What moved God?"

According to Richard Dawkins,

> All three of these ideas [the first three of Aquinas's five ways] rely upon the idea of a regress and invoke God to terminate it. They make the entirely unwarranted assumption that God himself is immune to the regress.[359]

Dawkins and other atheists like him sometimes make a caricature of Aquinas and claim he is arguing, "Everything needs a cause. Therefore, there had to be a first cause called

God. God is the exception and has no cause of his own." But Aquinas never makes such a simplistic argument. He says that everything in motion only moves because it has a potential to move. Since nothing can move itself, an object can only move if its potential to move is activated by something outside of it. For example, water has the potential to freeze if the air temperature lowers enough to act upon the water. Likewise, the air has a potential to become colder if something else acts upon it (like changes in air pressure).

But what makes God different from anything else is that he has no potential but is pure motion itself (or what Aquinas calls *act*). Nothing acts on God in order to bring about effects in the world. Instead, God brings about these effects by his own power. God can act on his own because, once again, there is nothing potential about God. Aquinas is not saying everything has a cause except for God, as if God were one object among many in the universe. Instead, he logically arrives at the conclusion that since all things have potential in them, there must be something which has no potential but instead moves everything. God is not an "exception to the rule," he's an entirely different "rule" or kind of being.

This refutes Dawkins's claim that there is no good reason to say God does not require a mover of his own. Asking the question, "If everything needs to be moved, then what moved God?" is like asking the question, "If every car on a train needs to be pulled, then what is pulling the locomotive?" It is because God is not acted upon by anything else that he is able to be pure being, or "act" itself, and cause everything else to exist and move in the world.

Objection #2: Why not an infinite number of movers?

Another popular objection goes like this: "Aquinas begs the question when he says that there cannot be an infinite number of movers and so there must be an unmoved mover that sets everything in motion. But why can't there just be movers or causes going back infinitely in time?[360]

To this objection Aquinas makes a distinction between causes that are *sequential* and causes that are *simultaneous.*[361] Sequential causation is like a chain of dominoes. After you knock over the first domino you start a chain reaction of dominoes hitting other dominoes. In fact, you could destroy the first domino after you've knocked it over, since it is no longer needed to keep the whole set of dominoes falling. Aquinas believed that sequential causes in the past, like a set of dominoes, could have occurred for all eternity, though their existence would still be dependent upon God, just as a set of dominoes requires a first mover in order to cause the whole sequence to begin. Aquinas simply did not believe that one could prove by reason alone that past sequential causal chains were not infinite or had a beginning in the past.[362]

Aquinas argues instead that God explains the existence of simultaneous causation even if such a causal chain were infinite. An example of this kind of causation would be a golfer hitting a golf ball. The act of the golfer hitting the ball is not as simple as we might think. The golf ball is moved by the golf clubhead, but the clubhead is simultaneously moved by the swing of the shaft, which is moved from the handle, and the handle is simultaneously moved by the flexing of the golfer's muscles, which cannot flex without nerve signals from the golfer's brain stimulating them, and so on. Aquinas argues that such a chain of causes cannot be infinite because the causation is all happening at the same time. Once again, this is like the train with an infinite number of boxcars that are all moving at the same time. In that case, there has to be an unmoved mover that causes all this simultaneous motion to exist at all.[363] Likewise, there must be an "uncaused cause" that sustains the elaborate chain of simultaneous causes in our universe. We call this uncaused cause God.

Objection #3: Modern physics shows that Aquinas is wrong.

Some atheists claim that an object can move without being moved by anything else, which seems to contradict the principles in Aquinas's First Way. They say Newton's First Law of Motion shows that an object in motion tends to stay in motion unless it is acted upon by an outside force. For example, if a person throws a baseball in space and there is nothing to cause the ball to slow down, then the ball would move forever in the same direction at a constant speed. Since it can move in this direction as a result of its own inertia, then this would be a case of something moving itself and so would refute Aquinas.[364]

But inertia only shows that an object can *maintain* motion it receives from something else, not that it can generate motion on its own. If the object slows down, then its potential to decelerate would need to be actualized by something else (like friction with another object).[365] Likewise, the object's initial acquiring of speed would also need to be actualized by something outside of it. Thus, the critic has not shown that Aquinas's principle of motion (which is a philosophical truth about reality) is contradictory to the scientific principle of inertia found in modern physics. A collection of objects giving and receiving motion from one another would still require a mover that is not moved by anything.

Objections to the Kalām Cosmological Argument

In this section, I'll examine the most common objections to the kalām cosmological argument. Since this is such a simple argument (in comparison to the arguments of Aquinas or Leibniz), atheists tend to attack it relentlessly online and in popular books. Though the objections can sometimes seem daunting, if you take them one at a time you can see that they aren't as overpowering as you might think. But before we examine the objections to the KCA, it will be helpful to review the argument one more time:

P1. Whatever begins to exist must have a cause for its existence.

P2. The universe began to exist.

C. Therefore, the universe has a cause for its existence.

As with any other deductive argument, in order to show that the KCA fails, the critic must show either that one of the premises is false or that the argument commits a fallacy in its reasoning. In this chapter we will examine objections to the causal principle summarized in premise one as well as objections to the philosophical and scientific evidence for the beginning of the universe. Then I'll examine charges that the argument commits a fallacy or error in its reasoning. First, let's examine three objections to premise one, "Whatever begins to exist must have a cause for its existence."

1. "Nothing has no rules, so something can come from it."

An atheist once told me, "If the universe came from nothing, then premise one doesn't apply to it. Since there are no limits on nothing, no rules for it to follow, then nothing could do anything. If it could do anything, then it could cause the universe to exist."

This is an interesting objection, but it misses something important: Only a real, existing thing can be described as having properties like "no constraints" or "capable of doing anything." It may be true in a sense that "nothing" has no rules or constraints, but neither does it have powers or properties.[366]

This objection also misunderstands how natural laws work. The law of cause and effect doesn't *command* matter to follow certain rules. It doesn't issue a citation if events happen without a cause. It just *describes* how things usually happen and thus aids human beings in our scientific descriptions of the world. If there were a state of nothing, or a state without anything for a scientific law to describe, then it is not the case that *anything* could happen. It is the case that *nothing* would happen.

2. "I can imagine something coming from nothing."

David Hume once argued that we can imagine a blank space and then an object appearing in that blank space (like an empty hat with a rabbit appearing in it). If we just add the title "something coming from nothing" to this mental picture, then—voila!—it's possible that something can indeed come from nothing.

But because something can be imagined doesn't mean it can really happen.[367] The Catholic philosopher Elizabeth Anscombe wrote in response to Hume, "Indeed I can form an image and give my picture that title. But from my being able to do that, nothing whatever follows about what is possible to suppose 'Without contradiction or absurdity' as holding in reality."[368] Anscombe is saying that all we are imagining in our minds is "nothing" and then we are imagining "something." But we can't really imagine, or see in our minds, something *coming* from nothing or show that such an idea is not absurd. Hume himself even denied the idea that things could come into existence without a cause:

> But allow me to tell you that I never asserted so absurd a Proposition as that anything might arise without a cause: I only maintain'd that our Certainty of the Falsehood of that Proposition proceeded neither from Intuition nor Demonstration but from another Source.[369]

Just because something can be imagined, then, it doesn't follow that it can really happen. The critic needs to supply evidence that something really can come from nothing. Imagination doesn't supply that evidence, but perhaps science can?

3. "Quantum physics shows that something can come from nothing."

Physics describes how objects move and behave in the world. But traditional physics has a limit when it comes to describing really small objects. For that we need quantum physics (sometimes called quantum mechanics), which explains the nature and motion of atoms as well as the particles that make up atoms. Because these particles are so small, they tend to act in strange ways.[370] For example, scientists have observed so-called "virtual particles" emerging, apparently without a cause, from a vacuum. Some people argue that since this phenomenon shows that "something can come from nothing," it follows that our entire universe could have emerged as a similar "quantum fluctuation" in a vacuum.

However, this phenomenon does not refute the fact that something cannot come from nothing, because the quantum vacuum is not "nothing." It is a field with a very low energy level that can fluctuate. Unlike nothing, it has properties and can be positively described, which makes it more than capable of producing something like a virtual particle. Philosopher and theoretical physicist David Albert writes:

> [V]acuum states—no less than giraffes or refrigerators or solar systems—are particular arrangements of *elementary physical stuff*. . . . [T]he fact that particles can pop in and out of existence, over time, as those [quantum] fields rearrange themselves, is not a whit more mysterious than the fact that fists can pop in and out of existence, over time, as my fingers rearrange themselves. And none of these poppings—if you look at them aright—amount to anything even remotely in the neighborhood of a creation from nothing.

An atheist could counter that maybe the particles do come from the vacuum, and not pure nothing, but since they come from the vacuum without any causal process, without any way to predict when they come into existence, then we have something that happens without a cause.[371] Why couldn't our Big Bang have happened in the same way?

There are three things to consider here. First, it's possible for *events* not to have causes (such as a ball to rolling to the right instead of to the left when set on a perfectly sharp cone), but it doesn't seem possible for *things* not to have causes (such as the ball just appearing for no reason at all).[372]

Second, if our universe came to exist through a vacuum fluctuation, then why don't we observe more universes emerging from quantum vacuums today? Virtual particles don't seem to be good candidates for the first cause of the universe, because they immediately disappear back into the vacuum after they appear from it.[373] What reason do we have to believe that an entire universe as massive as ours could emerge from the vacuum in a lasting fashion?

Third, the quantum vacuum may be without causal determinacy, but it has causal *conditions* that lead to certain results; otherwise, scientists wouldn't be able to replicate quantum experiments. John Jefferson Davis writes:

> Quantum-mechanical events may not have classically deterministic causes, but they are not thereby uncaused or acausal. The decay of a nucleus takes place in view of physical actualities and potentialities internal to itself, in relation to a spatiotemporal nexus governed by the laws of quantum mechanics. The fact that uranium atoms consistently decay into atoms of lead and other elements—and not into rabbits or frogs—shows that such events are not causal but take place within a causal nexus and lawlike structures.[374]

In short, virtual particles do not come from nothing. They come from a pre-existing vacuum that possesses certain behaviors, even if we cannot measure or understand those behaviors. This phenomenon simply does not show that something can come into existence from nothing without a cause.

Now let's examine some objections the philosophical argument that shows the past cannot be infinite in duration.

1. "If the past can't be infinite, then God can't be infinite."

The philosophical argument for the beginning of time says that you can't form an actual infinite set of things by adding one member at a time—thus there could not be an infinite number of days before today.[375] Instead, there must be a finite number of days and therefore a beginning of time. Some critics use this to their advantage and say that if actual infinites can't exist, then God can't exist, because God is described as being infinite.[376]

But when theists say God is "infinite," that is just a short-hand way of saying that God exists without any limitation. To say that God has infinite power or wisdom doesn't mean that God has an actual infinite number of "power-units" or "bits of wisdom." Instead, this means that God's power and wisdom have no limit.[377]

Some people reply that God must nonetheless have an infinite number of thoughts; and so if we can't cross an infinite amount of days to arrive at the present, then God could never think about the infinite number of thoughts in his mind. However, there's no reason to assume that God must think in the slow, linear way that we do. Instead of being divided, God's knowledge is united in one perfect vision or moment of absolute wisdom and is not composed of an infinite number of smaller elements.[378]

2. "It's not impossible to traverse the infinite; we do it every day."

Other critics will argue that it is not impossible for there to be an infinite number of days before today. After all, there are an infinite number of points between you and any wall, but you cross them all when you walk toward the wall. If it is possible to traverse an infinite set of points in space, then it is possible to traverse an infinite set of points in time, and there could have been an infinite number of days before today.

Here we must be careful to not confuse an actual infinity with a potential infinity. You can cross the points between you and the wall because the distance in this case is only *potentially* infinite. Think back to the example of Aunt Mildred and the flower shop (p. 126). The distance between Mildred and the door is a finite number of feet, even though critics say there are an infinite number of points (i.e., the halfway point, the three-quarter point, etc.). However, the number of points is *potentially* infinite because the divisions are unequal and keep getting smaller as you divide them. This is why Mildred doesn't take an eternity to walk five feet. But the flowers Mildred counts aren't like this because they represent an actual infinite. They don't get smaller or easier to count over time, and so they create contradictions when one tries to count them all.[379] Just as Mildred can't count an actually infinite number of flowers, the universe could not have possessed an actually infinite number of days before today.

3. "The past isn't infinite, it just had no beginning."

A critic might object that the story about Mildred is a bad illustration, because Mildred starts at the *beginning* of a series and tries to count all the way to infinity, which is impossible. But if the past were truly infinite, then there simply would be *no beginning* at all. There would just be a past that has always existed.[380] In that case one could count an infinite number of events, because there would be an infinite amount of time before the present moment in order to do so.

But as J. P. Moreland writes, "It is precisely the lack of a beginning that causes most of the problems in traversing the past to reach the present. If there were no beginning, then reaching the present moment would be like counting to zero from negative infinity."[381]

The defender of the KCA can still ask, "If the universe had no beginning, then how many days were there before today?" If there were a finite number of days, then one should be able to count backward after some time (even a long time) and find the first day and hence the beginning of the universe.

If there were an infinite number of days, then an actual infinite exists, and you can't form an actual infinite by adding one day at a time to the collection of past days. It can't be the case that there is just no beginning and all the days prior to today appeared instantly, because events occur in a sequence such as yesterday, today, and tomorrow. They don't all occur at once but are formed by successive addition.[382] Since the collection of past days can never form an infinite number of days by adding one day at a time (since there would always be one more day before the last day), it follows that the past is finite and the universe began to exist.

4. "If the past can't be infinite, then the future in heaven can't be infinite."

If we say the future in heaven has "no end" then why can't we say that the past on earth "had no beginning?" Would the prohibition on an infinite past imply that an infinite future in heaven isn't possible either?

Here we must distinguish again the difference between actual and potential infinites. An infinite future in heaven with God is a potential infinite. This just means that there will forever be another moment, another day of bliss to enjoy with God. There will never be a moment number "infinity" that will be the last moment. In contrast, an infinite past is an actual infinite of completed events. An infinite past must be an actual infinite while an infinite future must be a potential infinite because time is *asymmetrical* and moves in one direction.[383] A person in the present moves forward into the future and never reaches the end of time. However, the past does not "grow" away from the present like the future does. Instead, the number of past events must be fixed: If there were an infinite number of them, one could never reach the end of the past events and arrive at the present moment. Since time moves in one direction, or is asymmetrical, it follows that there must be a beginning to time and the universe itself.

Now that we've reviewed the major objections to the philosophical arguments for the universe having a beginning, let's examine two objections to the scientific evidence for premise two.

1. "Nothing ever begins to exist."

I remember a high school theology teacher once seeking my help when one of her students challenged the kalām argument in class. She said, "I don't know how to answer this. He says that the first law of thermodynamics shows that matter and energy cannot be created or destroyed but only changed. Therefore the past is eternal and nothing was ever created."

It is not true, however, that the first law of thermodynamics says that matter and energy have "always existed." The first law only claims that, in a physical reaction, matter and energy can't be created or destroyed by other physical reactions. Matter and energy can only be changed. For example, paper turns to ash when it is burned, but the basic atomic parts of the paper don't stop existing. They just rearrange and form another substance.

But the first law of thermodynamics must be balanced against the second law, which shows that the universe could not have existed forever. The first law of thermodynamics applies to physical processes within a closed system, taking for granted that the system it describes actually exists. When the universe did not exist, there was no physical system for the First Law to describe. But the causal principle "out of nothing, nothing comes" is a *metaphysical* principle about reality itself and accurately describes the impossibility of anything (especially the universe) popping into existence without a cause.

However, an act of creation from nothing would not be a violation of the First Law, because it would not involve matter being created within an already existing physical system. Moreover, even within an existing physical system the First Law would not constrain an omnipotent being who could, without logical contradiction, suspend the law in order to create something from nothing (just as he could suspend the Second Law in order to stop the universe's increase in entropy).

What this student was arguing was that instead of observing things "beginning to exist," we've only seen new objects come into existence when old objects are destroyed and their parts are rearranged. According to him, the universe is like a giant tub of Legos that can be rearranged to cause spaceships and buildings to come into existence, but the Legos themselves (or the fundamental particles of the universe) have always existed. But even if the universe is like a giant tub of Legos that get rearranged over time, we have evidence that the whole universe, including all the fundamental particles that make it up, came into existence in the finite past.[384] This fact requires an explanation in the same way that a brand-new tub of Legos appearing in a child's bedroom requires an explanation.

2. "The universe does not exist."

Another radical escape for the critic is to say that the universe *never* began to exist, since it contains the same amount of positive and negative energy. Those two amounts of energy cancel each other out, and so technically the amount of energy in the universe is the same that was present in the nothingness before the Big Bang.

I once heard an atheist explain this to some Christian high school students, and he literally used the phrase, "the universe doesn't actually exist." Therefore, he claimed, he didn't *have* to explain where the universe came from. Judging from the confusion on their faces, the statement seemed so nonsensical to these students that I thought their brains were going to overheat and shut down.

Nonetheless, let's take a closer look at this argument. If you add up the positive and negative energy in the universe, the amount indeed equals zero, or is "charge-neutral." Since a state of nothingness would also be charge-neutral, then the critic claims it makes sense to say that our universe came to exist from this state without a cause.[385] But just because the sum of the universe's positive and negative energy is zero, and the universe's energy prior to its beginning was "zero," this does not mean that those two states are the same kind of thing.

Imagine Bob just opened new checking and savings accounts whose total balances are combined into one figure which, since the accounts are new, is zero dollars. Let's say one day his checking account is mysteriously overdrawn by $5,000, and at the same time his savings account received a $5,000 deposit. Bob calls the bank and asks, "What caused this surplus of money and corresponding debt to come into existence in my accounts?" The bank teller responds, "Well, sir, neither really came into existence, because the positive money in your savings account cancels out the overdrawn negative money in your checking account. Therefore, neither the debit nor the credit needs to be explained, because the total balance is still zero dollars." But of course, Bob would demand an explanation for the sudden appearance of this positive and negative money. Just as the mysterious addition of an equal surplus and debt to a bank account requires an explanation, the appearance of a universe with its many kinds of negative and positive energy from nothing requires an explanation as well.

So we've seen that there are no good reasons to deny either the causal principle in premise one or the fact of the universe's beginning in premise two. But just because the premises are true does not mean that the kalām cosmological argument succeeds. One way the argument may fail to prove its conclusion is because it contains a fallacy or error in its reasoning. Philosophers call arguments with fallacies *invalid* arguments while arguments that have no errors in the reasoning are called *valid* arguments. Arguments that are valid and have only true premises are called *sound* arguments. Let's examine three alleged fallacies in the KCA and see if the argument is valid, let alone sound.

Fallacy #1: Begging the question, or circular reasoning

An argument "begs the question" when it asserts in one of the premises what it is trying to prove in the conclusion, or it proposes a circular argument. Here's a classic example:

P1. The Bible is the Word of God.
P2. The Word of God can never be wrong.
P3. The Bible says God created the universe.
C. Therefore, God created the universe.

This argument begs the question, because the only reason someone has to believe the first premise, "The Bible is the word of God," would be that he already believed the conclusion, "God created the universe." But this is the premise the argument tries to prove, and it only does so by "arguing in a circle."

Some critics say the KCA "begs the question" because the first premise assumes that "everything that begins to exist has a cause" yet the conclusion of the argument was that the universe has a cause.[386] If the argument assumes in the first premise that everything has a cause, including the universe, then it is assuming what it is trying to prove. As a result, the argument would be invalid, even if all the premises were true.

But the kalām argument commits no such fallacy, because the evidence for the first premise—"Everything that begins to exist has a cause"—does not depend on the conclusion, "The universe has a cause for its existence." You could believe that the universe was eternal, for instance, and still believe that when something comes into existence, such as an object within the universe, it requires a cause for its existence. Instead, the first premise is based off the well-established metaphysical principle "Out of nothing, nothing comes" and is confirmed by everyday observation. This argument begs the question no more than the argument that because all men are mortal, and Socrates is a man, then Socrates is mortal. It's simply a standard deductive argument.[387]

Fallacy #2: Reasoning from composition

The fallacy of composition occurs when someone says that what applies to every part of an object also applies to the whole object. For example, just because every cell in my body is likewise invisible to the naked eye, it doesn't follow that my entire body is invisible. An atheist may claim that just because everything in the universe has a cause for its existence, it doesn't follow that the universe itself must have a cause for its existence.

But the KCA does not claim that because everything in the universe has a cause, the universe itself has a cause. Rather, the KCA offers independent evidence for the claim that all things that begin to exist have a cause for their existence, such as the intuition "something cannot come from nothing." Furthermore, sometimes what is true of parts is also true of wholes. For example, if every cell in my body is made of matter, then it follows that my entire body is made of matter. The critic would have to provide further evidence that the combination of the universe's parts would transform it from being uncaused to being caused, just as the combination of human cells in my body transforms it from being invisible to being visible. In the absence of such evidence, the theist is justified in believing that things that begin need a cause and the universe is simply something that began and thus needs a cause.

Fallacy #3: Equivocation

If peanut butter is better than nothing, and nothing is better than heaven, then is peanut butter better than heaven? Obviously this is bad reasoning because the word "nothing" is used in two different ways, which is a fallacy called *equivocation*. Some critics claim that the KCA equivocates on the phrase "begins to exist."[388] They say that in premise one, the phrase "whatever begins to exist" means "anything that comes to be from preexisting matter." Whereas in premise two, "began to exist" means "comes to be from nothing." So the argument ends up saying:

P1. Whatever begins to exist from preexisting matter has a cause.
P2. The universe began to exist from nothing.
C. Therefore, the universe has a cause.

The critic might then say that there is no reason to think the universe needs a cause, because it came to be from nothing while everything else comes from pre-existing matter. But this is not a fallacy because we can define "begins to exist" so that instead of having two meanings (or being equivocal) it has only one meaning (or is univocal). We would say something begins to exist at a certain time if there was no other time before it when it ever existed.[389] For example, the Empire State Building began to exist in the year 1931 because there was no other year before 1931when it did exist.

Likewise, when we say the universe began at the first moment of time (let's call that Moment Zero), then all we are saying is, "The universe began to exist at Moment Zero because there was never a moment before Moment Zero when the universe existed." This allows us to answer the charge of equivocation by reformulating the argument in this way:

P1. Whatever exists at a certain time and never existed before that time has a cause.

P2. The universe existed 13.7 billion years ago and never existed before that time.

C. Therefore, the universe has a cause.

The critic might complain that of course there was no moment when the universe existed before Moment Zero. There were no moments at all! But this fact does not change the proposed definition of "begins to exist," and since "begins to exist" has the same definition in both premises, the charge of equivocation is refuted.

Advanced Cosmology

Cosmology is the study of the universe and its ultimate origins. In this section I'll examine more advanced challenges to the idea that the origin and fine-tuning of the universe provide evidence for the existence of God.

A Big Crunch for a Big Bang

Some atheists say that the universe might expand from a Big Bang and then re-collapse into a "Big Crunch." After the "crunch" back into the nothingness, the universe might expand again into another Big Bang. According to the cyclic model of the universe, this process will go on forever into the future and has gone on forever into the past. But the cyclic model can only succeed if the density of matter in the universe is greater than what scientists call the *critical density*. If it is greater, then gravity will overpower matter and pull it back into a big crunch. But if the density of matter is less than critical density, then gravity won't be strong enough to pull the matter back into a big crunch, and the universe will expand forever.

So, will there be a "Big Crunch," or will the universe expand forever? It appears to be the latter, since so-called "dark matter" and "dark energy" make up 96 percent of the matter in the universe. This strange matter has enough mass and gravitational force of its own to keep the universe expanding forever.[390]

Victor Stenger writes in his book *God and the Folly of Faith* that "most cosmologists currently do not expect that the big crunch will happen. The best guess based on current observation and theory is that the universe is open; that is, it will expand forever."[391] After billions of years, the universe will cool as every star in the universe uses up the finite amount of nuclear fuel it has and burns out. Then the universe will reach heat death and become a cold, lifeless place that will never collapse into a "Big Crunch."

But even if our universe did "bounce" from a previous big crunch, the evidence from physics shows that such a universe, in the words of Fr. Robert Spitzer, "could not have been bouncing forever."[392] That is because whenever a universe collapses or experiences a "Big Crunch," an intense buildup of disorder is created that carries over into the next cycle. According to physicist Richard Tolman, this increased disorder would cause future big bang cycles to be longer, because the energy being carried over after the big crunch creates more outward pressure in the next cycle.

Think of a retirement account where the amount of money gets larger and larger each month the account is active. Since the amount of money gets larger into the future, it logically follows that the amount of money would get smaller and smaller into the past until it reached zero, or the time the account began to exist. Likewise, a cyclic universe may have longer lifetimes in future cycles. But the past cycles would get shorter and shorter until the cycles became infinitely short in length (or zero). This would be the point when the universe began to exist.[393]

Was the Big Bang the beginning?

Some critics say the Big Bang model doesn't explain the beginning of the universe. They sometimes quote physicist Brian Greene:

A common misconception is that the Big Bang provides a theory of cosmic origins. It doesn't. The Big

Bang is a theory, partly described in the last two chapters, that delineates cosmic evolution from a split second after whatever happened to bring the universe into existence, but *it says nothing at all about time zero itself.* And since, according to the Big Bang theory, the bang is what is supposed to have happened at the beginning, the Big Bang leaves out the bang. It tells us nothing about what banged, why it banged, how it banged, or, frankly, whether it really banged at all.[394]

But the use of this isolated quote reflects a misunderstanding of what the Big Bang is supposed to explain. When the universe emerged from the Big Bang, it was very small, and at sub-atomic levels the theory of general relativity stops working, or it produces nonsensical solutions to the theory's equations. That is why physicists are searching for a "quantum theory of gravity" that will allow them to apply what we know about gravity to the moments after the Big Bang. Until such a theory is found, scientists can't study what happened at the first moment of time. But that doesn't mean such a moment did not happen, or that the universe never began to exist.

Greene writes later in his book that just as Newton's equations can tell you the trajectory of a baseball without telling you how its motion began, Einstein's equations can describe an expanding universe without explaining how it got started. But in 1979 an American cosmologist developed a theory that allowed us to explore the beginning of the universe more than ever before. Greene writes:

For many years, cosmologists took the initial outward expansion of space as an unexplained given, and simply worked the equation forward from there. *This is what I meant earlier when I said that the big bang is silent on the bang.* Such was the case until one fateful night in December 1979, when Alan Guth . . . showed that we can do better. . . . Guth's discovery—dubbed *inflation-ary cosmology* . . . provided the Big Bang with a bang.[395]

According to Greene, inflationary cosmology explains the universe's expansion, but it too cannot explain what happened at the creation of the universe itself. According to the inflationary universe hypothesis, our universe didn't expand at a slow, constant rate from the Big Bang. Stephen Hawking says the expansion of the universe would be like a penny expanding to the size of the entire Milky Way galaxy (or 100,000 light years across) in a few seconds.[396]

Some cosmologists have proposed that our universe will not only be eternally growing into the future (or inflating) but that it has been inflating and growing for all time. Therefore, our universe never "began to exist." Chaotic inflation theorist Andrei Linde explains what he calls "eternal inflation." He writes, "From this perspective, inflation is not a part of the big bang theory, as we thought 15 years ago. On the contrary, the big bang is a part of the inflationary model."[397]

Bursting your inflationary bubble

Some inflationary theorists have argued that our universe could be just one "bubble" from an even larger "bubble universe" or multiverse. Inflation theorists like Linde claim that the Big Bang was only the beginning of *our* universe but not the beginning of a bigger universe that we branched off from 13.7 billion years ago. Bubble universes are similar to the bubbles kids blow out of soap solution. Sometimes when a bubble is blown, it expands, and then a second bubble forms off the first one. Inflation theorists used to believe that this "bubble formation process" could have happened with our universe and continued forever into the past. Thus the wider universe we came from would have had no beginning for God to create.

However, in 2003 three cosmologists, Arvin Borde, Alexander Vilenkin, and the original pioneer of inflation, Alan Guth, published a theorem that disputes the idea of eternal inflation.[398] Vilenkin colorfully describes Guth in his 2006 book *Many Worlds in One: The Search for Other Universes*. He says that Guth had a tendency to fall asleep in meetings with other scientists, but upon waking could summarize every point the other scientists had made.[399] In other words, Borde, Guth, and Vilenkin are very smart individuals, and they are also not sympathetic to Christians. This refutes the idea that the following quote from Vilenkin is just a piece of Christian propaganda. Vilenkin writes:

> It is said that an argument is what convinces reasonable men and a proof is what it takes to convince even an unreasonable man. With the proof now in place, cosmologists can no longer hide behind the possibility of a past eternal universe. There is no escape: they have to face the problem of a cosmic beginning.[400]

What is especially remarkable about this theorem is that it applies in almost any universe, or even a multiverse (like the bubble universe scenario we just discussed). Borde, Vilenkin, and Guth found that (with rare exceptions) if a universe or multiverse is expanding, that universe or multiverse must have had a beginning.

The Borde-Vilenkin-Guth Theorem

Borde, Vilenkin, and Guth used relatively simple math (their original paper is only four pages long) to determine that any universe that is on average expanding could not have been expanding forever. Their theorem (called the Borde-Vilenkin-Guth, or BVG, theorem) shows that in an expanding universe the relative velocity of objects would keep getting faster the more one goes backward in time. But this acceleration into the past can't go on forever. That is because, according to modern physics, nothing can have a relative velocity faster than the speed of light, or 186,000 miles per second. Therefore, in order to stop this increase in relative velocity, there must have been a past-boundary, or "wall" that designates the beginning of our universe.

Of course, atheists aren't content to let the Borde-Vilenkin-Guth theorem go unchallenged (nor should they be content and not put up a good fight!). For example, Victor Stenger emailed Vilenkin and asked him, "Does your theorem prove the universe has an absolute beginning?" Some Internet websites, as well as Stenger's book *The Folly of Faith*, only quote this part of Vilenkin's response: "No. But it proves that the expansion of the universe must have had a beginning. You can evade the theorem by postulating that the universe was contracting prior to some time." What is left out of Vilenkin's response is the fact that contracting models of the universe are highly unstable and would be just as mysterious as a universe that began to exist from nothing. In the rest of the response to Stenger, Vilenkin says:

> This sounds as if there is nothing wrong with having contraction prior to expansion. But the problem is that a contracting universe is highly unstable. Small perturbations would cause it to develop all sorts of messy singularities, so it would never make it to the expanding phase. That is why Aguirre & Gratton and Carroll & Chen had to assume that the arrow of time changes at t = 0. This makes the moment t = 0 rather special. I

would say no less special than a true beginning of the universe.[401]

Theories of time

One popular though advanced way to undermine the kalām argument is to say that there could be an infinite series of events before today because the past, present, and future all exist at the same "time" in one infinite timeless block or chain. This is called the B-theory, or static theory of time. Under this view, the universe never "began to exist," because nothing begins to exist. The competing view is the A-theory of time, which says that the future is not real and temporal becoming is an objective fact about reality. Even if the static or B-theory of time turns out to be correct, the contingency argument would still succeed, since it answers the timeless question "Why is there something rather than nothing?"

There are several arguments that have been put forward in defense of the A-theory of time, which appears to be the theory of time the KCA must rely on in order to succeed as an argument.[402] First, tensed statements that cannot be rewritten without their tense (like the statement "It is now noon") are powerful evidence for the view that temporal distinctions are real. Second, the A-theory of time makes sense of our concept of existence. Consider the question "Do dinosaurs exist?" If the B-theory of time is true, then dinosaurs that existed 65 million years ago are just as real as the birds that evolved from them and exist today. Dinosaurs still exist, but at a "different" though equally real time.

Space does not permit me to address the arguments for a B-theory of time in this work, because they raise a host of issues related to special relativity and divine timelessness. However, even if the B-theory was preferable for scientific or theological reasons, the kalām argument may still have a future through Mark Nowacki's substance-based defense of the argument.[403]

Is fine-tuning a myth?

Victor Stenger writes in his book *The Fallacy of Fine-Tuning* that the argument from fine-tuning rests on fundamental mistakes apologists and even some non-religious scientists make about the laws of nature and their constants. It would take an entire book to refute Stenger, but a few examples should show the kinds of errors he makes.

First, Stenger says that gravity is not fine-tuned to our existence, because gravity is an essential feature of the universe. Stenger says that if there were no gravity, for example, this would violate something he calls "point-of-view invariance," or the idea that any model of the universe must be the same in every direction.[404] But my research on the concept of "point of view invariance" has found that the term, at least in the context of astrophysics, appears only in Stenger's writings. This seems to make sense, because Stenger is an anti-realist who rejects the idea that the laws of nature even have an independent existence.

He writes in *God the Failed Hypothesis*, "So where did the laws of physics come from? They came from nothing!"[405] Stenger writes in *The Fallacy of Fine-Tuning* that these laws are simply "human inventions" and that the only thing that matters to him is if his model is coherent (which is similar to the view put forward by Hawking and Mlodinow in their 2009 book *The Grand Design*).[406] However, as Robin Collins has pointed out, one could posit a universe without gravity where all objects move away from each other and do not attract. This model would be symmetrical, physically possible and still life-prohibiting (i.e., there is nothing contradictory in its description as a model), thus showing that fine-tuning is still necessary, and the laws of physics are not arbitrary descriptions of a theoretical model.[407]

In addition, Stenger's online program Monkey God, which is described at the end of his book on fine-tuning, claims that a person could adjust the constants of physics (at least eight sample ones) and still have a 60 percent chance that a life-permitting universe will come into existence. But as astronomer Luke Barnes has pointed out, "Of these eight criteria, three are incorrect, two are irrelevant, and one is insufficient. Plenty more are missing. Most importantly, all manner of cherry-picked assumptions are lurking out of sight." It seems that Stenger's program is fine-tuned to produce life just like our own universe! For example, Stenger uses an equation with a logarithmic prior that Barnes says "spuriously inflates the value of [life-permitting universes] by over-representing very small values of a parameter [in the fundamental constants]. This point alone renders Monkey God's calculations meaningless."[408]

Stenger has responded to Barnes, but I have not found his response convincing. He answers Barnes's charge that Monkey God oversimplifies fine-tuning by asking rhetorically, "Does he really expect me to simulate entire universes?"[409] One should especially note that Stenger claims that one source of contention between him and Barnes is philosophical, with Barnes being described as a Platonist and Stenger saying he is a "common-sense realist"—though I would more accurately describe Stenger as an "anti-realist."

Does the multiverse disprove God?

There is some evidence that our universe is the only one that exists. Apparently the strength of magnetic quadropoles is much lower than it would be if there were an infinite multiverse. One study found that, "In an infinite flat space, waves from the Big Bang would fill the universe on all length scales ... the first observable harmonic is the quadropole ... WMAP found a quadropole only about 1/7 as strong as would be expected in an infinite flat space. The probability that this could happen by mere chance has been estimated at about a fifth of one percent."[410]

Another proposal that provides differing constants without a multiverse is the idea that the constants of physics could change and have different values throughout the universe. As a result, the life-permitting values would eventually emerge at some location (e.g., our galaxy). But cosmologist Sean Carroll claims that if the constants smoothly varied across the universe, then the mass of the corresponding scalar field would be, in his words, mind-bogglingly small, making such a proposal very implausible. Chad Orzel claims that data originally measured by *both* telescopes in John Webb's original study on the matter showed no shift. Individual telescope data from that study that did show a shift in the fine-structure constant may be better explained by variations in the telescopes themselves and not the fine-structure constant.[411]

I see your multiverse and raise you a Boltzmann Brain.

Even if the multiverse did exist, that would not automatically refute the fine-tuning argument. According to the Copernican principle, our place in the cosmos is not special. Prior to the work of Copernicus, many people believed that the earth resided at the center of the universe and all the planets revolved around it. However, Copernicus and Galileo demonstrated that our planet actually resides in a typical solar system within a typical galaxy somewhere in a much larger universe. Therefore, if a multiverse did exist, we should expect that our particular universe would be much like any other universe within this entire multiverse or "world ensemble."

It is more likely that if ours were a randomly generated universe in the multiverse, we would expect our universe to be a very small fluctuation within the multiverse. In fact, it's more likely that any "intelligent observer" would just be a single sentient brain that popped into existence from the quantum vacuum (with a bunch of false memories) than it would be a normal observer in a huge and ordered universe like ours. Philosophers and physicists call these typical observers "Boltzmann brains."[412] Critics of the fine-tuning argument often say that if there is a multiverse, then someone had to win the fine-tuning "cosmic lottery," and that someone is us.

But the Boltzmann brain problem shows that the winner of the lottery didn't have to be our kind of life; in fact, the odds overwhelmingly say it would not be us. This causes physicists to ask, "If we do live in a typical multiverse, then why aren't we a typical Boltzmann brain?" Since we know that we are not Boltzmann brains (unless you disappear after reading this sentence), then we are justified in concluding that our universe is a designed one that beat all the odds via some outside help.

Works Cited

Aikin, Scott, and Robert Talisse. *Reasonable Atheism: A Moral Case for Respectful Disbelief.* Amherst, NY: Prometheus Books, 2011.

Al-Ghazali, Abu Hamid Muhammad. *The Incoherence of the Philosophers.* Translated by Michael E. Marmura. Provo, Utah: Brigham Young University, 2000.

Aquinas, Thomas. *Summa Theologicae.*

Arkes, Hadley. *First Things: An Inquiry into the First Principles of Morals and Justice.* Princeton: Princeton University Press, 1986.

Asch, Solomon. *Social Psychology.* Englewood Cliffs, NJ: Prentice-Hall, 1952.

Augustine. *City of God and Christian Doctrine.*

————. *Confessions.* Oxford: Oxford University Press, 2008.

————. *On Free Choice of the Will.* Indianapolis: Hackett Publishing Company: USA, 1993.

Barker, Dan. *Godless: How an Evangelical Preacher Became one of America's Leading Atheists.* Berkeley: Ulysses Press, 2008.

Bell, John. *Speakable and Unspeakable in Quantum Mechanics.* New York: Cambridge University Press, 1987.

Bonhoeffer, Dietrich. *Letters and Papers from Prison.* New York: Touchstone, 1997.

Carrier, Richard. *Sense and Goodness without God: A Defense of Metaphysical Naturalism.* Bloomington, IN: Author House, 2005.

Carroll, Sean. *From Eternity to Here: The Quest for the Ultimate Theory of Time.* London: Plume, 2010.

Christina, Greta. *Why Are You Atheists So Angry? 99 Things that Piss Off the Godless.* Charlottesville, VA: Pitchstone Publishing, 2012.

Coyne, Jerry. *Why Evolution Is True.* Oxford: Oxford University Press, 2009.

Craig, William Lane. *Reasonable Faith.* Wheaton, IL: Crossway Books, 2008.

Craig, William Lane, and J. P. Moreland, eds. *The Blackwell Companion to Natural Theology.* Sussex: Blackwell Publishing, 2009.

Craig, William Lane, and Walter Sinnott-Armstrong. *God? A Debate Between a Christian and an Atheist.* Oxford: Oxford University Press, 2004.

Copan, Paul, and William Lane Craig, eds. *Come Let Us Reason: New Essays in Christian Apologetics.* Nashville: B&H Publishing, 2012.

Dacey, Austin, and Lewis Vaughn. *The Case for Humanism: An Introduction.* Rowman and Littlefield Publishers, 2003.

Danielou, Jean. *Introduction to the Great Religions.* Translated by Albert J. La Mothe, Jr. Notre Dame: Fides, 1967.

Davies, Paul. *God and the New Physics.* New York: Touchstone, 1983.

Davis, John Jefferson. *Frontiers of Science and Faith: Examining Questions from the Big Bang to the End of the Universe.* Downers Grove, IL: InterVarsity Press, 2002.

Dawes, Gregory. *Theism and Explanation.* New York: Routledge, 2009.

Dawkins, Richard. *The Blind Watchmaker.* New York: Norton, 1986.

———. *The God Delusion*. New York: Houghton Mifflin Company, 2006.

———. *The Greatest Show on Earth: The Evidence for Evolution*. New York: Free Press, 2009.

Dennett, Daniel. *Breaking the Spell: Religion as a Natural Phenomenon*. New York: Penguin Books, 2006.

Donnelly, John, ed. *Language, Metaphysics, and Death*. New York: Fordham University Press, 1994.

Eddington, Arthur S. *The Nature of the Physical World*. New York: Macmillan, 1928.

Epstein, Greg. *Good Without God: What a Billion Non-religious People Do Believe*. New York: HarperCollins, 2009.

Everitt, Nicholas. *The Non-existence of God*. New York: Routledge, 2004.

Farrell, John. *The Day Without a Yesterday: Einstein, Lemaître, and the Birth of Modern Cosmology*. New York: Thunder's Mouth Press, 2005.

Feser, Edward. *Aquinas: A Beginner's Guide*. Oxford: One-World, 2009.

Greene, Brian. *The Fabric of the Cosmos: Space, Time, and the Texture of Reality*. New York: Random House, 2004.

Groothius, Douglas. *Christian Apologetics: A Comprehensive Case for Biblical Faith*. Downers Grove, IL: InterVarsity Press, 2011.

Harris, Sam. *The End of Faith: Religion, Terror, and the Future of Reason*. New York: W.W. Norton Company, 2004.

———. *Letter to a Christian Nation*. New York: Vintage Books, 2008.

———. *The Moral Landscape: How Science Can Determine Moral Values*. New York: Free Press, 2010.

Hawking, Stephen. *A Brief History of Time.* New York: Bantam Books, 1998.

Hawking, Stephen, and Leonard Mlodinow. *The Grand Design.* New York: Random House Publishing, 2011.

Hume, David. *Dialogues Concerning Natural Religion.* Millis, MA: Agora Publications, 2004.

————. *An Enquiry Concerning Human Understanding.*

————. *A Treatise of Human Nature.* New York: Dover Publications, 2003.

Johnson, B. C. *The Atheist Debater's Handbook.* Amherst, NY: Prometheus Books, 1983.

Kaku, Michio. *Parallel Worlds: A Journey through Creation, Higher Dimensions, and the Future of the Cosmos.* New York: Anchor Books, 2005.

Kant, Immanuel. *The Critique of Pure Reason.*

Keller, Timothy. *The Reason for God: Belief in an Age of Skepticism.* New York: Riverhead Books, 2008.

Kenny, Anthony. *The Five Ways: St. Thomas Aquinas' Proofs of God's Existence.* London: Routledge and Kegan Paul, 1969.

Kreeft, Peter, and Fr. Ronald Tacelli. *Handbook of Christian Apologetics.* Downers Grove, IL: InterVarsity Press, 1994.

LePoidevin, Robin. *Arguing for Atheism: An Introduction to the Philosophy of Religion.* New York: Routledge, 1996.

Leslie, John, ed. *Modern Cosmology and Philosophy.* Amherst, NY: Prometheus Books, 1999.

Lewis, C. S. *The Abolition of Man.* New York: HarperCollins, 1974.

————. *A Grief Observed.* New York: HarperCollins, 1961.

————. *Mere Christianity*. New York: Simon and Schuster, 1952.

————. *Miracles*. New York: HarperCollins, 1996.

————. *The Problem of Pain*. New York: HarperOne, 2001.

Locke, John. *An Essay Concerning Human Understanding*.

Loftus, John. *Why I Became an Atheist: A Former Preacher Rejects Christianity*. Amherst, NY: Prometheus Books, 2012.

Mackie, J. L. *The Miracle of Theism: Arguments for and against the Existence of God*. Oxford: Oxford University Press, 1982.

Martin, Michael. *Atheism: A Philosophical Justification*. Philadelphia: Temple University Press, 1990.

————, ed. *The Cambridge Companion to Atheism*. New York: Cambridge University Press, 2007.

Mencken. H. L. *A Mencken Crestomathy: His Own Selection of His Choicest Writings*. New York: Random House, 1982.

Moreland, J. P., and Kai Nielsen. *Does God Exist? The Debate Between Theists and Atheists*. Amherst, NY: Prometheus Books, 1993.

Nagel, Ernst, *The Structure of Science*, 2nd ed. Indianapolis: Hackett, 1979.

Nowacki, Mark. *The Kalam Cosmological Argument for God*. Amherst, NY: Prometheus Books, 2007.

Nielsen, Kai. *Reason and Practice*. New York: Harper & Row, 1971.

Nietzsche, Friedrich. *The Gay Science*. New York: Dover Publications, 2006.

Otto, Rudolph. *The Idea of the Holy*. Oxford: Oxford University Press, 1958.

Paley, William. *Natural Theology*. Oxford: Oxford University Press, 2006.

Paulos, John Allen. *Irreligion: A Mathematician Explains Why the Arguments for God Don't Add Up*. New York: Hill and Wang, 2009.

Penrose, Roger. *The Road to Reality*. New York: Vintage Press, 2004.

Pinker, Steven. *The Blank Slate: The Modern Denial of Human Nature*. New York: Penguin Books, 2002.

Plantinga, Alvin. *God, Freedom, and Evil*. Grand Rapids: Wm. B. Eerdmans Publishing Co., 1977.

————. *Warranted Christian Belief*. Oxford: Oxford University Press, 2000.

Ratzinger, Joseph Cardinal. *Introduction to Christianity*. Ignatius Press: San Francisco, 1990.

Rees, Martin. *Just Six Numbers: The Deep Forces that Shape the Universe*. New York: Basic Books, 2000.

Rosenberg, Alex. *The Atheist's Guide to Reality: Enjoying Life without Illusions*. New York: W. W. Norton & Company, 2011.

Russell, Bertrand. *Dear Bertrand Russell: A Selection of His Correspondence with the General Public, 1950–1968*. London: Allen & Unwin, 1969.

Sagan, Carl. *The Cosmic Connection: An Extra Terrestrial Perspective*. New York: Cambridge University Press, 2000.

————. *The Demon Haunted World: Science as a Candle in the Dark*. London: Headline Book Publishing, 1996.

Sennett, James, and Douglas Groothius, eds. *In Defense of Natural Theology: A Post-Humean Assessment*. Downers Grove, IL: InterVarsity Press, 2005.

Shafer-Landau, Russ. *Whatever Happened to Good and Evil?* Oxford: Oxford University Press, 2004.

Shermer, Michael. *The Believing Brain. New York:* Henry Holt and Co., 2012.

―――. *The Science of Good and Evil: Why People Cheat, Gossip, Share, Care, and Follow the Golden Rule*. New York: Henry Holt and Co., 2004.

Shook, John. *The God Debates: A 21st Century Guide for Atheists Believers and Everyone in Between*. Oxford: Wiley-Blackwell, 2010.

Sinnott-Armstrong, Walter, ed. *Moral Psychology Volume 2.: The Cognitive Science of Morality: Intuition and Diversity.* Cambridge: Massachusetts Institute of Technology, 2008.

Smith, Christian, and Melinda Denton. *Soul Searching: The Religious and Spiritual Lives of American Teenagers*. New York: Oxford University Press, 2005.

Smith, George. *Atheism: The Case Against God*. Amherst, NY: Prometheus Press, 1979.

Smolin, Lee. *The Trouble with Physics: The Rise of String Theory, The Fall of a Science, and What Comes Next*. New York: Mariner Books, 2007.

Snyder, Daniel Howard, and Paul K. Moser, eds. *Divine Hiddenness: New Essays*. Cambridge: Cambridge University Press, 2002.

Spitzer, Fr. Robert. *New Proofs for the Existence of God: Contributions of Contemporary Physics and Philosophy*. Grand Rapids: Wm. B. Eerdmans, 2010.

Stenger, Victor. *The Fallacy of Fine Tuning: Why the Universe Is Not Designed for Us.* Amherst, NY: Prometheus Books, 2011.

———. *God and the Folly of Faith.* Amherst, NY: Prometheus Books, 2012.

Swinburne, Richard. *The Existence of God.* Oxford: Oxford University Press, 2004.

Vilenkin, Alexander. *Many Worlds in One.* New York: Hill and Wang, 2006.

Vujivic, Nick. *Life without Limits.* New York: Doubleday, 2010.

Wielenberg, Erik. *Value and Virtue in a Godless Universe.* New York: Cambridge University Press, 2005.

Zimmerman, Dean and Peter Van Inwagen, *eds. Metaphysics: The Big Questions.* Oxford: Blackwell, 1998.

Endnotes

Introduction

1. Proverbs 15:1.

2. See Jonathan Rauch, "Let It Be: Three Cheers for Apatheism," *The Atlantic Monthly.* May 2003.

3. 1 Peter 3:15-16

Chapter 1: Theism, Atheism, and the God Debate

4. The astute reader may wonder why I use the pronoun "he" instead of "it" to describe a generic God. I use "he" because it is the traditional pronoun used to refer to God (even for atheists) and my faith tradition identifies God as a He. Furthermore, the masculine pronoun is a more fitting image of God creating the world from outside of himself like how a father creates a child as opposed to a mother who passively receives the male seed and would represent both the creator and the created, which could lead one to conceive of God in a pantheistic way. I owe this observation to Kreeft and Tacelli in their *Handbook of Christian Apologetics* (97-98). I also think that the pronoun "it" doesn't affirm God's personhood and can be misconstrued to refer to a God that is little more than an idea such as "The American Dream" which is real, but has no existence outside of human minds.

5. CCC 42.

6. For example, Thomas Jefferson created his own version of the Gospels called *The Life and Morals of Jesus of Nazareth*, also called the Jefferson Bible, which excised the supernatural elements in the canonical Gospels. While Jefferson believed God existed, he denied the central tenants of Christianity. See Gregg L. Frazer, *The Religious Beliefs of America's Founders: Reason, Revelation, Revolution* (University Press of Kansas, 2012).

7. Jean Danielou. *Introduction to the Great Religions* (Fides, 1967) 13. While *pantheism* claims that God and the universe are identical, *panentheism* claims that God is the animating force or "soul" of the universe. According to the Pontifical document *Jesus Christ: The Bearer of the Water of Life*, pantheism teaches that, "God is the 'life-principle', the 'spirit or soul of the world', the sum total of consciousness existing in the world." The document also affirms that, "There is no space in this view for God as a distinct being in the sense of classical theism."

8. For a good book on the subject I recommend Krista Tippett's *Einstein's God: Conversations about Science and the Human Spirit* (Penguin Books: New York, 2010).

9. It's hard to define naturalism without being circular and using the word "natural" in the definition. John Shook defines it as, "the philosophical conclusion that the only reality is what is discovered by our intelligence using the tools of experience, reason, and science." John Shook. *The God Debates: A 21st Century Guide for Atheists, Believers and Everyone in Between* (Wiley-Blackwell: Oxford, 2010) 14. Anyone who happens to conclude that God exists using experience, reason, or science is simply mistaken, I guess.

10. According to the *Pew Forum on Religion and Public Life*, 25% of all Americans and 33% of Americans under age the age of 30 do not belong to any particular religion. Only 2.4% of Americans are atheists, though some recent studies place the number as high as five percent. See "Nones' on the Rise: One-in-Five Adults Have No Religious Affiliation," October 9, 2012, available online at http://www.pewforum.org/uploadedFiles/Topics/Religious_Affiliation/Unaffiliated/NonesOnTheRise-full.pdf

11. C. S. Lewis. *Mere Christianity* (Simon and Schuster: New York, 1952) 152.

12. Christian Smith and Melinda Denton. *Soul Searching: The Religious and Spiritual Lives of American Teenagers* (Oxford University Press: New York, 2005) 162-164.

13. Harris writes, "In fact, it is difficult to imagine a set of beliefs more suggestive of mental illness than those that lie at the heart of many of our religious traditions." Sam Harris. *The End of Faith: Religion, Terror, and the Future of Reason* (W.W. Norton Company: New York, 2004) 70.

14. Richard Dawkins. *The God Delusion* (Houghton Mifflin Company: New York, 2006) 354.

15. Tom Flynn, "Why I Don't Believe in the New Atheism." Available online at: http://www.secularhumanism.org/index.php?sectio n=library&page=flynn_30_3 While ridicule of religion has a long history (such as in the works of Thomas Paine and Robert Ingersoll) the mainstream appeal of such polemics has been a more recent phenomenon.

16. The term comes from Thomas Huxley who used it in an 1869 address at a meeting of the Metaphysical Society in London.

17. Michael Shermer seems to be an example of a strong agnostic. He writes, "I once saw a bumper sticker that read "Militant agnostic: I don't know and you don't either." This is my position on God's existence: I don't know and you don't either." Michael Shermer, *The Believing Brain* (Henry Holt and Co: New York, 2012) 175.

18. According to the Catechism, "Agnosticism can sometimes include a certain search for God, but it can equally express indifferentism, a flight from the ultimate question of existence, and a sluggish moral conscience. Agnosticism is all too often equivalent to practical atheism."—CCC 2128

19. Address of his Holiness Benedict XVI at the Meeting For Peace in Assisi, Assisi, Basilica Of Saint Mary of the Angels Thursday, 27 October 2011. available online at http://www.vatican.va/ holy_father/benedict_xvi/speeches/2011/october/documents/ hf_ben-xvi_spe_20111027_assisi_en.html

20. Austin Dacey and Lewis Vaughn. *The Case for Humanism: An Introduction* (Rowman and Littlefield Publishers, 2003) 162.

21. CCC 31.

22. Even logical proofs like Aquinas's five ways rely on evidence from the natural world that needs to be interpreted (such as Aquinas's description of change) which, as a result, can be rationally doubted. The only proofs for God that resemble mathematical proofs are complex versions of the ontological argument like Robert Maydole's version in *The Blackwell Companion to Natural Theology* (2009).

23. Harris writes, "religious faith is simply *unjustified* belief in matters of ultimate concern." (2004) 65.

24. CCC 1814.

25. For more on personal experience of God, see chapter 16.

26. "First Vatican Council." Available online at: http://www.ewtn. com/library/councils/v1.htm

27. See a similar discussion in Peter Kreeft and Fr. Ronald Tacelli's Handbook of Christian Apologetics (InterVarsity Press: Downers Grove, 1994) 33-37. Russ Shafer-Landau is an atheist who defends objective morality, but he concedes that while he arrives at his unpopular belief through reason, it seems that the only students of his who immediately share a belief in objective morality are committed theists who usually arrive at the same conclusion by faith. (Russ Shafer-Landau. *Whatever Happened to Good and Evil?* (Oxford University Press: Oxford, 2004) 30.

28. For atheist de-conversions see Dan Barker. *Godless: How an Evangelical Preacher Became One of America's Leading Atheists.* (Ulysses Press: Berkeley, 2008) and John Loftus. *Why I Became an Atheist: A Former Preacher Rejects Christianity* (Prometheus Books: Amherst, 2012). For a story of conversion from atheism to theism see Kevin Vost. *From Atheism to Catholicism: How Scientists and Philosophers Led Me to the Truth.* (Our Sunday Visitor: Huntington, 2010).

29. William Lane Craig vs. Arif Ahmed: "Is Belief in God More Reasonable than Disbelief?" Cambridge University (2005). Available

online at: http://www.apologetics315.com/2009/10/william-lane-craig-vs-arif-ahmed-is.html

30. "Penn Jillette gets the gift of a Bible." Available online at http://www.youtube.com/watch?v=ZhG-tkQ_Q2w

Chapter 2: Getting rid of bad attitudes

31. This is also called the Dunning-Kruger effect.

32. Joseph Cardinal Ratzinger. *Introduction to Christianity*. (Ignatius Press: San Francisco, 1990) 20.

33. For people's views on evolution see the Pew Research Center July 2009 study available online at: http://www.people-press.org/2009/07/09/section-5-evolution-climate-change-and-other-issues/ Also, according to the theory of evolution we did not evolve from monkeys but we and primates like monkeys share a common evolutionary ancestor.

34. St. Augustine. *On the Literal Interpretation of Genesis* 1:19-20.

35. William Lane Craig/Peter Williams vs. Arif Ahmed/Andrew Copson "This House Does Not Believe that God is a Delusion" Cambridge Union Society (October 20, 2011). Available online at: http://www.reasonablefaith.org/media/craig-williams-vs-ahmed-copson-cambridge

36. Scott Aikin and Robert Talisse. *Reasonable Atheism: A Moral Case for Respectful Disbelief* (Prometheus Books: Amherst, 2011) 41.

37. While Hitler did invoke God and Christianity in his public speeches as part of a propaganda campaign, his private views on religion seem to be very different and much more critical. For a good book on Hitler's personal views about religion I recommend *Hitler's Table Talk* which records Hitler's private conversations among his inner circle between 1941-1944.

38. That is why the majority of arguments put forward by Christopher Hitchens in his book *God Is Not Great* simply aren't relevant to what I am arguing in this book.

39. While atheists can be moral, atheism itself is still a sin because it refuses to give God the respect he deserves. However, the *responsibility* an atheist has for the sin of atheism can vary widely. Even the failures of Christians can mitigate the blame an atheist has for not worshipping God. The Catechism states that, "The imputability of this offense can be significantly diminished in virtue of the intentions and the circumstances. Believers can have more than a little to do with the rise of atheism. To the extent that they are careless about their instruction in the faith, or present its teaching falsely, or even fail in their religious, moral, or social life, they must be said to conceal rather than to reveal the true nature of God and of religion." (CCC 2125).

40. Greta Christina. *Why Are You Atheists So Angry? 99 Things That Piss Off the Godless* (Pitchstone Publishing, 2012).

41. For example, in 2011 high school student Jessica Ahlquist (an outspoken atheist) received death threats from Christians because she advocated for a prayer to be removed from her public high school's auditorium. State Representative Peter Palumbo even called Ahlquist an "evil little thing" in a local radio interview. See Abby Goodnough, "Student Faces Town's Wrath in Protest Against a Prayer," *The New York Times*, January 26, 2012

42. Neil Gross and Solon Simmons, "How Religious are America's College and University Professors?" Social Science Research Council, February 06, 2007. Available online at: http://religion.ssrc.org/reforum/Gross_Simmons.pdf

43. For the Hindu view on creation see Michael Cremo. *Forbidden Archaeology: The Hidden History of the Human Race* (Bhaktivedanta Book Publishing, 1998).

44. For a good treatment of this period of history see James Hannam. *The Genesis of Science: How the Christian Middle Ages Launched the Scientific Revolution* (Regnery Publishing, Washington, DC, 2011).

45. See "Religious Differences on the Question of Evolution," The Pew Forum on Religion in Public Life, February 4, 2009, available

at http://www.pewforum.org/Science-and-Bioethics/Religious-Differences-on-the-Question-of-Evolution.aspx. There is also a growing acceptance of evolution among evangelicals. One prominent example would be Francis Collins, the current head of the National Institutes of Health and the leader of the team who mapped the human genome. His case for the compatibility of Christianity and the theory of evolution can be found in his book *The Language of God: A Scientist Presents Evidence for Belief* (2009).

46. For an affirmation of both God's act of creation and the reality of evolution see Pope Benedict XVI *In the Beginning . . . A Catholic Understanding of Creation and the Fall* (Our Sunday Visitor: Indiana, 2010) 50. For a perspective from a Catholic scientist see Kenneth Miller, *Finding Darwin's God: A Scientist's Search for Common Ground Between God and Evolution* (HarperCollins: New York, 1999).

47. Dietrich Bonhoeffer. *Letters and Papers from Prison.* (Touchstone: New York, 1997) 311.

48. The only question for these philosophers is whether freedom simply doesn't exist (also called hard determinism) or if one can be determined by outside forces and yet still be "free," though in a qualified sense of the word. This latter view is called compatibilism (or soft determinism) because it is thought that free will and determinism can be compatible with each other.

49. For example see Timothy O'Connor, *Persons and Causes: The Metaphysics of Free Will* (Oxford University Press: New York, 2000).

Chapter 3: Is atheism true?

50. William Lane Craig vs. Lewis Wolpert "Is God a Delusion?" Westminster Hall, London, January 1, 2009. Available at http://www.reasonablefaith.org/media/craig-vs-wolpert-westminster-hall-london.

51. For more on the existence of moral truths see chapter 13.

52. This belief is called Platonism. I don't support the view that abstract objects exist in a self-sufficient way apart from God but am instead inclined toward the view that they exist either as thoughts in God's mind (conceptualism), as an essential part of God's nature,

or they don't really exist and are just useful fictions (nominal-ism/fictionalism). For a good survey of the controversy see Lin-nebo, Øystein, "Platonism in the Philosophy of Mathematics," *The Stanford Encyclopedia of Philosophy (Fall 2011 Edition)*, Edward N. Zalta (ed.) http://plato.stanford.edu/archives/fall2011/entries/platonism-mathematics/>. One might argue that mathematical endorsement of Platonism undermines the KCA's prohibition of really existing actual infinites. To this objection I defer to J.P. Moreland "A Response to a Platonistic and a Set Theoretic Objection to the Kalām Cosmological Argument," *Religious Studies* 39, no. 4 (2003): 373-390.

53. Jim Holt. "Proof" *The New York Times*, Sunday Book Review, January 13, 2008. Available online at http://www.nytimes.com/2008/01/13/books/review/Holt-t.html?_r=0

54. An atheist could counter that while they agree truth does not come *only* from science, science is still the most *reliable* way to discover truth. But this begs the question because science is limited to discovering truths about the natural world. The atheist has not been able to prove that other kinds of truths (such as religious or philosophical truths) do not exist. If they did exist, science would not be the most reliable way to discover those truths because they lie outside of the purview of the scientific method.

55. Nicholas Everitt. *The Non-existence of God*. (Routledge: New York, 2004) 213-226.

56. C. S. Lewis. *Miracles*. (HarperCollins: New York, 1996) 79

57. See Michael Murray. "Deus Absconditis" in *Divine Hiddenness: New Essays,* eds. Daniel Howard Snyder and Paul K. Moser (Cambridge University Press: Cambridge, 2002) 62.

58. Hitchens made the comparison between God and North Korean dictator Kim Jong Il in a 2010 debate with Prime Minister and recent Catholic convert Tony Blair. See Paul Harris, "Christopher Hitchens 1 – 0 Tony Blair" *The Guardian* 11/27/10. Available online at: http://www.guardian.co.uk/world/2010/nov/27/christopher-hitchens-tony-blair-debate

59. The argument from "divine hiddenness" was formally developed by J. L. Schellenberg in his 1993 book *Divine Hiddenness and Human Reason*. Some atheists claim God's silence is evidence he doesn't exist because it would be absurd to think that so many people who don't believe in God will automatically be damned through no fault of their own, such as people who lack knowledge of Jesus or even the Western concept of God. But only some Christian sects teach the impossibility of salvation for those who do not know Christ. The Catholic Church teaches that even people in other religions who have no knowledge of Christianity have the possibility of salvation. In the Vatican II document *Lumen Gentium*, the Second Vatican Council wrote, "For they who without their own fault do not know of the Gospel of Christ and His Church, but yet seek God with sincere heart, and try, under the influence of grace, to carry out His will in practice, known to them through the dictate of conscience, can attain eternal salvation" (Paragraph 16). One might object that this makes missionary efforts useless, but the Church only teaches the possibility, not the certainty, of salvation for the ignorant and so evangelism is still incredibly important.

60. Richard Swinburne. *The Existence of God*. (Oxford University Press: Oxford, 2004) 272. This also explains why God made his existence obvious to the Israelites in the Old Testament and the Apostles in the New Testament so that they could accomplish a great good of cooperating with God in order to lead other humans to salvation by sharing the knowledge of God.

61. Sam Harris. *Letter to a Christian Nation*. (Vintage Books: New York, 2008) 17.

62. Some critics cite the mildly apocryphal story of the 18th-century scientist Pierre Laplace and the French emperor Napoleon as evidence that science has done away with God. According to the account, Napoleon asked Laplace where God fits into his new model of the solar system to which Laplace allegedly responded, "Sir, I have no need for that hypothesis." In a 1999 public lecture entitled "Does God Play Dice??" Stephen Hawking commented on

the event and said, "I don't think that Laplace was claiming that God didn't exist. It is just that He doesn't intervene, to break the laws of Science." Available online at: http://www.hawking.org.uk/does-god-play-dice.html

63. John Allen Paulos. *Irreligion: A Mathematician Explains Why the Arguments for God Don't Add Up.* (Hill and Wang: New York, 2009) 42.

64. Bertrand Russell. *Dear Bertrand Russell: A Selection of his Correspondence with the General Public, 1950–1968* (Allen & Unwin: London: 1969).

65. This also explains why we dismiss beings, like the Flying Spaghetti Monster, that have no evidence for them *and* are implausible (which counts as evidence against them). We might say that the FSM doesn't exist, for example, because we know that spaghetti is a man-made food composed of flour and water and is not a natural part of any organism, much less a sentient all-powerful one.

66. Kai Nielsen, *Reason and Practice* (New York: Harper & Row, 1971), 43-44.

Chapter 4: Did man invent God?

67. See Arthur Fairbanks. *The First Philosophers of Greece* (Paternoster House: London, 1898) 78 and Lesher, James, "Xenophanes", *The Stanford Encyclopedia of Philosophy (Fall 2011 Edition),* Edward N. Zalta (ed.) http://plato.stanford.edu/archives/fall2011/entries/xenophanes/

68. St. Clement of Alexandria quotes Xenophanes in the *Miscellanies*, Book V, Chapter XIV.

69. Modern arguments that God is a human invention come from Fuerbach's *The Essence of Christianity* (1841), Marx's contribution to *Critique of Hegel's Philosophy of Right* (1843), which famously said religion was "the opium of the people," and Freud's *The Future of an Illusion* (1927). In the mid-twentieth century the French Catholic philosopher Maurice Blondel provided an excellent rebuttal to

these views. See Fr. John Cihak "The Threshold of Faith" *This Rock* Volume 11, No. 4, April 2000. See also Plantinga, 2000 135-163.

70. This thesis is argued in Justin Barrett's 2004 book *Why Would Anyone Believe in God?*

71. Jerry Coyne. *Why Evolution Is True* (Oxford University Press: Oxford, 2009) 248.

72. Shermer, 174.

73. Persinger claims that the Swedish team did not replicate the experiment properly, but the Swedish team claims that they followed a pre-established set of mutually-agreed upon guidelines. See Marcus Larsson, et al. Reply to M. A. Persinger and S. A. Koren's response to Granqvist et al. "Sensed presence and mystical experiences are predicted by suggestibility, not by the application of transcranial weak magnetic fields" Neuroscience Letters Volume 380, Issue 3, 3 June 2005, Pages 348–350

74. Shook, 103-104. Shook goes on to give several reasons to think that religious experiences should not count as evidence for God. These are interesting but do not need to be discussed here as I am merely critiquing the "argument for atheism from the artificial inducement of religious experiences" which Shook also considers fallacious. I am not defending an argument for theism from general religious experience.

75. Published originally in Mencken's essay "Memorial Service" which can be found in H.L. Mencken *A Mencken Crestomathy: His Own Selection of His Choicest Writings* (Random House: New York, 1982) 95.

76. Plato shows in the *Euthyphro* that the quarreling among the Greek gods counts against their existence. Aristotle writes in the *Metaphysics*, "From old-and extremely ancient times there has been handed down to our later age intimations of a mythical character to the effect that the stars are gods and that the divine embraces the whole of nature. The further details were subsequently

added in the manner of myth. Their purpose was the persuasion of the masses and general legislative and political expediency. For instance, the myths tell us that these gods are anthropomorphic or resemble some of the other animals and give us other, comparable extrapolations of the basic picture." Aristotle. *The Metaphysics*. (Penguin Press: New York, 1998) 380. In Book XII, Aristotle writes of the true God that he "is a living being, eternal, most good, so that life and duration continuous and eternal belong to God; for this is God."

77. The few notable exceptions would be David Berlinsky who wrote *The Devil's Delusion: Atheism and its Scientific Pretensions* and Bradley Monton who wrote *Seeking God in Science: An Atheist Defends Intelligent Design,* both of which were published in 2009.

78. See Bobby Henderson. *The Gospel of the Flying Spaghetti Monster*. (Villi Books: New York, 2006) or visit their "church" online at www.venganza.org

79. 1 Corinthians 13:11, cited in George Smith. *Atheism: The Case Against God* (Prometheus Press: New York, 1979) 273.

80. 2 Timothy 3:14.

81. Spoiler alert: since spaghetti is a material object, and the creator existed prior to the creation of all matter as well as the space where matter resides, then the creator can't be made of spaghetti or any other kind of pasta.

82. Swinburne, 23-51.

83. Bart J. Bok, Lawrence E. Jerome, and Paul Kurtz, "Objections to Astrology: A Statement by 186 Leading Scientists," *The Humanist*, September/October 1975.

84. Carl Sagan. *The Demon Haunted World: Science as a Candle in the Dark* (Headline Book Publishing: London, 1996) 285.

85. Swinburne 45-51.

Chapter 5: Is God a contradiction?

86. The Baltimore Catechism, Lesson One, Question Two. Available online at http://www.catholicity.com/baltimore-catechism/lesson01.html

87. Matthew 10:29-30.

88. Some critics will object that if God knows the future then humans can't be free. First, this would not prove atheism but rather that humans either had no free will or that God doesn't know the future. Secondly, the Christian tradition offers two possible solutions to the paradox. Followers of St. Thomas Aquinas (or *Thomists*) argue that God perceives the past, present, and future in one eternal moment. Under this view, God observes the future happening for him right "now." He is seeing me, at what is the "present" for him, freely choose to wear the red shirt tomorrow. God's knowledge of the future doesn't *determine* that I wear the red shirt tomorrow any more than your watching me decide to wear the shirt on that day determines that I will wear it. The other solution is called *Molinism* and it claims God knows what I would do in every possible world that could exist. Prior to creating the world, God merely chose to make one of those possible worlds the actual world. Under this explanation, I am free because God does not determine what I freely do in all of these possible worlds. He just chooses to make what I freely did in one of those possible worlds become actual. There are more to these solutions than what I can adequately summarize in this note. Just keep in mind that regardless of which solution one chooses, God's knowledge of the future doesn't cause what we do.

89. Arguments like these seem to be a derivative of an approach put forth by Michael Martin in his 1974 article "A Disproof of the God of the Common Man" Martin admits that philosophers avoid this objection by defining omniscience in terms of propositional knowledge, but he claims this is just an informal argument against an informal conception of God. See *The Impossibility of God,* eds. Michael Martin and Ricki Monnier (Prometheus Books: New York, 2003) 232-241.

90. For a more complete description of omnipotence see Thomas Flint and Alfred Freddoso's essay "Maximal Power," in the book *Philosophy of Religion: a Reader and Guide* (New Brunswick, N.J.: Rutgers University Press, 2002), edited by William Lane Craig. I also recommend Brian Davies. *An Introduction to the Philosophy of Religion*. (Oxford University Press: Oxford, 1993) 189-197. Interestingly enough, omnipotence is the only divine attribute that is mentioned in the Nicene Creed.

91. A critic might object that the act of lying or sinning is not an impossible task (we do those things all the time) and God's failure to do likewise counts against his omnipotence. The critic might also object that saying God can only do what is logically possible for God to do is a meaningless definition. Is a rock omnipotent because it can do anything that is logically possible for a rock to do? That is why Flint and Fredosso's paper I cited above is so helpful. They frame omnipotence not in God being able to do anything, but in God being able to actualize any logically possible state of affairs. Since the state of affairs involving a perfect being acting imperfectly is a contradiction that no being could actualize, God's failure to actualize such a state of affairs does not show he is not omnipotent.

92. St. Thomas Aquinas. *Summa Theologica*. "Whether God is Omnipotent?" Question 25, Reply to objection two.

93. St. Augustine. *City of God and Christian Doctrine*, Book V, Chapter 10.

94. The Catholic Encyclopedia entry on the "Nature and Attributes of God" puts this point well, "According to our finite manner of thinking we conceive this presence of God in things spatial as being primarily a presence of power and operation—immediate Divine efficiency being required to sustain created beings in existence and to enable them to act; but, as every kind of Divine action *ad extra* is really identical with the Divine nature or essence, it follows that God is really present everywhere in creation not merely *per virtuten et operationem*, but *per essentiam*. In other words, God Himself, or the

Divine nature, is in immediate contact with, or immanent in, every creature—conserving it in being and enabling it to act. But while insisting on this truth we must, if we would avoid contradiction, reject every form of the pantheistic hypothesis. While emphasizing Divine immanence we must not overlook Divine transcendence." Toner, Patrick. "The Nature and Attributes of God." The Catholic Encyclopedia. Vol. 6. New York: Robert Appleton Company, 1909. 12 Jun. 2013

95. Theodore M. Drange. "The Incompatible Properties Argument: A Survey," *Philo* Issue 2, 1998, pp. 49-60

96. If this mind were created in God's image, then it could move itself to act without being acted upon in the same way that God is an unmoved mover. For modern defenses of libertarian free will see Robert Kane. *The Significance of Free Will* (1998) and Timothy O'Connor. *Persons and Causes: The Metaphysics of Free Will* (2000).

97. Alex Rosenberg. *The Atheist's Guide to Reality: Enjoying Life without Illusions* (W.W. Norton & Company: New York, 2011) 193.

98. See Brian Leftow's *Time and Eternity* (2009) and Paul Helm's *Eternal God: A Study of God Without Time* (2002) for a defense of a timeless God.

99. I suggest the reader review St. Thomas Aquinas for what I mean by the phrase "satisfies the demands of justice." I chose these words very carefully and am not implying that Jesus was a penal substitution for sin. He satisfied the demands of justice through his death, though he was not punished for each person's individual sin. See St. Thomas Aquinas, the *Summa Theologica*, First Part of the Second Part, Question 87, "Whether anyone is punished for another's sin?," Answer 8.

100. According to the Catechism, "St. Bonaventure explains that God created all things 'not to increase his glory, but to show it forth and to communicate it,' for God has no other reason for creating than his love and goodness: 'Creatures came into existence when the key of love opened his hand.' " (CCC 293)

101. I admit this survey is very brief and atheists have mounted other arguments from logical contradiction which I do not have the space to address in this book. A well-thought-out collection can be found in the anthology *The Impossibility of God*, eds. Michael Martin and Ricki Monnier (Prometheus Books, New York, 2003). For a more in-depth treatment of this topic from a theistic perspective, see Edward Wierenga. *The Nature of God: An Inquiry Into Divine Attributes* (Cornell University Press: Ithaca, 1989) and Richard Swinburne, *The Coherence of Theism* (Oxford University Press, 1993). For the classic treatment of the nature and attributes of God, see St. Thomas Aquinas, *Summa Theologicae Part I–Treatise on the One God (Questions 2-26)*.

102. Richard Carrier. *Sense and Goodness without God: A Defense of Metaphysical Naturalism* (Author House: Indiana, 2005) 275-276.

Chapter 6: Does evil disprove God?

103. C. S. Lewis. *A Grief Observed* (HarperCollins Publishers: New York, 1961) 18.

104. David Hume. *Dialogues Concerning Natural Religion.* (Agora Publications: MA: 2004) 119.

105. B. C. Johnson. *The Atheist Debater's Handbook* (Prometheus Books: New York, 1983) 105.

106. Available on YouTube at http://www.youtube.com/watch?v=Vg-qgmJ7nzA&feature=youtu.be&t=31s

107. Critics who say God must make the best possible world and since this world could be better it follows that God does not exist make the same mistake Leibniz made—there is no "best of all possible worlds." One could make a world better and better and never reach the best just as one could count forever and never reach "the highest possible number." One would only approach an infinite limit. All God is required to do is to make a good world and the critic is in no position to argue our world is not good.

108. *Candide*, Chapter Five, Paragraph Eight.

109. In Article 2, Reply to Objection 1, Thomas says, "Evil is distant both from simple being and from simple 'not-being,' because it is neither a habit nor a pure negation, but a privation." In Reply to Objection 2, he says, "being conveys the truth of a proposition which unites together subject, and attribute by a copula, notified by this word "is"; and in this sense being is what answers to the question, "Does it exist?" and thus we speak of blindness as being in the eye; or of any other privation. In this way even evil can be called a being." He goes on to make clear that evil is not a "positive thing in itself," but it does exist. I owe this observation to Tim Staples.

110. I owe this approach to the problem to William Lane Craig, though I am not aware if it is original to him.

111. J. L. Mackie, "Evil and Omnipotence," *Mind,* Vol. 64, No. 254. (Apr. 1955).

112. Now, God's good reasons don't satisfy some ethical demand or rule that exists outside of him, but are instead reasons that correspond to his essentially loving nature.

113. Sometimes our human tendency to anthropomorphize objects can get the better of us. In P. W. Singer's book *Wired for War: The Robotics Revolution and the 21st Century*, Singer describes military units praising the heroic actions of their bomb-disposal robots and even awarding them rank and medals (see 337-339 of the book). But this can probably be chalked up to the stress of war and its effect on the human psyche, similar to Tom Hanks developing a friendship with a volleyball in the film *Castaway.* The main point still stands that when we are thinking rationally, humans don't considered inanimate objects heroic or virtuous.

114. God can even use these evils to achieve his will. In Genesis 50:20, Joseph tells his brothers who sold him into slavery, "Even though you meant harm to me, God meant it for good, to achieve this present end, the survival of many people."

115. John Loftus. *Why I Became an Atheist: A Former Preacher Rejects Christianity* (Prometheus Books: New York, 2012) 240-241.

116. Swinburne writes, "Such a world would be a toy-world; a world where things matter, but not very much; where we can choose and our choices can make a small difference, but the real choices remain God's. The objector is asking that God should not be willing to be generous and trust us with his world, and give us occasional opportunities to show ourselves at our heroic best." (Swinburne, 264).

117. St. Augustine of Hippo. *On Free Choice of the Will.* (Hackett Publishing Company: USA, 1993) 81.

118. Also, a human being without free will would be like a triangle without three-sides. Being free seems essential to what it means to be human since a human is a kind of substance that possesses a rational nature.

119. CCC 302.

120. Paul Draper. "Pain and Pleasure: An Evidential Problem for Theists," *Nous* 23 (1989): 331-350.

121. J. L. Mackie. *The Miracle of Theism: Arguments for and against the Existence of God* (Oxford University Press: Oxford, 1982) 154. See Alvin Plantinga. *God, Freedom, and Evil* (Wm. B. Eerdmans Publishing Co.: Grand Rapids, 1977) for his approach to overcoming the logical problem of evil.

Chapter 7: Does pointless suffering disprove God?

122. Michael Murray uses a similar example to this in his book *Nature Red in Tooth and Claw: Theism and the Problem of Animal Suffering.* A real-life example did occur in 1998 when eleven members of a Congolese soccer team were all killed by lightning while the opposing team was left unharmed. See "Africa Lightning kills football team." *BBC News,* October 28, 1998. Available online at: http://news.bbc.co.uk/2/hi/africa/203137.stm

123. See William Rowe. "The Problem of Evil and Some Varieties of Atheism." *American Philosophical Quarterly* 16 (4): 335–41, October 1979.

124. I changed the word "gratuitous" to "pointless" as this will help the reader understand what Rowe means in more accessible language. See Rowe, 1979, Ibid.

125. What I am offering are *defenses* of God against the problem of evil or possible reasons as to why evil exists and is compatible with God. The term *theodicy* (which I am not offering) refers to the task of pinpointing the exact reason God allows evil, and not just the possible reasons.

126. Associated Press. "90 nations offer aid to help U.S. with Katrina" 09/07/05 See http://www.msnbc.msn.com/id/9231819/ns/us_news-katrina_the_long_road_back/t/nations-offer-aid-help-us-katrina/

127. Of course, some of the so-called natural evils that atheists use to indict God are actually *moral* evils that are the result of human failures. For example, it's popular on the internet to show a picture of a shriveled African child dying from starvation and then rhetorically ask, "So you still believe a loving God exists?" But famines in the modern world usually aren't God's fault, they're ours. According to the 2012 Copenhagen Consensus Project, there is enough food on the planet to feed everyone; we just don't share it with everyone who needs it. Even when we do send food and aid to countries suffering from famine, the food and aid are often stolen and sold by corrupt government officials. In fact, one of the worst famines in the history of the world took place between 1959 and 1961 because of the economic policies being promoted in Communist China.

128. Johnson, 99.

129. Ibid, 104.

130. Mark Vuletic. "The Tale of the Twelve Officers" (2002) Published online at The Secular Web http://www.infidels.org/library/modern/mark_vuletic/five.html

131. The no-see-um example is from Plantinga. See also Alvin Plantinga. *Warranted Christian Belief.* (Oxford University Press, Oxford, 2000) 466-467.

132. Philosopher William Alston lists several reasons related to our ignorance and weaknesses as human beings which show that we are not in a good position to know God is not justified in permitting the present amount of suffering in the world. See William Alston. "The Inductive Argument from Evil and the Human Cognitive Condition." *Philosophical Perspectives*, Vol. 5, Philosophy of Religion. (1991) 29-67.

133. This approach is based on a logical maneuver called *Moore's Shift* that was developed by G. E. Moore in his 1939 essay "Proof of an External World."

134. Genesis 18:25.

135. Timothy Keller. *The Reason for God: Belief in an Age of Skepticism* (Riverhead Books: New York, 2008) 27.

136. Ibid. 28.

137. Philippians 4:13.

138. John Stuart Mill. *Utilitarianism* (Dover Publications, 2007) 8.

139. C. S. Lewis. *The Problem of Pain* (HarperOne: New York, 2001) 93.

140. Nick Vujivic. *Life without Limits* (Doubleday: New York, 2010) 34-35.

Chapter 8: Why is there something rather than nothing?

141. Derek Parfit. "The Puzzle of Reality: Why does the universe exist?" *Metaphysics: The Big Questions,* eds. Dean Zimmerman and Peter Van Inwagen (Blackwell: Oxford, 1998).

142. William Lane Craig. *Reasonable Faith* (Crossway Books: Illinois, 2008) 106.

143. Don't take this to mean that all arguments for the existence of God are deductive. For example, Oxford philosopher Richard Swinburne in his 2004 book *The Existence of God* makes several

persuasive inductive arguments for the existence of God, though I disagree with him on some key issues (especially the nature of God and morality and the understanding of God's necessity).

144. Available online at http://www.bringyou.to/apologetics/p20. htm

145. Cited in Craig, 2008 107.

146. Strong versions of the PSR hold that everything needs an explanation, but philosophers have criticized the strong version of the PSR because of so-called brute facts or states of affairs that may have no explanation (such as why the Sun rises in the east instead of the west). However, there is no reason to think that a *material object* could just exist without an explanation like an immaterial fact can, and so the limited PSR can still apply. See Alexander Pruss's *The Principle of Sufficient Reason: A Reassessment* (2006) for a defense of the strong version of PSR.

147. Sir Arthur Conan Doyle. *The Sign of the Four* (Penguin Books: London, 1982) 51.

148. I owe this observation to Alexander Pruss in his article "The Leibnizian Cosmological Argument" which is published in *The Blackwell Companion to Natural Theology* (2009).

149. Pope John Paul II, General Audience, July 10, 1985.

150. This is what is meant by St. Thomas Aquinas when he says that God's essence (what he is) is identical to existence (that he is), or God is the ground of being and existence itself.

151. A critic could object that I am trying to say that God by definition exists, therefore God exists. That is not what I am arguing. Instead, I am saying that *if* God exists, then the reason God exists would be found within him and not outside of him. The contingency argument does not claim God exists by definition (or a priori). Rather, the ontological argument tries to prove God exists in this way. The contingency argument says God, or a necessary being, is the only sufficient explanation for the contingent universe we

observe. Therefore, his existence is an inferred explanation of this observed, or a posteriori, fact.

152. A critic could object that in some cases we can imagine impossible states of affairs (like cases involving time-travel) therefore just because we can imagine the universe not existing does not mean such a state of affairs could actually happen. But in cases like time-travel the impossibility is not explicit and has to be discovered through logical reasoning. If such impossibility exists in us imagining "nothing," then it is up to the critic to demonstrate the logical contradiction that implicitly exists just as he would demonstrate such an implicit contradiction in the time-travel case.

153. But if I can imagine a universe without God, does it follow that God's existence is not necessary? The problem is that God by definition is a being that must exist, that's what the term God means. Imagining God not existing is on par with imagining that the unproven Goldbach's conjecture (all even numbers greater than two are the sum of two prime numbers) could either be true or false, even though logically it can only be true or only be false. Any imagining to the contrary won't change this fact since the conjecture is a necessary mathematical truth. Metaphysical possibility is tricky, but since the universe is not defined by the need to exist while God is, this allows us to make an easier leap from the epistemic possibility of the universe's non-existence to the metaphysical possibility of its non-existence.

154. A critic could object that this is the fallacy of composition, but a former apologist writing on John Loftus's blog counters that argument and writes, [S]ince the existence of the collection of dependent beings is a positive fact, then it follows from PSR alone—i.e., without the need to rely on an inference from dependence of the parts to dependence of the whole—that there must be a sufficient reason for why the collection exists. Exapologist, "Leibnizian Cosmological Argument Part I," *Debunking Christianity Blog.* Available online at http://debunkingchristianity.blogspot.com/2007/10/leibnizian-cosmological-argument-part-i.html Loftus objects to

the Leibnizian argument in his 2012 book by citing philosophy professor Felipe Leon as saying that the argument only proves that a factually necessary being exists and even this being would need an explanation, thus causing explanatory overkill. But the first premise says only that everything which exists is either contingent (has an explanation outside of itself) or is necessary (has an explanation within itself), not that everything has an external explanation. If God is factually necessary (which I don't think is the case) and exists as a result of his own nature, then that just is the explanation of the universe, which is one that atheists sometimes co-opt for the universe itself if they are not given defeaters for that belief. Therefore, I believe the argument is sound.

155. Craig, 109.

156. Natalie Wolchover. *Science & God: Will Biology, Astronomy, Physics, Rule Out Existence of Deity?* The Huffington Post. 09/18/12 Available online at: http://www.huffingtonpost.com/2012/09/18/science-god-biology-astronomy-physics-deity_n_1894010.html

157. Carrier, 73.

158. David Hume. *Dialogues Concerning Natural Religions* (Empire Books: USA, 2012) 68.

159. Richard Gale. "The Failure of Classical Theistic Arguments," *The Cambridge Companion to Atheism,* ed. Michael Martin (Cambridge University Press: New York, 2007) 94.

160. Most philosophers agree that if abstract objects like numbers exist, then they would exist as a result of their own nature. But unlike God who is a mind with intentions and an ability to exercise those intentions, abstract objects like numbers have no intentions and cannot cause anything to happen in the material world. Therefore, God is the only candidate for a causal explanation of the contingent world that is itself necessary in existence.

161. Stephen Hawking and Leonard Mlodinow. *The Grand Design.* (Random House Publishing: New York, 2011) 5.

162. David Albert. "On the Origin of Everything: A Universe from Nothing by Lawrence Krauss," *New York Times* Book Review 03/23/12. Available online at: http://www.nytimes.com/2012/03/25/books/review/a-universe-from-nothing-by-lawrence-m-krauss.html?_r=0

163. Ross Andersen. "Has Physics Made Philosophy and Religion Obsolete?" *The Atlantic* 04/23/12. Available online at http://www.theatlantic.com/technology/archive/2012/04/has-physics-made-philosophy-and-religion-obsolete/256203/. Andersen says, "But debating physics with Augustine might not be an interesting thing to do in 2012." To which Krauss replies, "It might be more interesting than debating some of the moronic philosophers that have written about my book."

164. Massimo Pigliucci. "Lawrence Krauss: another physicist with an anti-philosophy complex," *Rationally Speaking* 04/25/12. Available online at: http://rationallyspeaking.blogspot.com/2012/04/lawrence-krauss-another-physicist-with.html

Chapter 9: Did the universe begin to exist?

165. Al-Ghazali. The Incoherence of the Philosophers. (Brigham Young University, USA, 2000) 28. Even before Al-Ghazali, the argument seems to have had its first defender in the sixth century Christian philosopher John Philoponus and his work *On the Eternity of the World Against Aristotle* (though he did not use the term "kalām" in his arguments).

166. See St. Bonaventure's commentaries on Peter Lombard's Sentences for his version of the *Kalām* argument. (II Sent. D.1,p.1,a.1,q.2)

167. Craig's major books include *The Kalām Cosmological Argument* (1979), *The Cosmological Argument from Plato to Leibniz* (1980), *Time and Eternity* (2001), and his co-authored volume with Jim Sinclair "The *Kalām* Cosmological Argument" in the 2009 *Blackwell Companion to Natural Theology*. Craig has also published numerous scholarly papers on the argument that are available on his website www.reasonablefaith.org.

168. The phrase was first expressed in book one of the Roman philosopher Titus Lucretius's work *De Rerum Natura*.

169. John Locke: *An Essay Concerning Human Understanding*: Book Four: Chapter Ten, Paragraph Three.

170. And of course, don't be cute and say an iron ship is a kind of iron bar that floats. We never observe an object float in normal water that weighs more than the amount of water it displaces.

171. Victor Stenger. *The Fallacy of Fine Tuning: Why the Universe is not Designed for Us* (Prometheus Books: New York, 2011) 116.

172. My description of the passage of time as involving the traversal of discrete moments is not without controversy. This argument I am proposing appears to rest on what is called the A-theory of time. For more on this distinction, see "Theories of time" in the "Advanced Cosmology" appendix.

173. Another way to argue against an infinite past is to argue that an actual infinite is impossible in the real-world and therefore an actually infinite past cannot exist regardless of how it is formed (even if God caused it to appear instantaneously). Craig's favorite example of this is Hilbert's Hotel with its infinite rooms that are all occupied but can still accommodate new guests. See William Lane Craig and James Sinclair, "The Kalām Cosmological Argument." *The Blackwell Companion to Natural Theology.* eds. William Lane Craig and J.P. Moreland (Blackwell Publishing: Oxford, 2009) 103-117.

174. David Hume, *An Enquiry Concerning Human Understanding*, Section XII, Part II. Hume, the hyper-skeptic he was, wrote that we should even be skeptical of our skepticism towards these absurdities! However, he was still baffled as to how one could form such an absurd belief about reality in the first place.

175. Not only do we understand infinities, but the impossibility of so-called supertasks seems to demonstrate that infinite sets in the real world create unresolvable contradictions. See Laraudogoitia, Jon Pérez, "Supertasks," *The Stanford Encyclopedia of Philosophy (Spring*

2011 Edition), Edward N. Zalta (ed.), URL = <http://plato.stanford.edu/archives/spr2011/entries/spacetime-supertasks/>.

176. Edward Kasner and James Newman. *Mathematics and the Imagination*. (Dover Publications, 2001) 61.

177. Some critics may be concerned that this argument presupposes that God is not eternal in the Boethian sense of that term (that God contains his entire existence in one timeless moment that has neither beginning nor end), which appears to be the sense of the term "eternal" that is used by the First Vatican Council to describe God. These critics may argue that the A-theory of time, which the KCA seems to rely upon, with its ever-changing temporal distinctions, would make it impossible for God to exist outside of time and still interact with his creation. For an intriguing defense of divine timelessness within an A-theory of time, see Edward Wierenga, "Omniscience and Time, One More Time: A Reply to Craig" Faith and Philosophy Volume 21, Issue 1, January 2004.

178. In his commentary on the Sentences of Peter Lombard, Aquinas claimed that past moments have no real existence and so an infinite number of them do not cause a contradiction. But some scholars believe Aquinas erred on this point. The Thomistic philosopher Fernand Van Steenberghen wrote, "the infinite series of past events implied by the hypothesis of an eternal world is clearly an infinite in act, not in potency. Indeed, it is a realized and achieved infinite, already produced in reality." See Fernand Van Steenberghen, *Thomas Aquinas and Radical Aristotelianism* (Catholic University of America Press: Washington, D.C., 1980) 16-17. Cited in Mark Nowacki. *The Kalām Cosmological Argument for God* (Prometheus Books: New York, 2007) 144. Nowacki goes on to provide a substance-based defense of the KCA that strengthens the claim that actual infinites are factually impossible. Aquinas also argued in the *Summa Theologica* (Book I, Question 46, Article 6) that traversal implies moving between two terms and any term in an infinite past will only be a finite distance from the present and thus can be traversed. However, traversing a

series only implies traversing all of its members because a series could be without a first member. Furthermore, this commits the fallacy of composition by supposing that just because any member in an infinite set is a finite distance away, the entire set can be traversed as a finite distance. See Spitzer, 177-180, for a good discussion of Aquinas on this point.

179. St. Thomas Aquinas. *Summa Contra Gentiles.* Book I, Chapter VIII, Paragraph 30.

180. I understand that the increase in entropy is statistically certain but not absolutely certain. It is possible, though astronomically unlikely, for the balls to reassemble into the rack formation. But I wouldn't bet your life on such an event happening.

181. "The total entropy of the observable universe is correspondingly higher, and is $S\_obs = 3.1+3.0-1.7 \times 10^{104}$ k. We calculate the entropy of the current cosmic event horizon to be $S\_CEH = 2.6+-0.3 \times 10^{122}$ k, dwarfing the entropy of its interior, $S\_CEHint = 1.2+1.1-0.7 \times 10^{103}$ k." See Chas A. Egan and Charles H. Lineweaver. "A Larger Estimate of the Entropy of the Universe" (Cornell University Library, Cosmology and Extragalactic Astrophysics, 2010). Available online at http://arxiv.org/abs/0909.3983

182. Lawrence Krauss and Glenn Starkmann, "Life, The Universe, and Nothing: Life and Death in an Ever-Expanding Universe," Cornell University Library, Astrophysics, 1999. Available online at http://xxx.lanl.gov/abs/astro-ph/9902189

183. Or has it?! Stenger writes in *God: The Failed Hypothesis,* "I seem to be saying that the entropy of the universe was maximal when the universe began, yet it has been increasing ever since. Indeed, that's exactly what I am saying." (Prometheus Books: New York, 2007, 120). Stenger justifies this claim by saying that at the Big Bang the universe was a black hole and was at the maximum entropy possible for an object at that size. But one major problem with Stenger's argument is that, as Roger Penrose observes, if the universe collapsed

it would experience an increase in entropy even though it is returning to its previously small size that once possessed "maximum" entropy (Roger Penrose, *The Emperor's New Mind: Concerning Computers, Minds, and the Laws of Physics* (New York: Oxford University Press, 1989 239) Other cosmologists like Sean Carroll have calculated that the universe is at 10^{101} entropy, not 10^{120} as Stenger claims (Carroll, 63). I owe this observation to Robin Collins in his article "Stenger's Fallacies" which is available online at http://home.messiah.edu/~rcollins/Fine-tuning/Stenger-fallacy.pdf

184. Paul Davies. *God and the New Physics* (Touchstone: New York, 1983) 11.

185. Arthur S. Eddington. *The Nature of the Physical World*. (New York: Macmillan. 1928) 74.

186. For more information see John Farrell. *The Day Without a Yesterday: Einstein, Lemaitre, and the Birth of Modern Cosmology*. (Thunder's Mouth Press: New York, 2005) 115. Farrell cautiously notes that, "there is some confusion as to the extent of Einstein's enthusiasm for Lemaitre's primeval atom theory . . . Encouraging as Einstein was, it's unlikely that he regarded Lemaitre's primeval atom theory as the last word on the subject — and unlikelier still that he would have employed the word 'creation' to describe it."

187. This observation is known as Hubble's Law.

188. Quoted in *Michio Kaku. Parallel Worlds: A Journey through Creation, Higher Dimensions, and the Future of the Cosmos. (Anchor Books, New York, 2005) 69-70.*

189. Fr. Lemaitre learned about Penzias and Wilson's discovery three weeks before he passed away from leukemia in 1966.

190. While the Big Bang is still the majority view, it is incomplete. Scientists have proposed new mechanisms such as "inflation" to account for irregularities in this standard model such as the flatness problem or the horizon problem. Scientists also need a quantum theory of gravity to account for the universe's structure at the Big

Bang itself because relativity theory becomes incapable of describing the singularity prior to what is called the Planck time, or 10^{-43} seconds. For a more thorough treatment of this subject see the advanced cosmology appendix.

191. Lisa Grossman, "Why physicists can't avoid a creation event." New Scientist Magazine. 01/11/12 In their original paper Mithani and Vilenkin write, "Did the universe have a beginning? At this point, it seems that the answer to this question is probably yes." Audrey Mithani and Alexander Vilenkin. "Did the universe have a beginning?" (Cornell University Library, High Energy Physics – Theory, 2012) Available online at http://arxiv.org/abs/1204.4658. Leonard Susskind offers a critique of the paper but even he ultimately concludes, "there is a beginning, but in any kind of inflating cosmology the odds strongly (infinitely) favor the beginning to be so far in the past that it is effectively at minus infinity." Of course, Susskind has left the realm of speculation in physics and has entered philosophical speculation about the nature of an infinitely far away beginning and whether or not the present could exist if this was the case. See Leonard Susskind, "Was There a Beginning?" Cornell University Library, High Energy Physics – Theory, 2012) Available online at http://arxiv.org/abs/1204.5385.

192. Rees, 10.

193. Even Bertrand Russell makes this objection, he writes, "If everything must have a cause, then God must have a cause. If there can be anything without a cause, it may just as well be the world as God, so that there cannot be any validity in that argument." Bertrand Russell. *Why I am not a Christian* (Simon and Schuster, New York, 1957) 6-7.

194. St. Augustine. *Confessions.* (Oxford University Press, Oxford, 2008) 229. Augustine admits it's a joke he's heard other people tell in order to evade the force of the question.

195. Kai Nielsen, *Reason and Practice* (New York: Harper & Row, 1971), 48.

Chapter 10: Is God the first cause?

196. Excerpt from *Darwin's Dangerous Idea* quoted in Daniel Dennett. *Breaking the Spell: Religion as a Natural Phenomenon* (Penguin Books: New York, 2006) 244.

197. Quentin Smith. "A Cosmological Argument for a Self-Caused Universe," The Secular Web (2008) Available online at: http://www.infidels.org/library/modern/quentin_smith/self-caused.html. Smith doesn't argue that the universe brought itself into existence but that the universe's existence prior to the present can be infinitely divided leaving out a first moment due to the lack of time at the Big Bang singularity and creating a series that explains its own existence. I can't go into depth to examine the argument here, but I believe that such a series is not possible as is illustrated in Alexander Pruss's Grim Reaper paradox which is summarized in a footnote in Craig and Sinclair, 113.

198. Excerpt from *Darwin's Dangerous Idea* quoted in Daniel Dennett. *Breaking the Spell: Religion as a Natural Phenomenon* (Penguin Books: New York, 2006) 244.

199. George Smith. *Atheism: The Case Against God* (Prometheus Press: New York, 1979) 237.

200. Carrier, 253-254.

201. See also Kreeft and Tacelli, 60.

202. Douglas Groothius. *Christian Apologetics: A Comprehensive Case for Biblical Faith* (InterVarsity Press: Illinois, 2011) 237.

203. Furthermore, Aquinas's first proof for the existence of God (which I discuss in appendix I) leads to the conclusion that God is pure act; therefore, he cannot be caused to do anything (e.g., feel pain, be saddened, die, etc.) and therefore must exist along with the universe.

204. For the nit-picky reader, know that I am using the word "prior" in this sentence to mean logical priority and not temporal priority

because obviously there was no moment "prior" to the first moment of time and space.

205. For a more in-depth explanation see William Lane Craig and James D. Sinclair. "The *Kalām* Cosmological Argument" *The Blackwell Companion to Natural Theology*, eds. William Lane Craig and J.P. Moreland. (Blackwell Publishing: Sussex, 2009) 191-194.

206. Immanuel Kant, *The Critique of Pure Reason* Chapter II, Section II.

207. Dawkins, 77.

208. Aquinas would argue that his cosmological argument does show God is good because evil is simply a deficiency or a lack of being (for Aquinas goodness and being are interchangeable transcendentals) and since God is pure act, there is no deficiency or potentiality in him. Consequently he is fully being itself and as such fully good.

Chapter 11: Is the universe fine-tuned for intelligent life?

209. Translation found in Joseph Fitzmyer. *Spiritual Exercises Based on Paul's Epistle to the Romans* (Wm. B. Eerdmans Publishing: Grand Rapids, 2004) 21.

210. Romans 1:20.

211. William Paley. *Natural Theology* (Oxford University Press: Oxford, 2006) 7.

212. I should note that other design arguments, such as Aquinas's fifth way which focuses on Aristotelian final causation were and still are immune to the problems evolutionary theory poses for Paley's argument.

213. Richard Dawkins. *The Greatest Show on Earth: The Evidence for Evolution* (Free Press: New York, 2009) 116-133.

214. http://www.vatican.va/holy_father/benedict_xvi/speeches/2007/july/documents/hf_ben-xvi_spe_20070724_clero-cadore_en.html.

215. "Communion and Stewardship: Human Persons Created in the Image and Likeness of God." International Theological Commission, 2004. Available online at: http://www.vatican.va/roman_curia/congregations/cfaith/cti_documents/rc_con_cfaith_doc_20040723_communion-stewardship_en.html

216. CCC 283.

217. See Vilenkin (2008), Rees (2000), Hawking (2011) as well as Lawrence Kraus. *A Universe from Nothing* (Free Press: New York, 2012) 76.

218. This deductive version of the argument comes from William Lane Craig. However, the strongest treatment of the argument is an inductive version that is promoted by Robin Collins. Collins argues that the fine-tuning we observe best confirms a theistic hypothesis over a single universe atheistic hypothesis or even a multiverse atheistic hypothesis. See his essay, "The Teleological Argument" in *The Blackwell Companion to Natural Theology* (2009).

219. William Lane Craig. *Reasonable Faith* (Crossway Books: Illinois, 2008) 193.

220. Martin Rees. *Just Six Numbers: The Deep Forces that Shape the Universe.* (Basic Books: Great Britain, 2000) 33-34.

221. "Gravity mysteries: Why is gravity fine-tuned?" *New Scientist Magazine,* Issue 2712, June 10, 2009. Available online at: http://www.newscientist.com/article/mg20227123.000-gravity-mysteries-why-is-gravity-finetuned.html

222. Ibid.

223. Rees, 54-55.

224. Rees, 99.

225. Vilenkin, 10. Not all cosmologists believe this is fine-tuned, though. University of Alberta physicist Donald Page has argued that if the cosmological constant were fine-tuned, then it would have a slightly less than negative value in order to promote the evolution of

intelligent life, and not the positive value it currently has (see Don Page, "Does God so Love the Multiverse?" *The Blackwell Companion to Science and Christianity*. eds. Alan Padgett and J. B. Stump, 2012). But this conclusion is premature. First, if I get ten straight flushes in a row and said I wasn't cheating because if I were cheating I would aim for ten royal flushes, you would not believe me. The incredible odds against even a suboptimal cosmological constant must still be accounted. Second, God may have overriding reasons for a positive value in the cosmological constant, such as a desire to stop a big crunch from occurring but keeping the universe in existence forever.

226. Lisa Dyson, Matthew Kleban, and Leonard Susskind. "Disturbing Implications of a Cosmological Constant" Cornell University Library, High Energy Physics—Theory, 2002). Available online at http://arxiv.org/abs/hep-th/0208013 Lawrence Krauss says that the cosmological constant, "remains unsolved and is perhaps the most profound unsolved fundamental problem in physics today." (Krauss, 73).

227. Roger Penrose. *The Road to Reality* (Vintage Press: New York, 2004) 729, 763. Fr. Spitzer provides an excellent summary and writes, "Penrose begins by calculating the total entropy of our universe, which represents the logarithm of the total phase-space volume of possible universes in a creation event. The total entropy of our universe is equal to the total number of baryons (protons and neutrons) in the universe (10^{80}) x the entropy per baryon (10^{43}), which yields a total entropy of 10^{123}. Since 10^{123} (total entropy) is the logarithm of the total phase-space volume, the total phase-space volume of possible universes for a creation event (V) is the exponential of 10^{123}, namely $10^{10^{123}}$." (58)

228. Loftus, 92.

229. See the Advanced Cosmology appendix, "Is fine-tuning a myth?"

230. Lenny Esposito vs. Richard Carrier, "Does God Exist?" UC–Riverside Debate, May 23, 2012.

231. Farrel, 168-169.

232. Leslie, 105.

233. Carl Sagan. *The Cosmic Connection: An Extra Terrestrial Perspective* (Cambridge University Press: New York, 2000) 46.

234. Collins, 225.

235. Dawkins, 147.

236. Gregory Dawes. *Theism and Explanation* (Routledge: New York, 2009) 16.

237. Erik Wielenberg. "Dawkins's Gambit, Hume's Aroma, and God's Simplicity," *Philosophia Christi,* Vol. 11, No. 1, 2009.

238. According to media accounts, The Higgs Boson was allegedly discovered in July 2012 but as of this writing a boson that could be the Higgs is still being investigated at CERN (see http://m/phys.org/news/2013/-01-cern-chief-firmer-higgs-boson.htm). If the particle does exist, it would only serve to confirm the standard model of particle physics. However, the fine-tuning argument presupposes that the standard model of particle physics is correct and the Higgs itself would not be the reason the unified forces broke symmetry after the Big Bang. In addition, the Higgs Boson is not called the "God Particle" because it created the universe. The name comes from Leon Lederman's 1993 book called *The God Particle: If the Universe is the Answer, What is the Question,* which ascribes the nickname based on the importance of the particle in scientific models and because it was so "gosh darn" hard to locate.

239. See the DVD "Collision: Christopher Hitchens vs. Douglas Wilson" (2009). When asked which argument for theism is the best one, Hitchens remarked, "I think [atheists] pick the fine-tuning one as the most intriguing."

240. Richard Dawkins. *The Blind Watchmaker* (New York: Norton, 1986) 6.

241. See Feser, 110-120 for an excellent defense of Aquinas's fifth way from design. I have not included the Fifth way in this book

because if Aquinas's metaphysics aren't defended at length, then the argument comes off like Paley's design argument and can be refuted by the evolution objection.

Chapter 12: What explains the fine-tuning?

242. Ernst Nagel, *The Structure of Science*, 2d ed. (Indianapolis: Hackett, 1979), pp. 53-54.

243. "The original hope of physicists to produce a single theory explaining the apparent laws of our universe as the unique possible consequence of a few simple assumptions may have to be abandoned. Where does that leave us? If m-theory allows for 10^{500} sets of apparent laws, how did we end up in this universe, with the laws that are apparent to us?" Stephen Hawking and Leonard Mlodinow. *The Grand Design* (Random House Publishing: New York, 2011) 119.

244. "See the podcast "Luke Barnes—11 Responses to Fine Tuning," *Conversations from the Pale Blue Dot Podcast.* Available Online at: http://www.archive.org/download/ConversationsFromThePaleBlueDot040-LukeBarnes/040-LukeBarnes.mp3 Physicists agree and write, "[E]ven if all apparently anthropic coincidences could be explained in terms of some grand unified theory, it would still be remarkable that the relationships dictated by physical theory happened also to be those propitious for life." Bernard Carr and Martin Rees, "The Anthropic Principle and the Structure of the Physical World," *Nature* 278 (1979) 612.

245. Dawkins, 173.

246. Sean Carroll. *From Eternity to Here: The Quest for the Ultimate Theory of Time* (Plume: London, 2010) 38.

247. Based off an example from Leslie, 111.

248. This principle was most famously argued by Brandon Carter. "Large Number Coincidences and the Anthropic Principle in Cosmology." *Modern Cosmology and Philosophy,* ed. John Leslie (Prometheus Books: New York, 1999) 131-139.

249. Leslie, 13-14.

250. See the appendix for an alternative scenario where the constants fluctuate in different parts of space.

251. Assume for simplicity that the odds of getting a royal flush are one in a million (it's closer to one in 650,000). The odds of getting 50 royal flushes in a row would be $(1/10^6)^{50}$ which leave us with $1/10^{300}$. This comes nowhere near Penrose's number for the odds of a low-entropy universe $(1/10^{10^{123}})$ and is still smaller than the odds of the five other constants and conditions being added together.

252. Barnes podcast "Luke Barnes – 11 Responses to Fine Tuning," *Conversations from the Pale Blue Dot Podcast*. Available online at: http://www.archive.org/download/ConversationsFromThePaleBlueDot040-LukeBarnes/040-LukeBarnes.mp3

253. Barker uses this rebutter in his public debates and describes it in his book on pages 107-108.

254. Dawkins, 174-175.

255. Jenny Hogan. "Hawking concedes black hole bet" *New Scientist Magazine*, July 21, 2004. Available online at: http://www.newscientist.com/article/dn6193-hawking-concedes-black-hole-bet.html

256. Shawn Pogatchnik. "Hawking's New Black Hole Theory" *Associated Press*, July 15, 2009 Available online at: http://www.cbsnews.com/2100-205_162-630203.html

257. Quarks get their name from Cal. Tech physicist Murray Gell-Mann who liked the line, "Three quarks for Muster Mark!" from James Joyce's novel *Finnegans Wake*.

258. Quoted in Lee Smolin. *The Trouble With Physics: The Rise of String Theory, The Fall of a Science, and What Comes Next* (Mariner Books: New York, 2007) 125.

259. Michael Riordan. "Stringing physics along," *Physics World*, February 1, 2007. Available online at: http://physicsworld.com/cws/article/print/2007/feb/01/stringing-physics-along.

260. Max Tegmark. "The Multiverse Hierarchy" (Cornell University Library, *Popular Physics*, 2009). Available online at http://arxiv.org/abs/0905.1283

261. Fr. Robert Spitzer. *New Proofs for the Existence of God: Contributions of Contemporary Physics and Philosophy* (Wm. B. Eerdmans: Grand Rapids, 2010) 70-71. Even adjustments to the model like "slow rolling" involve fine-tuning and just push the problem back one step further.

262. Some researchers have claimed that abnormal "cold-spots" in the Cosmic Microwave Background Radiation could be signs of a collision with another bubble universe. But Cambridge astronomers led by Kendrick Smith have put forward a convincing proposal that the cold spot is just a measurement anomaly and there is no indication of a CMBR disruption or, by further stretch, another universe. See Kendrick M. Smith and Dragan Huterer, "No evidence for the cold spot in the NVSS radio survey" (Cornell University Library, Astrophysics, 2011). Available online at http://arxiv.org/abs/0805.2751

263. George Ellis. "Does the Multiverse Really Exist?" *Scientific American,* July 19, 2011.

264. Paul Davies, "Stephen Hawking's Big Bang Gaps" *The Guardian,* September 3, 2010. Available online at http://www.guardian.co.uk/commentisfree/belief/2010/sep/04/stephen-hawking-big-bang-gap

265. Hume, 45.

266. James Sennett evaluates this objection and proposes a "candidate Gods" approach that bolsters the conclusion that the traditional God of theism via a process of elimination. He writes, "the choice between the God of theism and the gods of slapstick is a philosophical no-brainer." James Sennett. "Hume's Stopper and the Natural Theology Project," In Defense of Natural Theology: A Post-Humean Assessment. ed. James Sennett and Douglas Groothius (InterVarsity Press: Downers Grove, 2005) 97.

Chapter 13: Do moral truths exist?

267. In Book 11, Chapter 4 of *The Brothers Karamazov*, Dmitri remarks to Alyosha, "Without God and immortal life? All things are lawful then."

268. Romans 2:14-15.

269. My formulation is similar to one offered by New Zealand philosopher Glenn Peoples.

270. Craig, 2008, 173.

271. Craig writes, "Objective moral values are not the same thing as objective moral duties. It is not the case that just because something is good we must do it. It is good to become a teacher, or a doctor, or a fireman, but you can't do all of them." William Lane Craig. *Reasonable Faith* (Crossway Books: Illinois, 2008) 173.

272. Steven Pinker. *The Blank Slate: The Modern Denial of Human Nature* (Penguin Books: New York, 2002) 273.

273. Shook tries to escape this dilemma by saying that while morals are not absolute, they are objective within the societies that create them. He writes, "An objective moral truth is made true by the natural fact that a society of people share a common culture which includes that accepted truth among its social rules." (Shook, 112) Shook criticizes the "nasty" alternative of moral subjectivism where there are no moral truths except what individuals decide are moral. However, Shook's proposal is just as nasty for he says that there are no "absolute moral truths" except what large groups of individuals decide are moral.

274. See David Hume. *A Treatise of Human Nature*. "Book III: Of Morals" (Dover Publications: New York, 2003).

275. Burkhard Bilger, "The Possibilian," *The New Yorker* April 25, 2011. Available online at: http://www.newyorker.com/reporting/2011/04/25/110425fa_fact_bilger

276. An anonymous referee points out that repeated exposure to atrocities can cause some people to reject their sense of morality and accept the normalness of evil acts. This is true, but it no more disproves the existence of objectively evil acts than repeated exposure to sunlight that damages someone's vision disproves the objective reality of the external world.

277. Some critics claim that Paul Slovic's research has shown that our moral intuitions are faulty and can't be trusted. Slovic found that people are more apt to give less money to charitable causes when those causes seek to help larger numbers of people. We are even less willing to act against genocide because we are numb to the huge numbers of people being killed. Therefore, moral intuitions can't be trusted. But even Slovic agrees that our moral intuition is what primarily tells us genocide is wrong. He writes, "Our gut feelings will give us the moral intuition that genocide is wrong, but moral reasoning will cause us to lay out reasons to act." We must simply use our reasoning to guide our conflicting intuitions in these cases where we want to help, but we also want to use our finite resources in a prudent way. "Why nations fail to act in the face of genocide," *ScienceDaily,* May 19, 2008. Available online: http://www.science-daily.com/releases/2008/05/080515145348.htm

278. Walter Sinnott-Armstrong. "Framing Moral Intuitions" in *Moral Psychology (Volume 2): The Cognitive Science of Morality: Intuition and Diversity,* ed. Walter Sinnott-Armstrong (Massachusetts Institute of Technology: Cambridge, 2008) 47.

279. William Lane Craig vs. Louise Antony "Is God Necessary for Morality," University of Massachusetts–Amherst, April 10, 2008.

280. In an April 18, 2005 homily Pope Benedict said, "Today, having a clear faith based on the Creed of the Church is often labeled as fundamentalism. Whereas relativism, that is, letting oneself be "tossed here and there, carried about by every wind of doctrine," seems the only attitude that can cope with modern times. We are building a dictatorship of relativism that does not recognize anything

as definitive and whose ultimate goal consists solely of one's own ego and desires." Available online at http://www.vatican.va/gpII/ documents/homily-pro-eligendo-pontifice_20050418_en.html

281. Solomon Asch, *Social Psychology* (Prentice-Hall: Englewood Cliffs, NJ, 1952) 378-79. Asch is cited approvingly by Victor Stenger in his book *God: The Failed Hypothesis* (196).

282. C. S. Lewis. *The Abolition of Man* (HarperCollins: New York, 1974) 83.

283. Even atheists recognize this point. Michael Martin writes, "many moral disputes may be the result of nonculpable ignorance of nonmoral facts, such as whether a particular economic policy would increase the standard of living." (Martin, 39).

284. Paul Raffaele. "Sleeping with Cannibals." *Smithsonian Magazine*. September, 2006 page 2. Available online at: http://www. smithsonianmag.com/travel/cannibals.html?c=y&page=1

285. In 2006, the nation of Iran hosted an entire conference dedicated to the view that the mainstream historical account of the Holocaust was wrong. See "Iran defends Holocaust conference" BBC News December 11, 2006. Available online at: http://news. bbc.co.uk/2/hi/middle_east/6167695.stm

286. C. S. Lewis, *Mere Christianity*, 24.

287. Anthropologist Erwin Frank says of infanticide, "This is their way of life and we should not judge them on the basis of our values. The difference between the cultures should be respected." Jemimah Wright, "Girl survived tribe's custom of live baby burial," *The Telegraph* June 22, 2007. Available online at http://www.telegraph. co.uk/news/worldnews/1555339/Girl-survived-tribes-custom-of-live-baby-burial.html. In Richard Robbin's book on anthropology he seems ambivalent about the morality of Sati, or the practice of burning wives on their husband's funeral pyres in India and says that ultimately there is no easy way to determine if an action is evil

enough that it should be stopped by the force of law. Richard Robbins. *Cultural Anthropology: A Problems-Based Approach*, Fifth Edition (Wadsworth: Belmont, 2009) 14–15.

288. See Harris, 2004, 179.

289. Some critics who advance this argument are theists like Richard Swinburne. They say that even if God did not exist, moral truths would still exist because they are necessary truths that must exist. But what this objection misses is that necessary truths can have their foundation in other necessary truths. For example, the reason 2+2=4 is true in every possible world (or is necessarily true) is because the foundational truths of mathematics (in this case the axioms of Peano arithmetic like 1=1) are true in every world. Likewise, the reason moral truths are necessary is because they are grounded in God's nature, which is also necessary.

290. J. L. Mackie. *The Miracle of Theism: Arguments for and against the Existence of God* (Oxford University Press: Oxford, 1982) 115.

291. William Lane Craig and Walter Sinnott-Armstrong. *God? A Debate Between a Christian and an Atheist* (Oxford University Press: Oxford, 2004) 47.

292. Erik Wielenberg. *Value and Virtue in a Godless Universe* (Cambridge University Press: New York, 2005) 26.

293. Luke Muehlhauser. "Many Atheists are Hypocrites about Morality," *Common Sense Atheism*, May 9, 2010. Available online at: http://commonsenseatheism.com/?p=8859

294. See the PhilPapers survey conducted by David Chalmers and David Bourget at http://philpapers.org/surveys/results.pl According to the survey, 56 percent of professional philosophers endorse moral realism and nearly three quarters of philosophers are atheists. However, the majority of philosophers (72%) who specialize in the philosophy of religion and extensively study the arguments for and against the existence of God are theists.

295. See also Kreeft and Tacelli, 74.

Chapter 14: Can moral truths be explained naturally?

296. "When we ask why we are moral I am asking the question in the same manner that an evolutionary biologist might ask why we are hungry (to motivate us to eat) or why sex is fun (to motivate us to procreate)." Michael Shermer. *The Science of Good and Evil: Why People Cheat, Gossip, Share, Care, and Follow the Golden Rule.* (Henry Holt and Co., New York, 2004) 8.

297. A notorious example of this is Randy Thornhill and Craig T. Palmer's book *A Natural History of Rape: Biological Bases of Sexual Coercion* (2001) which was later criticized in the 2003 anthology *Evolution, Gender, and Rape.*

298. C.S. Lewis. *Mere Christianity* (Simon and Schuster: New York, 1952) 23.

299. For a more academic treatment of this popular idea See Erich Fromm. *Man for Himself: An Inquiry into the Psychology of Ethics.* (Henry Holt and Co., New York, 1947).

300. See John Paul II "Veritatis Splendor" *Papal Encyclical* 1993. Paragraph 58.

301. It is estimated that one in every 25 people is a sociopath, or is someone who does not possess the normal empathy and conscience that other people have. See Martha Stout, *The Sociopath Next Door* (Broadway Books, USA, 2005)

302. See the Catholic Catechism paragraphs 1783-1785 for more on the formation of conscience.

303. Available online at http://www.africa.upenn.edu/Articles_ Gen/Letter_Birmingham.html

304. As recently as 2009 women in Afghanistan who protested a law which required them to submit to their husband's sexual requests were stoned by an angry mob in the nation's capital city of Kabul. See "Women protesting at 'pro-rape' law attacked by Afghan men" *The Independent* April 16, 2009 Available online at http://

www.independent.co.uk/news/world/asia/women-protesting-at-pro-rape-law-attacked-by-afghan-men-1669296.html

305. Harris writes, "It seems clear that what we are really asking when we consider whether a certain state of pleasure is "good" is whether is conducive to, or obstructive of some deeper form of well-being." Sam Harris. *The Moral Landscape: How Science Can Determine Moral Values* (Free Press, New York, 2010) 12. Humanist Chaplain Greg Epstein agrees on this point and writes, "The simplest way to put this is: our ethics come from human needs and interest. What do human beings need to flourish?" Greg Epstein *Good Without God: What a Billion Non-religious People Do Believe* (HarperCollins, New York, 2009) 34.

306. Harris's argument is really just an updated version of the utilitarianism proposed by John Stuart Mill (which itself is an updated version of Epicurus's hedonism). Harris tries to make his work break new ground by incorporating his expertise in neuroscience to argue that moral goodness is not a philosophical question but is a strictly scientific one that relates to brain states.

307. Rosenberg, 2011, 330.

308. Despite Harris' protests in his book, I'm not convinced science can even identify what it means for humans to "flourish" or achieve "well-being." Harris tries to answer this objection by saying the terms are imprecise yet recognizable in the same way as the term "healthy" is in the field of medicine. But I don't see how Harris can separate physical health from the fullest concept of flourishing or wellbeing, the idea that a person becomes virtuous. If Harris is only focusing on mental states personal feelings, then I don't see how he is not investigating psychology instead of morality.

309. Harris, 2010, 189-190.

310. I owe this insight to William Lane Craig in his 2011 debate with Harris.

311. Hadley Arkes, *First Things: An Inquiry into the First Principles of Morals and Justice* (Princeton University Press: Princeton, 1986) 109 -110. Kant's universalizing principle is called the *categorical imperative.* For secular writers who base ethics off of Kant, it may be of interest to know that Kant was one of the first proponents of the moral argument for the existence of God. See Immanuel Kant's *Critique of Practical Reason and Groundwork for the Metaphysic of Morals,* Book II, Chapter II.

312. This is also called "Ideal Observer Theory" and is argued by Michael Martin in *Atheism, Morality and Meaning* (Prometheus Books: New York, 2002) 50-72.

313. "'S Korea child 'starves as parents raise virtual baby,' " BBC News March 5, 2010. Available online at http://news.bbc.co.uk/2/hi/8551122.stm

314. See Michael Tooley. *Abortion and Infanticide* (Oxford University Press: USA, 1985) and Peter Singer. *Practical Ethics* (Cambridge University Press: Cambridge, 2011). Singer writes, "if a right to life must be based on the capacity to want to go on living, or on the ability to see oneself as a continuing mental subject, a newborn baby cannot have a right to life (Singer, 152). Philosophers who defend abortion have trouble refuting Singer's claim infants do not have a right-to-life without making arguments that inadvertently grant a right-to-life to fetuses waiting to be born. Philosophers who oppose abortion may have trouble refuting Singer because Singer's views, though repulsive, are very consistent and thus not easily susceptible to a reductio ad absurdum argument.

315. The Institute is briefly mentioned under a different name in James Patrick Kelly and John Kessel's anthology *Digital Rapture: The Singularity Anthology* (Tachyon Publications: San Francisco, 2012) 7.

316. I caution critics not to be cute and say that when we fly in an airplane we violate the law of gravity. Gravity is still enforced, but now we must obey another law called Bernoulli's principle in order to stay airborne. Airplanes and their passengers and crew who

disobey the law of Bernoulli will find themselves subject to the law of gravity with less than positive consequences.

317. Atheistic moral Platonism is also undermined by the fact that even if virtues like love, justice, and courage existed as abstract objects, vices like hate, bigotry, and cowardice would also exist as abstract objects. What reason is there for me to follow one abstract object, love, when I could just as easily follow another such as "hate?" In order to distinguish between moral values that just exist platonically, there must be some overriding feature of the universe that compels me to pick one value over another (like Lewis's sheet music for the piano keys).

Chapter 15: Can moral truths be explained supernaturally?

318. Leah Libresco. "This is my last post for the atheist portal," *Unequally Yoked*, June 18, 2012. Available online: http://www.patheos.com/blogs/unequallyyoked/2012/06/this-is-my-last-post-for-the-patheos-atheist-portal.html

319. Michael Shermer, *The Science of Good and Evil: Why People Cheat, Gossip, Care, Share, and Follow the Golden Rule.* (Henry Holt and Co.: New York, 2004) 154-155.

320. Shermer, 57-58.

321. Loftus, 108.

322. See Paul Copan. *Is God a Moral Monster?: Making Sense of the Old Testament God* (Baker Books: Grand Rapids, 2011).

323. See Exodus 21:16, 26-27.

324. See Josiah Freedman's *Bible Defense of Slavery* (1853).

325. Consider Anscombe's example of a sheriff who must choose between allowing a mob to kill an innocent imprisoned man or refusing the mob and allowing many other people to be killed in a riot. If morality is about securing the greater good, then it seems

that the innocent man should be killed. But this seems to be grossly unfair and immoral.

326. Harris, 52-53.

327. It's important to remember that not all evil actions are intrinsically evil because we can conceive of situations where those evil acts would not be wrong. For example, killing a human being is not intrinsically wrong because most people agree it is acceptable to kill a human being in self-defense when all other non-lethal options to preserve life have failed. However, other actions like rape or torture can never be justified in any circumstance and so are wrong because of what those actions simply are.

328. Asking "If God commanded rape would rape be moral?" is like asking, as Craig says, "If a square-circle existed could you find its area by multiplying its sides?" Since square circles are impossible (just like evil Gods) then the question is meaningless and can't be answered.

329. Islam teaches that God, who is called Allah, is not bound by any moral or logical standards and would even be within his right to send faithful Muslims to Hell. For further information, see Daniel Brown, "Islamic Ethics in Comparative Perspective," *The Muslim World*, Volume 89, Issue 2, 1999 181–192.

330. William Alston, "What Euthyphro should have said" in *Philosophy of Religion: A Reader and Guide,* ed. William Lane Craig (Rutgers University Press: New Jersey, 2002) 283.

331. CCC 271.

332. The original meter bar is kept at the International Bureau of Weights and Measures in Paris. However, what is now used to determine the length of a meter is the path a beam of light travels during a certain fraction of a second in a vacuum.

333. If goodness is just what God commands, then isn't saying God is good just the same thing as saying that "God is God?" Would this make calling God "good" a meaningless tautology? This objection confuses moral semantics (what moral terms mean) with moral

ontology (what makes moral claims real or true). God could be the foundation of morality without being identical to the meaning of morality. For example, saying Superman is Clark Kent is not a tautology like Clark Kent is Clark Kent. These terms have different meanings (man of steel vs. mild-mannered reporter) even while they have the same referent, Kal-El of the late planet Krypton. Another way to put it is that the terms differ in *sense* but not in *referent*. Aquinas followed this approach and argued that "being" and "goodness" refer to the same thing. Or something is good if it is a fullness of its being, but we could distinguish what it means to be "good" with what it means to just "be."

334. Robin LePoidevin. *Arguing for Atheism: An Introduction to the Philosophy of Religion* (Routledge: New York, 1996) 79.

335. William Lane Craig. *Reasonable Faith* (Crossway Books: Illinois 2008) 181-182.

336. According to Aquinas, "Goodness and being are really the same, and differ only in idea." See St. Thomas Aquinas, *Summa Theologicae*, Book I, Question V, Article I, "Goodness in general."

Chapter 16: What about personal experience?

337. C. S. Lewis. *Mere Christianity* (Touchstone: New York, 1996) 135.

338. Rudolf Otto. *The Idea of the Holy* (Oxford University Press: Oxford, 1958).

339. Alvin Plantinga uses this example in his book *Warranted Christian Belief* (450). Loftus says that the analogy Plantinga uses is a bad one and that sometimes our basic beliefs are mistaken. He uses the example of waking up covered in blood and being told you killed someone and that the police have witnesses to prove it (Loftus 193-194). But here Loftus confuses a basic belief with a basic desire. I have a basic desire not to kill an innocent person and if I am told I did so while sleepwalking, I will probably be skeptical. But I can't say I "know I didn't do it" because in that state I had no basic beliefs. In fact, no one ever remembers "not doing something." They

instead remember *doing something else* instead of what they were accused of doing. Furthermore, my desire to be innocent could not be vindicated because I would have no basic belief to retreat to. Following Plantinga, I wouldn't be able to say something like, "I was hiking Mount Baker at the time. It couldn't be me!"). But the experience of God is not like the experience of not committing a crime or of not doing anything else. It is more like the experience of the external world that could only be overwhelmed by an incredibly powerful defeater.

340. A. J. Ayer, "What I saw when I was dead," in *Language, Metaphysics, and Death,* ed. John Donnelly (Fordham University Press: New York, 1994) 228.

341. According to adherents.com, eight percent of modern people have no religion and also do not believe in any kind of theism. Since secular non-religion is a comparatively modern phenomenon, it should be a fair estimate to say that 95% of people who have ever lived have believed in some form of the divine, whether it is theism, pantheism, or a combination of the two.

342. Paul Doland. "The Case against Faith: A Critical Look at Lee Strobel's *The Case for Faith"* (4th ed., 2006), The Secular Web. Available online at http://www.infidels.org/library/modern/paul_doland/strobel.html

343. See Alvin Plantinga. *Warranted Christian Belief* (Oxford University Press: Oxford, 2000) 188. Personally, I think most people come to belief in God through experience and simpler versions of the traditional arguments for theism. For example, the cosmological argument for a layperson usually gets summarized as, "Well, how else did everything get started unless God caused everything?"

Conclusion: Beyond the God Debate

344. Quote originally derived from http://www.imdb.com/title/tt0118884/quotes and later modified.

345. Friedrich Nietzsche. *The Gay Science* (Dover Publications: New York, 2006) 90.

346. Jean Paul Sartre. "Existentialism Is a Humanism" (1946).

347. See Dennett, 21. If Dennett is a "bright" does that make a believer like me a "dim"? I'm not persuaded by Dennett's response that I could just call myself a "super" in order to feel better about myself not being a "bright." If anything, going around saying, "I'm a super!" would actually make me feel dim. I'm a theist, Dennett's an atheist. The normal terms work just fine.

348. Richard Dawkins, Michael Shermer, and Matt Ridley vs. William Lane Craig, Douglas Geivett, and Rabbi David Wolpe. "Does the Universe Have a Purpose?" Puebla, Mexico, November 13, 2010. Available online at http://www.youtube.com/watch?v=p6tIee8FwX8

349. Interview with Stone Phillips, Dateline NBC, Nov. 29, 1994.

350. A critic is bound to say that I haven't proven that Christianity is true and so this claim is unsupported. Well, that doesn't make it any less true. I have devoted a future book to defending Christian theism. I'm still comfortable sharing the Gospel message for the reader to consider even if I don't have all the evidence proving such a belief is true contained in this book. Would a doctor who knows that a treatment will save a patient's life refrain from telling him about it just because he left information about the effectiveness of the drug trials at home?

351. Louise M. Antony. "Good Minus God," *The New York Times* December 18, 2011 Available online at http://opinionator.blogs.ny-times.com/2011/12/18/good-minus-god/

352. Blaise Pascal. "On the Necessity of the Wager," in *The Pensées* (1669) Pensées is French for "thoughts."

353. This is also true for the theist who simply believes in a generic God while investigating the claims of the world's different religions.

354. "It is appointed that human beings die once, and after this the judgment."—Hebrews 9:27

355. Stephen Hawking. *A Brief History of Time*. (Bantam Books: USA, 1998) 190.

Appendix I: St. Thomas Aquinas's cosmological arguments

356. Edward Feser. *Aquinas: A Beginner's Guide* (OneWorld: Oxford, 2009) 62-63.

357. St. Thomas Aquinas, *The Summa Theologicae*, Question 2, Article 3.

358. Philosophical atheists, and even theists like Alvin Plantinga (1977, 79-80), say the Third Way commits the *quantifier shift fallacy*. The quantifier shift fallacy occurs when a quantifier in an argument (like "every" and "one") shifts in the premises. For example, just because every wife has one husband, it does not follow that there is one husband who has every wife. Likewise, just because every object goes out of existence at a certain moment, it does not follow that there is a certain moment where everything goes out of existence. See Feser 93-98 for a complete answer to this objection based on the inherent tendency of objects that are composites of matter and form to stop existing over time.

359. Richard Dawkins. *The God Delusion* (Houghton Mifflin Company: New York, 2006) 101.

360. Michael Martin. *Atheism: A Philosophical Justification*. (Temple University Press: Philadelphia, 1990) 99.

361. The formal terms are *per se* causation (simultaneous causation) and *per accidens* (sequential) causation. See Feser 69-70.

362. I discuss this view in light of the kalām cosmological argument in chapter nine. For a contemporary interaction with Aquinas that reaches a different conclusion than him on the possibility of an infinite past, see Fr. Robert Spitzer. *New Proofs for the Existence of God: Contributions of Contemporary Physics and Philosophy* Wm. B. Eerdmans: Grand Rapids, 2010) 177-180.

363. Feser anticipates the objection that the causes we observe have a short-lag time and so they aren't really simultaneous. He writes, "some critics place too much significance on the physical details of the examples Aquinas gives in the course of the proof, failing to see that their point is merely to illustrate certain basic metaphysical principles rather than to support broad empirical or quasi-scientific generalizations . . . when we talk about one thing being moved by another, which is moved by another, etc., in a causal series ordered per se, this is shorthand for saying that a certain potency is reduced to act by something whose potency is itself reduced to act by something whose potency is itself reduced to act by... and so forth (Feser 68, 73).

364. Anthony Kenny, *The Five Ways: St. Thomas Aquinas' Proofs of God's Existence* (Routledge and Kegan Paul: London,1969) p. 28.

365. See Edward Feser. "The medieval principle of motion and the modern principle of inertia," *Proceedings of the Society for Medieval Logic and Metaphysics*, Volume 10, 2012 4–16.

Appendix II: Objections to the Kalām Cosmological Argument

366. See also William Lane Craig. "Objections so Bad I couldn't Have Made Them Up (or, the World's 10 Worst Objections to the *Kalām* Cosmological Argument" in *Come Let Us Reason: New Essays in Christian Apologetics,* eds. Paul Copan and William Lane Craig (B&H Publishing: Nashville, 2012) 59.

367. For example, one can imagine that it is possible to go back in time and kill one's own grandfather, which would create a logical contradiction or paradox.

368. G. E. M. Anscombe, "Whatever has a beginning of existence must have a cause—Hume's argument exposed," *Analysis* 34 (1974) 150.

369. "David Hume to John Stewart (Tuesday Forenoon, February 1754)," *The Letters of David Hume: Volume 1,* ed. J.Y.T. Grieg (Oxford University Press: New York, 1932) 187.

370. For example, in the famous "double slit experiment," an electron seems to act like both a particle and a wave depending on what kind of barrier it passes through. Even more puzzling, the electron may act like a wave until it is measured by an observer where, at that point, the wave-function collapses and it acts like a particle instead.

371. Even the indeterminacy of quantum events is not a proven fact but one of many possible interpretations of the mathematical formulas in quantum mechanics (usually the Copenhagen interpretation). Victor Stenger admits, "Other viable interpretations of quantum mechanics remain with no consensus on which, if any, is the correct one"; hence, we have to remain "open to the possibility that causes may someday be found for such phenomena." Victor Stenger, *Has Science Found God?* (Amherst, N.Y.: Prometheus, 2003), 188–89, 173 (cited in Craig, 114). These interpretations represent what scientists think their mathematical formulas actually depict happening in the real world. Some interpretations of quantum physics describe events without causes, but others, such as that offered by the late David Bohm, include no uncaused events. Under Bohm's view (or the deBroglie-Bohm interpretation) the way particles behave or act is completely determined by the physical events that happened earlier in time. The quantum events *appear* to be random, but they still have a determined cause. Under this interpretation, virtual particles would have a reason or cause for coming into existence from the vacuum even if we aren't aware of it. The eminent quantum physicist John Bell has praised this interpretation for its use of non-locality. Bell writes about the difficulty quantum researchers have in developing models that include truly free or random observers. He says, "It is a merit of the de Broglie–Bohm version to bring this [nonlocality] out so explicitly that it cannot be ignored." John Bell, *Speakable and Unspeakable in Quantum Mechanics* (Cambridge University Press: New York, 1987) 115.

372. Of course, the entire force of this objection can be averted by reforming the kalām argument, as William Lane Craig did in his 2013 debate with Alex Rosenberg, in the following way:

P1. If the universe began to exist, then it has a transcendent cause.

P2. The universe began to exist.

C. Therefore, the universe has a transcendent cause.

373. Gordon Kane. "Are virtual particles really constantly popping in and out of existence? Or are they merely a mathematical book-keeping device for quantum mechanics?" *Scientific American,* October 9, 2006. Available online at: http://www.scientificamerican. com/article.cfm?id=are-virtual-particles-rea

374. See John Jefferson Davis. *Frontiers of Science and Faith: Examining Questions from the Big Bang to the End of the Universe* (InterVarsity Press: Downers Grove, 2002) 55-56.

375. Another way to argue that the past is finite (which I have not argued for in this book due to space limitations) is to argue that actual infinites cannot exist at all, regardless of how they are formed. Craig argues this way when he uses thought experiments like infinite libraries or Hilbert's Hotel. To see this approach I recommend William Lane Craig and James D. Sinclair. "The *Kalām* Cosmological Argument," *The Blackwell Companion to Natural Theology*, eds. William Lane Craig and J.P. Moreland (Blackwell Publishing: Sussex, 2009) 106-117.

376. A similar objection occurs when critics say if actual infinites can't exist then Big Bang singularities that are finitely dense cannot exist either. However, Quentin Smith addresses this terminological issue and writes, "If the universe is finite, and the Big Bang singularity a single point, then at the first instant the entire mass of the universe is compressed into a space with zero volume. The density of the point is $n/0$, where n is the extremely high but finite number of kilograms of mass in the universe. Since it is impermissible to divide by zero, the ratio of mass to unit volume has no meaningful and measurable value and *in this sense is infinite.*" Thus the singularity would represent a limit approaching infinity, or an incredibly high immeasurable number, and not an actual infinity. Smith also says that philosophers often misunderstand physicists when they use the word

"infinite." See William Lane Craig and Quentin Smith. *Theism, Atheism, and Big Bang Cosmology* (Clarendon Press: Oxford, 1993) 210.

377. See also Fr. Robert Spitzer. *New Proofs for the Existence of God: Contributions of Contemporary Physics and Philosophy* (Wm. B. Eerdmans: Grand Rapids, 2010) 198-200.

378. See St. Thomas Aquinas, "That God Does Not Understand By Composing and Dividing," *Summa Contra Gentiles*, Book 1, Chapter 58.

379. A critic could object that there really are an actual infinite number of points in the distance traversed, not a potential infinite. But without additional proof that actual infinites exist, the critic is simply assuming what they are trying to prove. One is just as rational to assume that distance is finite and mathematical points are mental constructs that are added over a physical distance and have no real existence of their own.

380. Stenger makes this objection and writes, "saying the universe is eternal simply is saying that it has no beginning or end, not that it had a beginning an infinite time ago" (Victor Stenger. *The Fallacy of Fine Tuning: Why the Universe is not Designed for Us* (Prometheus Books: New York, 2011) 112.

381. J. P. Moreland and Kai Nielsen. *Does God Exist? The Debate Between Theists and Atheists* (Prometheus Books: New York, 1993) 230. Another variant of this objection holds that the past is not actually infinite because the distance measured between any past day and the present will always be finite. But just because every part of the past sequence of events has the property of being a finite distance from the present, it by no means follows that the whole past sequence of events has the property of being a finite distance from the present. This is the fallacy of composition. For example, just because every beam in a fence has a width of five inches, surely the fence itself is not only five inches long.

382. As I've stated earlier, while this statement may seem obviously true, it actually isn't. The idea that time forms as a result of successive

moments that come into existence rests on a hotly debated theory of time called the A-theory or dynamic theory of time. Under an alternative view called the B-theory or static theory, time is essentially another spatial dimension and all moments past, present, and future are equally real and do not come into existence sequentially. For more on this important subject see the section, "Theories of time" in the Advanced Cosmology appendix.

383. Physicists also refer to this as the "arrow of time," or the idea that temporal events are ordered in a particular direction while spatial events are not.

384. Even if the critic's belief that only fundamental particles exist were true, that would not refute the KCA. Craig reformulates the KCA to accommodate this view in this way:

P1. If the fundamental particles arranged universe-wise began to exist, they have a cause.
P2. The fundamental particles arranged universe-wise began to exist.
C. Therefore, the fundamental particles arranged universe-wise have a cause.

See William Lane Craig. "Objections So Bad I Couldn't Have Made Them Up (or, the World's 10 Worst Objections to the *Kalām* Cosmological Argument*" in *Come Let Us Reason: New Essays in Christian Apologetics,* eds. Paul Copan and William Lane Craig (B&H Publishing: Nashville, 2012) 61. For a critique of mereological nihilism, the view this objection endorses, see Roderick Chisolm. "Parts as Essential to Their Wholes" *The Review of Metaphysics* Vol. 26, No. 4, June 1973.

385. Stephen Hawking made this argument in the first episode of the television series *Curiosity* (original airdate August 7, 2011).

386. Dan Barker makes a more serious claim that the KCA begs the question. He says that in premise one the phrase "whatever begins to exist has a cause" implies there are two types of things in the universe, things which begin to exist and things which do not begin

to exist. But if the set of "things which do not begin to exist" only contains God, then premise one just means "Whatever begins to exist has a cause or it is God," thus the argument begs the question. But the KCA only begs the question if the term "God" is put in the first premise, not a term that *refers* to God but has a different *meaning*. It's possible that the set of "things which never begin to exist" could be empty and the universe is eternal. But since that is not the case, it just logically follows that the universe has a cause for its beginning. If God is the only thing that never began to exist, then that is just the logical outcome of the argument. Furthermore, many mathematicians think abstract objects never began to exist, so the term "never began to exist" may not exclusively refer to God. Either way, Barker's objection does not refute the KCA (Barker, 131-134).

387. See also Craig, 2012, 55-56.

388. Critics also say the KCA equivocates on the word "cause," to mean both "cause to be from preexisting matter" and "cause to be from nothing." But this objection has already been answered when I said that we could reword the argument to say that whenever the fundamental particles arranged universe-wise begin to exist from nothing, they require a cause and since the fundamental particles arranged universe-wise did begin to exist from nothing, they require a cause.

389. William Lane Craig. "Objections So Bad I Couldn't Have Made Them Up (or, the World's 10 Worst Objections to the *Kalām* Cosmological Argument" in *Come Let Us Reason: New Essays in Christian Apologetics,* eds. Paul Copan and William Lane Craig (B&H Publishing: Nashville, 2012) 62.

390. See Edward J. Wollack, NASA, "What is the ultimate fate of the universe?" 08/19/2010. Available online at http://map.gsfc.nasa.gov/universe/uni_fate.html

Appendix III: Advanced cosmology

391. Victor Stenger. *God and the Folly of Faith* (Prometheus Books: New York, 2012) 205.

392. Fr. Robert Spitzer. *New Proofs for the Existence of God: Contributions from Contemporary Physics and Philosophy*. (Wm. B. Erdmans Publishing: Grand Rapids, 2010) 27.

393. In addition, the entropy from the previous cycle carries over into the next cycle. But if the universe had been "cycling" for eternity then the entropy wouldn't have reached a maximum level by now?

394. Brian Greene. *The Fabric of the Cosmos: Space, Time, and the Texture of Reality* (Random House: New York, 2004) 272.

395. Ibid. 280, 285.

396. Hawking, 129.

397. Andre Linde, "The self-reproducing inflationary universe." *Scientific American,* May 1998 103. Available online at: http://muktomona.net/science/physics/Inflation_lself_prod_inde.pdf Cited in William Lane Craig and James Sinclair, "The Kalām Cosmological Argument," *The Blackwell Companion to Natural Theology,* eds. William Lane Craig and J.P. Moreland (Blackwell Publishing: Oxford, 2009) 139.

398. Arvind Borde, Alan H. Guth, and Alexander Vilenkin. "Inflationary spacetimes are not past-complete" (Cornell University Library, General Relativity and Quantum Cosmology, 2003) Available online at http://arxiv.org/abs/grqc/0110012

399. Alexander Vilenkin. *Many Worlds in One.* (Hill and Wang: New York, 2006) 83.

400. Ibid. 176.

401. This exchange was posted by the Arizona Atheist who took part in the exchange between Stenger and Vilenkin. The emails took place between 5-20-10 and 5-24-10. They are available online at: http://arizonaatheist.blogspot.com/2010/05/william-lane-craigs-arguments-for-god.html. Craig references this exchange in his debate with Peter Millican at Birmingham University on October 21, 2011. This part of the exchange can be viewed online at http://youtu.be/dnRD5TJZ9FM?t=53m40s

402. The most compelling defense of divine temporality and an A-theory of time can be found in William Lane Craig's *Time and Eternity* (2001). For a good comparison of different accounts of God's relationship to time see Alan Padgett. *God and Time: Four Views* (Intervarsity Press: Downers Grove, 2001).

403. See Mark Nowacki. *The Kalām Cosmological Argument for God* (Prometheus Books: New York, 2007).

404. Victor Stenger. *The Fallacy of Fine Tuning: Why the Universe Is Not Designed for Us* (Prometheus Books: New York, 2011) 80.

405. Victor Stenger. *God: The Failed Hypothesis* (Prometheus Books: New York, 2007) 131.

406. Victor Stenger. *The Fallacy of Fine Tuning: Why the Universe Is Not Designed for Us* (Prometheus Books: New York, 2011) 52-53.

407. Robin Collins. "Stenger's Fallacies," 7-8. Available online at http://home.messiah.edu/~rcollins/Fine-tuning/Stenger-fallacy.pdf)

408. See Luke Barnes. "The Fine-Tuning of the Universe for Intelligent Life" (Cornell University Library, History and Philosophy of Physics, 2012). Available online at http://arxiv.org/abs/1112.4647.

409. Victor Stenger. "Defending the Fallacy of Fine-tuning," 11, avaialble online at: http://www.colorado.edu/philosophy/vstenger/Fallacy/DefendFallacy.pdf

410. Jean-Pierre Luminet, Jeffrey R. Weeks, Alain Riazuelo, Roland Lehoucq & Jean-Philippe Uzan. "Dodecahedral space topology as an explanation for weak wide-angle temperature correlations in the cosmic microwave background," Letters to Nature, Volume 425, October 9, 2003. Cited in James Daniel Sinclair. "At Home in the Multiverse?" *Contending with Christianity's Critics,* eds. Paul Copan and William Lane Craig (B&H Publishing Group: Nashville, 2009) 18.

411. See Sean Carroll. "The Fine Structure Constant Is Probably Constant." *Cosmic Variance,* 10/18/2010. Available online at

http://blogs.discovermagazine.com/cosmicvariance/2010/10/18/the-fine-structure-constant-is-probably-constant/

412. Dennis Overbye. "Big Brain Theory: Have Cosmologists Lost Theirs?" *The New York Times,* January 15, 2008. Available online at: http://www.nytimes.com/2008/01/15/science/15brain.html?pagewanted=all